Out in Public

CONFIGURATIONS

of WOMEN'S BODIES *in*

NINETEENTH-CENTURY

AMERICA

Out in Public

Alison Piepmeier

The University of North Carolina Press CHAPEL HILL & LONDON

Set in Cycles and Sabon types
by Tseng Information Systems, Inc.
Manufactured in the United States of America
The paper in this book meets the guidelines for permanence and durability of the Committee on Production Guidelines for Book Longevity of the Council on Library Resources.

Library of Congress
Cataloging-in-Publication Data
Piepmeier, Alison.
Out in public: configurations of women's bodies in nineteenth-century America / Alison Piepmeier.
p. cm.
Includes bibliographical references and index.
ISBN 0-8078-2904-8 (cloth: alk. paper)—
ISBN 0-8078-5569-3 (pbk.: alk. paper)
1. Body, Human—Social aspects—United States—History—19th century. 2. Body, Human—Symbolic aspects—United States—History—19th century. 3. Women—United States—Physiology. 4. Women—United States—History—19th century. 5. Women—United States—Public opinion. 6. Women in popular culture—United States—History—19th century. 7. Public opinion—United States—History—19th century. I. Title.
GT495.P54 2004
391.6'0973—dc22 2004009062

cloth 08 07 06 05 04 5 4 3 2 1
paper 08 07 06 05 04 5 4 3 2 1

To Lee, Kelly, Trey,

and Aaron Piepmeier

and to Walter Biffle

CONTENTS

ILLUSTRATIONS

ACKNOWLEDGMENTS

I am touched by the fact that, as I researched the lives and writings of these five nineteenth-century women, much of the help and support I received was from women. I came to feel sometimes that I am part of a community of women that stretches, now, over three centuries.

Out in Public began its life as my dissertation, and I was helped immeasurably by the careful readings and apt critiques of Cecelia Tichi, Teresa Goddu, Thadious Davis, Ronnie Steinberg, and the late Nancy Walker. I am fortunate to have had such hands-on mentors and excellent readers. Cecelia and Teresa, in particular, through their classes and their out-of-class coaching, helped me to fall in love with the nineteenth century (although Jack Sallee and Kurt Eisen deserve a nod here, too, since they were truly the first to pique my interest in nineteenth-century America). Cecelia merits special mention because she was with me from the very earliest days of my research into Sojourner Truth and Mary Baker Eddy. I thank her for her consistent support as well as for the example she continues to provide of how to balance academia and a real life. In the dissertation stage I also benefited from the help and friendship of generous, insightful colleagues. I'd like to thank Eliza McGraw and Carol Manthey for the months we spent drinking coffee and discussing our dissertations. Eliza and I have encouraged each other as we've gone through the gauntlet of the publishing world, and I'm thrilled that both our books will be coming out this year. I'm also grateful for the support I received from the Vanderbilt Dissertation Writer's Group under the leadership of Darlene Panvini.

As I moved the project through the intensive transformation from dissertation to book, I found still more support available to me. Cecelia Tichi and Ronnie Steinberg have continued to be wonderful mentors. The images interspersed throughout the book were originally Cecelia's suggestion. Thank you also to Deandra Little, whose attentive, sensitive readings of the introduction and Chapter 4 provided more help to me than I can say. Deandra has an impressive ability to see empathically into the heart of another person's project—be it one involving scholarship or teaching—and help the person she's working with recognize how to bring that project to fruition. I am grateful that she shared this gift with me. She has played an important role in my development as a scholar. Carla Peterson and Shirley Samuels provided excellent feedback on the manuscript and helped me to reconceptualize key aspects of the work; their rigorous and thorough readings were instrumental in my revision process. I am humbled to have benefited from the insights of such outstanding scholars. I am also grateful to have had the opportunity to work with Sian Hunter at the University of North Carolina Press; she has been an attentive and supportive editor, not to mention a delightful person. The production team at the Press was also top-notch.

I have had other kinds of excellent help along the way. Gayle Parrott has provided structure as well as encouragement and has helped me to navigate the world of the university so that I could stay focused on the world of nineteenth-century women. Jamie Adams at the Vanderbilt University Learning Resource Center photographed the majority of images featured in *Out in Public*.

Opportunities to present parts of this book in conference presentations and in print helped me to develop the ideas more fully. I presented the beginning thoughts on Chapter 4 at the Society for the Study of American Women Writers Conference in 2001, and I offered early thoughts on Chapter 5 at the Popular Culture Association/American Culture Association Conference in 2000; I received helpful feedback from the audience and other panelists at both venues. A version of Chapter 3 appeared in *Women as Sites of Culture*, ed. Susan Shifrin (London: Ashgate Press, 2002), and a version of Chapter 2 appeared in *Women's Studies: An Interdisciplinary Journal* 30 (2001).

I am truly grateful for the many friends who have provided personal support to me through this process. Writing a book can be unutterably exciting and also excruciatingly lonely, and I am blessed to have a community of friends and family who were with me through all the emotional ups and downs. Deborah Denson, Kathy Mattea, Connie McCaughelty, Christie McKaskle, Jennifer Parker, Peggy Reynolds, and Elizabeth Stelling provided many lifelines and helped me not to lose myself. Jay Crockett has been a consistent friend through many years. Rory Dicker and I spent part of the last two years editing another volume, and her friendship and collegiality helped me to feel like a grownup. Catherine Bush has been the quintessential friend. When Oprah's Book Club books rhapsodize about female friendships, they're talking about what Catherine and I have.

Through no effort of my own, I was born into an amazing family, one that values and encourages anything I want to try. My parents, Lee and Kelly Piepmeier, have been my biggest fans. I feel fortunate to be related to Trey and Aaron Piepmeier because I suspect that, if I wasn't, I wouldn't be interesting enough to hang out with them. And finally, thank you to Walter Biffle, who took me to *South Park: The Movie* the night before my dissertation defense, took a picture of me mailing in my revised manuscript, fixed me countless dinners, sang me songs, and let me explain parts of my argument to him at length. He, more than anyone else, knows what this book means to me. I am grateful to him for cherishing my efforts and my aspirations and for being my feminist co-conspirator and my life partner.

Out in Public

INTRODUCTION
Bodies in Public

> *But—oh, dear, I want to do such a quantity of "improper" things, that there is not the slightest real harm in doing. I want to see and know a thousand things which are forbidden to flounces—custom only can tell why—I can't. I want the free use of my ankles, for this summer at least, to take a journey; I want to climb and wade, and tramp about, without giving a thought to my clothes; without carrying about with me a long procession of trunks and boxes, which are the inevitable penalty of femininity as at present appareled. . . . I want to run my fingers through my cropped hair some fine morning without the bore of dressing it. . . . Wouldn't that be fine?*
> —Fanny Fern, "A Law More Nice Than Just, Number II," 1858

> *"Come, the curtain is down, so I may be myself for a few hours, if actresses ever are themselves."*
>
> *Still sitting on the floor she unbound and removed the long abundant braids from her head, wiped the pink from her face, took out several pearly teeth, and slipping off her dress appeared herself indeed, a haggard, worn, and moody woman of thirty at least. The metamorphosis was wonderful, but the disguise was more in the expression she assumed than in any art of costume or false adornment. Now she was alone, and her mobile features settled into their natural expression, weary, hard, bitter.*
> —Louisa May Alcott, *Behind a Mask*, 1866

Out in public: the phrase connotes visibility, freedom, agency. It suggests a body taking up space and moving through the world of commerce, government, or celebrity. Placed in the context of nineteenth-century womanhood, the phrase may also suggest transgression and deviance. Indeed, for nineteenth-century women, "outing" could be dangerous, implying a connection between publicity and sexual availability.[1] As this study will demonstrate, these multiple connotations are exactly the point: the "outing" of women's bodies in nineteenth-century America carried a range of possible meanings, the deployment of which depended on a network of factors including race, class, the particular historical moment, the context within print culture, and the framing narratives.

Recent scholarship on nineteenth-century womanhood has spoken less of a range or spectrum of possible meanings of women's public embodiment and has, instead, tended to view nineteenth-century social, political, and gender organization through interlocking sets of binary lenses: the public and private spheres, and agency and victimization. These lenses obscure as much as they reveal; although they help to bring certain aspects of gender construction in the nineteenth century into clarity, they also make much invisible. For instance, scholarship over the past thirty years has canonized the image of private, domesticated nineteenth-century womanhood; this scholarship has also familiarized us with some women who deviate from this model.[2] What needs to be more fully articulated and explored are the modalities of embodiment that make use of both public and private, that are neither fully victim nor agent, that—rather than being either appropriate or deviant—are multiple, transitional, strategic, playful, contested.

The epigraphs to this introduction document two versions of multivalent womanhood during one particular mid-century moment. Neither Fanny Fern's narrator nor Louisa May Alcott's gothic heroine Jean Muir is fully legible through the rubric of the public and private spheres. Fern's narrator voices a longing for a body that is *out*—out of the home, outdoors, free of the physical constraints of clothing and hairstyles that confine the bodies of appropriately feminine women at mid-century. She describes her desire to have an active and mobile body, with "free use of my ankles"; the hiding of the ankles in long hoop skirts comes to signify the larger restrictions placed on female mobility and selfhood. She offers an enthusiastic image of an assertive physicality, which could "climb and wade, and tramp about," and explicitly leave the domestic sphere to "take a journey." Her longing, however, voiced particularly in the last, plaintive question, "Wouldn't that be fine?," suggests that Fern's narrator is, in fact, behaving as a properly domesticated woman, not acting on her desires for a body that, tongue-in-cheek, she identifies as "improper." She longs for the public while existing in the private sphere—she straddles the two. Similarly, Muir is not clearly localized to either "sphere." The excerpt features her in utter privacy, locked in her bedroom; however, by publishing—and thus making public—Muir's systematic removal of the trappings of femininity that identify her as a properly domesticated woman, Alcott brings the public gaze to bear on Muir. Neither woman, then, is fully legible within the rubric of the public and private spheres. Although the two bodies presented here are quite different from one another—Jean Muir's "weary, hard, bitter" expression contrasts dramatically with Fern's narrator's delighted description of bodily freedom—the texts are linked through their representation of corporeal identities that oppose and undercut simplistic binary approaches.

Both excerpts reveal some of the mechanisms by which binaries such as the public and private spheres are maintained. For instance, through their descriptions of the accoutrements that literally produce womanhood, Fern and Alcott expose the performances that constitute traditional white, middle-class, nineteenth-century femininity and, in so doing, undercut any notion of natural or essential femininity. Fern wants to reject the "long procession of trunks and boxes, which are the inevitable penalty of femininity," and yearns for hair that does not require "dressing"; through her catalog of complaints, she presents femininity as a labored performance, requiring props and preparations. Alcott takes this critique a step further by detailing the accessories that go into Muir's performance: her hair, skin coloring, and even her teeth, all of which are removed, finishing with the very facial expression of happy innocence that Muir discards. In Alcott's text, even body parts are props that can be manipulated to produce femininity, and Muir explicitly identifies herself as an actress, indicting her actions within the private sphere as a play. Both excerpts document gender as an embodied performance requiring physical effort as well as the veiling, distortion, or manipulation of the female body.

These excerpts also reveal how performances of womanhood can become conflated with particular binary constructions so that "woman" becomes a kind of code word signaling domestic as opposed to public, and victim as opposed to agent. In other words, as they perform "womanhood," Fern's narrator and Muir also perform female domesticity and a lack of agency. The notion of the woman as a domestic being, unable to "tramp about," and without the ability to effect change in her own life, is crucial to the femininity the two characters perform. Muir's dilemma in *Behind a Mask* emphasizes this collapsing of proper womanhood with the private sphere as she must repeatedly demonstrate weakness of heart and body and a longing for domestic sanctity in order to be accepted as a proper woman by the Coventry family. Both texts reveal how gender becomes linked with a particular social, economic, and political model—womanhood and the private sphere—at the site of the female body.

One of the most striking elements in each of the epigraphs, however, is the extent to which Alcott and Fern demonstrate the inadequacy of these defining binaries. Even as they link womanhood with the private sphere and victimization, Alcott and Fern unveil the incomplete ways in which this linking is enacted, thereby revealing fissures in this discursive model. Just as Muir "wipe[s] the pink from her face . . . and slip[s] off her dress" to reveal another female body beneath the societal trappings, so, too, do Alcott's and Fern's texts reveal the imperfect construction of feminine privacy and victimization as well as the existence of *other bodies* than those the binary of appropriate woman and deviant would suggest. These characters—and their authors—are performing privacy even as they are undertaking public work; they pretend to be submissive while enacting agency. In so doing, they demonstrate that the binary categories themselves are inadequate and unstable. Dichotomies often function to contain complexity, but in these texts the containment is incomplete and is revealed to be mechanically and discursively constructed, not inherent in female gender identity.

The instability of categories is central to *Out in Public*. Indeed, the "out" of this book's title suggests categorical uncertainty: boundaries are fluid; containment is inadequate; what was thought to be "in" is "out." By "outing" nineteenth-century women—analyzing the writings of five prominent women and their discussions of their public embodiment from the 1830s through the 1890s—this study provides a view of nineteenth-century womanhood which emphasizes networks of power as well as continual, productive tensions between dominant discourses and women's corporeal and discursive strategies. For the past three decades, and even within recent scholarly work, binary oppositions have maintained their appeal—perhaps particularly so in scholarship surrounding gender. *Out in Public* contends that it is time to move beyond the binaries, and in so doing, positions itself within the field of poststructuralist feminist scholarship, taking its place alongside such texts as Carla Peterson's *Doers of the Word* (1995), Lora Romero's *Home Fronts* (1997), Lisa Duggan's *Sapphic Slashers* (2000), and Cathy Davidson and Jessamyn Hatcher's *No More Separate Spheres!* (2002). These texts are theoretically sophisticated and politically grounded, resisting an emphasis on nineteenth-century women's victimization and domestic entrapment as a necessary prerequisite of literary and historical value. Like these texts, *Out in Public* takes as its point of departure the acknowledgment that the familiar binaries foreclose many possible readings of nineteenth-century womanhood. These binaries limit the ability of critics to see or understand certain aspects of women's lives in the nineteenth century, such as Anna Cora Mowatt's claiming of physical pleasure as a means of resisting sexism, or Sarah Hale's strategic compliance with an ideal of domesticated womanhood even as she headed the country's most influential publication.

Recent scholarship has challenged the separate spheres model; because of this work, scholars are freer to consider the spheres not as a determining force but as one discourse among many that shaped the lives of women in the century. Indeed, previous scholarship makes it possible for this book to take as its point of departure a complex world in which Barnum's freaks may influence the constructed embodiment of a middle-class wife, or in which a fully domestic woman may also be a successful businesswoman. *Out in Public* furthers these critical projects, contending that our understanding of womanhood must acknowledge fluid interactions between public and private and the simultaneity of victimization and agency. In this context the concept of embodiment becomes particularly useful, because it facilitates new readings which may argue into visibility previously obscured aspects of women's lives.

Studying the female body in the nineteenth century offers a means of destabilizing the categories of public and private, victim and agent, and other bifurcated ideals that have come to dominate studies of nineteenth-century womanhood. The public embodiment of nineteenth-century women provides a way not simply to emphasize the public or women's agency but to trouble the binaries themselves. This text examines five women—Anna Cora Mowatt (1819–1871), Mary Baker Eddy (1821–1910), Sojourner Truth (1797–1883), Ida B. Wells (1862–1931), and Sarah Josepha Hale (1788–1879)—and the material as well as discursive configuration of their bodies, which refuse easy categorization. Although often veiled with the costumes of domesticity, privacy, victimization, and proper femininity, these bodies were out in public.

It is, of course, no longer a revelation that women participated in public life in the nineteenth century. Critics no longer must follow historian Mary Ryan and "go defiantly in search of women in public."[3] For the last fifteen years, much excellent scholarship by historians, literary critics, and others has documented women's activity in public life, from the business of literature to political activism, from factory labor to involvement in the Civil War. This documentation has been part of a larger critical project to problematize the separate spheres model from a variety of standpoints. For example, critics such as Hazel Carby and Carla Peterson have used race as a key factor to complicate the binaric spheres model, presenting criticism of the private sphere from the perspective of those excluded from it.[4] Critics have re-examined the market, politics, and the nation, larger structures assumed to be external to the private sphere, and have noted their existence within this sphere.[5] Further, those recent critics who have examined sentimentality and domesticity have often done so in new ways, assessing the role of sentimental literature in nation-building and in the formation of individual identity.[6]

The destabilization of the spheres is still fairly recent, however. It was a critical commonplace two decades ago to demarcate the boundaries between the public and private spheres and to discuss the inner workings of the feminine private sphere. Over the last thirty years, scholars have mapped out the terrain of the private sphere as defined by the middle-class home and the white woman's presence there, isolated or insulated from the economic and political workings of the public sphere, men's domain.[7] They have also explored the psychological and physical implications of women's entrapment within the domestic realm.[8] While this model was both compelling and useful within reclamation and recovery work, it has proven to be reductive, dichotomizing a complex set of power relations and conflating gender stereotypes and social structures. As Davidson explains, "for all the utopic appeal of loving female worlds, the binaric version of nineteenth-century American history is ultimately unsatisfactory because it is simply too crude an instrument —too rigid and totalizing—for understanding the different, complicated ways that nineteenth-century American society or literary production functioned."[9] Over the past fifteen years, critics have begun reassessing the spheres model and have proposed new strategies for examining the nineteenth century without recourse to the private and public spheres. Much interesting literary and historical writing of late has concerned this reevaluation, and this trend has been institutionalized in such texts as the 1998 *American Literature* special issue titled "No More Separate Spheres!" and the 2002 expanded book version of that collection of essays.[10]

Even with this excellent scholarship, however, the binaries linger and exert their influence on what is seen as normative and deviant for nineteenth-century women.[11] Critics note that "the separate spheres paradigm has come to seem as if hardwired to feminist recovery projects."[12] Furthermore, the binaries feed into one another in such a way that *current* gender stereotypes are often applied retroactively to the nineteenth century. Lora Romero has documented the ways in which our current notions of agency are implicated in and perpetuate nineteenth-century models, affecting our assessments of literary value. Certainly the same is true of our notions of victimization. Our concepts of gender affect our readings of the nineteenth century; binaries such as private/public and victim/agent—binaries then mapped onto woman/man—shape what critics are able to see. Indeed, nineteenth-century women's engagement with the public world can become invisible to scholars when that engagement is embedded in the context of a society that values women's situatedness in the home and of a scholarship that views women as victims. For instance, in a 2001 study of women's work in periodicals, the editors identify Sarah Hale as fervently wedded to the private sphere, asserting, "It is, of course, ironic that a successful, visible, self-supporting woman editor should encourage other women not to participate in the public sphere, but Hale adamantly segregated the sexes in her own writings and never wavered from her position."[13] This assertion documents the lingering power of the equation of public with male and private with female to shape what critics are able to see. As *Out in Public* will show, Hale, along with the other women studied here, did more than simplistically align herself with one sphere or the other; she strategically negotiated the discourses available to her to allow herself a fuller range of choices than this model provided. Indeed, the irony the editors note should be their clue to look further: Hale's adamancy and refusal to waver, which may initially seem to be signs of her commitment to the private sphere, can, instead, be read as tools in her complex negotiations.

Just as the dichotomy of public/private appeals to scholars as a means of categorizing and making sense of nineteenth-century gender roles and social relations, so, too, do the categories *victim* and *agent*. Power relations and their connection to gender are central concerns to feminist scholars. Complex power relations, however, can easily be flattened into the dichotomy of victim and agent, with men coming to stand for the agents and women for the victims; this tendency has been well documented by Mary Ryan, Lora Romero, Elizabeth Grosz, and others.[14] Just as the notion of public and private is reductive and inadequate, so, too, is a flattened reading of victim/agent. These binaries are interlocking, and where gender is concerned, they have come to fit together with such apparent neatness and familiarity as to seem inevitable.[15] As Dana Nelson notes, "The notion of 'the separate spheres' has been used for over a century to endow emerging cultural hierarchies with the obviousness of gender (male/female) opposition."[16] This obviousness often obscures the messy realities of power negotiations, off-the-cuff organizing, and strategic compliance that emerge in nineteenth-century women's writing.

A particularly useful theoretical strategy for addressing the victim/agent binary—and, by extension, for addressing other prevailing nineteenth-century binaries—emerges from late-twentieth-century feminist scholarship on the subject of violence against women. In the public debate surrounding violence against women, feminists are often accused of victimizing women through their attention to women's victimization; because of this complex dilemma, sophisticated thinking about oppression and agency has begun to be articulated in this field. Legal scholar Martha Mahoney notes that our current cultural and legal understanding of victimization is such that a victim is seen as *one who has no agency*; the terms are deployed in popular culture and in the courtroom as opposing and mutually exclusive, and each is defined by the absence of the other. She argues, "In this concept, agency does not mean acting for oneself under conditions of oppression; it means *being without oppression*, either having ended oppression or never having experienced it at all."[17] This cultural understanding is extraordinarily significant for women because, in a male-dominated society, women's lives are never lived in the utter absence of oppression. For nineteenth-century women this was even more clearly the case, and when considering women of color and of varying class backgrounds, it becomes crucial to develop ways of describing women's lives that do not reduce them simplistically to victimization.[18]

A significant consequence of a political, cultural, or critical context in which women are viewed as victims is that women's agency or their acts of resistance and empowerment can be not only obscured but rendered virtually invisible, impossible to read. Women's agency becomes culturally unreadable. Excavating the agency of nineteenth-century women is thus an effective political and historical act, not to reinvoke the simplistic victim/agent dichotomy from its other pole, but to destabilize the dichotomy. What this re-envisioning accomplishes is a decommissioning of the concepts themselves so that victimization and agency can be seen not as mutually exclusive but as interpenetrating. The question becomes not whether the women studied here are victims or agents, but how does agency—or how do *acts* of agency and resistance—emerge within a social, cultural, and perhaps a personal context of disempowerment and even oppression? What does agency look like in these contexts? Similarly, the question becomes not whether women were public or private beings but how women gained access to the power and authority of the public world without becoming transgressive figures. Further, we must question how these women's actions demonstrate the operations of the spheres discourses: they reveal that, although this discursive and societal model attempted to stabilize and contain shifting power relationships, it was inadequate and its containment only partial. These are the issues *Out in Public* takes up.

The female body is the site on which *Out in Public* will conduct this line of questioning. The body is the crux of many of the binaries I am considering: the female body is the defining feature of the private sphere and of the victim paradigm, often coming synechdochally to stand for domesticity and victimization. However, the body is also a site which is mobile and malleable, able to change in response to changing circumstances and able to be configured in terms of various spaces, from the home to the podium. Because of its mobility, the body becomes an excellent vehicle for the destabilization of categories; the body can demonstrate and enact the fluidity of boundaries via its literal physical movement, movement into and out of homes, movement in travel, and movement through sport. Additionally, the body "moves" through and is constructed by discourses—medicine, science, religion, the sentimental narrative, the tall tale—as well as legal categories—citizen or chattel. Furthermore, the female body destabilizes binary oppositions through such disruptive energies as pleasure, which are impossible to read and interpret through the familiar dichotomies.[19] Female embodiment is a site at which the lines dividing the private and public spheres begin to break down because the body serves as a bridge linking the individual, the material world, and larger structures of power. However, in its textual and material mobility and energy, the female body is not unbounded; as *Out in Public* will discuss, an examination of the body brings particular cultural limitations into focus even as it removes others. The body can therefore provide a valuable interpretive lens for the analysis of the nineteenth century and for the revision of familiar models of womanhood.[20]

Certainly in a scholarly arena shaped by poststructuralism, we recognize the body as discursively constructed.[21] The women I study form their bodies as they speak of them or write about them; much of the mobility and political strategy available to nineteenth-century women emerged from their ability to intervene in the textual construction of their corporeality. However, a discursively grounded approach to corporeality raises the question of essentialism versus constructionism, a question for which, Diana Fuss reminds us, the body is "the exemplary problem."[22] This study contends that a purely poststructuralist—and thereby constructionist—explanation of the body is not entirely adequate for describing the lives of nineteenth-century women; or perhaps it is more accurate to say that *Out in Public* utilizes a *careful* poststructuralist approach. It is tempting, when assessing the question of social construction versus essentialism, to resort to the same binary thinking that propels the victim/agent fallacy or the public/private spheres model, and to identify bodies within a kind of all-or-nothing mentality—indeed, to view discursive construction of bodies as a means of escape from or transcendence of materiality, to view discursive construction as somehow entirely "freeing." Binaries are activated here: the discursively constructed body can come to represent a kind of idealized agent. Susan Bordo warns against exactly this "prematurely celebratory" approach, an approach many poststructuralist readings take "when looking at bodily 'texts' without attention to the concrete contexts—social, political, cultural, and practical—in which they are embedded. And so they need to be reminded of the materiality of the body."[23] Bordo emphasizes the importance of recognizing not only historical context but also material and cultural limitations when assessing bodies.

As the following chapters will demonstrate, a completely constructionist or poststructuralist reading of the bodies of nineteenth-century women inadequately accounts for the real bodily limitations these women faced. Just as a nuanced analysis must attend to the ways in which victimization and agency coexist and interpenetrate in the lives of nineteenth-century women, so, too, must this analysis attend to the ways in which discursive construction of embodiment is enabled and constrained by particular historical, cultural, and even physiological contexts.[24] Each chapter addresses the limitations of the material body of a particular woman, offering a kind of revised poststructuralist assessment of the practical realities of embodiment as shaped by a particular social and historical context. So, for instance, although Sojourner Truth is able to manipulate her public reception, utilizing the discourse of tall tales to present her body as powerful, virtuous, and heroic, she is *not* able to make the public receive her as a small, white woman. This is not purely a failure of the idea of discursive construction; we know of many discursive frameworks in which a black person could be received as white, or a woman as a man,[25] or vice versa, but given the particular confluence of discursive, historical, and physiological factors at the site of Truth's public performance, it would have been very difficult for her to do this. Her ability to shape her body in public was constrained; she could not fully "transcend" her body, nor could any of the women here.

Although it may seem necessary to contrast the material and the discursive, or to subsume one within the other, the public corporeality of women like Truth demonstrates the intersection of material and discursive construction at the site of the body. Limitations of the sort Truth faced did not foreclose her bodily identity but, in fact, contribute to the materialization of the body and, as such, may be *productive* of bodily identity. Bordo defines materiality via the concept of limitations: "'Materiality,' in the broadest terms, signifies for me our finitude. It refers to our inescapable physical locatedness in time and space, in history and culture, both of which not only shape us . . . but also *limit* us. . . ."[26] Constraints such as those faced by Truth and the other women studied here in many cases allowed these women the grounds on which to construct their self-expressions. Certainly different women experienced different constraints, and embodiment was experienced differently for women of varying races and classes. However, there were no essentialized differences based on ethnicity: Truth and Wells, the two African American women considered in *Out in Public*, are able to mediate their embodiment as effectively as any of the other women I study; indeed, Wells, whose work on lynching addresses the most profound limitations of the material body of any of the women considered in the text, is perhaps best able to leverage those bodily limitations into political meaning. The question is not how or whether the women studied here transcended the body, the private sphere, or their victimization; the question is how they negotiated with and within the constraints of their historical moment in order to effect a measure of change.

The body rewards multidisciplinary approaches, and this study will therefore have recourse to the insights of many body scholars. The body operates on multiple levels in each of the following chapters, appearing in various configurations; each woman negotiates a different set of discourses in her attempt to define and shape her public embodiment, and each woman positions her physical self differently as a result. While this book cannot fully exhaust any woman's physical enactment, each chapter highlights a particular mechanism or set of discourses its subject brings into play. One discursive formulation merits particular mention because of its recurrence throughout this text: the freak. The freak—a discursively constructed identity created when a person is defined as a marginally human public spectacle—patrols the borders of all the bodily configurations presented here. Freaks are abjected figures. Julia Kristeva says of the abject, "It is . . . not lack of cleanliness or health that causes abjection but what disturbs identity, system, order. What does not respect borders, positions, rules. The in-between, the ambiguous, the composite."[27] The freak represents this very abjection, offering an extreme example of the blurring or interpenetration of categories that these women's bodily self-constructions are already invoking. The idea of the freak, however, serves both to acknowledge categorical instability and to *restabilize* categories by locating "freaks" as a separate—and ostensibly coherent—site. Thus the label "freak" becomes a point of no return, because the label serves the socially important function of containing the abjection of the freakish body. The containment, of course, is incomplete, but identification with the freakishly abject body still presented a threat of containment that the women presented here avoided.

Not all women whose bodies became visibly public were freaks, but all ran the risk of this designation. Women's visibility was potentially transgressive of and threatening to hegemonic ideals. Framing women's visibility in terms of a simplistic binary such as "appropriate" and "deviant," however, obscures the range of possible meanings women's public embodiment could evoke. For instance, in the epigraph to this introduction, Jean Muir's body borders on the freakish. Alcott presents a somewhat gruesome and certainly sensational spectacle of Muir removing her hair, skin color, and teeth, a spectacle suggestive of the disruption of order and identity that characterizes the abject. Because this scene is part of a gothic narrative, and because Muir is a pseudo-villainous protagonist, her body's visibility may be read as freakish.[28] Fern's narrator's body, on the other hand, is not freakish, although her invocation of bodily transformation—envisioning herself without her hair or clothing, and with an athletic physicality—certainly *could* be identified as freakish under the right set of discursive circumstances. The framing narrative and tone, however, communicate to the reader that this woman's bodily transgressions are harmless. Although these two bodies are each challenging a domestic, submissive model of female corporeality, they do not automatically become deviant. In fact, they signify differently, demonstrating the many configurations the body may assume and the complex ways bodies interact with and are constructed by texts.

The goal of my research is not to present the one correct identification of the body; rather, the body's complexity and unevenness is a function of the larger cultural discourses that apply pressures to women's shaping of their corporeality and make certain bodily possibilities more or less available to a given woman at a given time. As Foucault explains, the body is "imprinted by history" and is thus a site on which history is enacted.[29] The body's ability to function differently in different public configurations and different historical moments is one reason it is such a compelling subject of analysis.

Out in Public spans a historical period stretching from the 1830s to the last years of the nineteenth century. This seventy-year period was a crucial one for women; this was the time during which the abolition and woman-suffrage movements developed, and this period saw such legal innovations as the Married Women's Property Act of 1848, the *Dred Scott* decision of 1857, and *Plessy v. Ferguson* (1896). Beginning in the 1830s, women such as Maria Stewart and the Grimké sisters began speaking in public to male and female audiences, and women's higher education expanded throughout the century, beginning with the founding of Oberlin College in 1833. This was in many ways a time of national turmoil, with such crises as the conflict over slavery, the Civil War and Reconstruction, and women's rights. America's identity as a nation was formed and reformed, with increasing expansion of cities and growth of immigrant populations; while the nation began the century a rural, farming populace, by the last quarter of the century industrial output increased exponentially. The century also saw development of a self-consciously American literature and science. During this time the publishing world was revolutionized, and women's involvement played a huge role in this change (the number of bestsellers authored by women has been well documented).

In this time of national formation and transformation, the meanings of gender and ethnicity were malleable and contested, and this is therefore an ideal historical period to examine for an understanding not only of the nineteenth century but also of how the epistemology of gender and race were constructed. This study engages with breadth not only chronology but also vocation and, to a more limited extent, region and race. Changes in the period happened by fits and starts and thus are not easily represented through one case study; by considering a particular historical moment and set of key discourses in each chapter, *Out in Public* attempts to capture the complexity of the changes in this period. But there are also many connecting threads throughout the period, discursive continuities that tied together the lives of women as apparently disparate as Ida B. Wells and Mary Baker Eddy.

Out in Public participates in the critical reconfiguration of the nineteenth century by examining five women who were significant figures in nineteenth-century American culture but who have not received the critical attention allotted to such novelists as Harriet Beecher Stowe, Susan Warner, or Louisa May Alcott. Anna Cora Mowatt, Mary Baker Eddy, Sojourner Truth, Ida B. Wells, and Sarah Josepha Hale may initially appear to be marginal to the study of nineteenth-century American women's literature, which has often been preoccupied with women's fictional productions; however, their lives were culturally central and their writings document their configuration and deployment of important—and currently unfamiliar—models of womanhood. Their nonfiction writings provide an important counterpoint to the literature produced by their contemporaries. These women emerge from fields related to but not always central to nineteenth-century literary study, fields such as theater history, religious history, political oratory, and the history of periodicals. While scholars recognize Mowatt as a playwright, they generally approach Eddy only as the founder of a religion, Truth as an abolitionist and feminist speaker, Wells as a journalist, and Hale as the editor of *Godey's Lady's Book*. While accurate, these identifications are too limited and are thus reconfigured here. I consider the women not only in their most familiar roles but also embedded in rich cultural and discursive contexts.

Out in Public is less a straightforward literary history of nineteenth-century women's public embodiment than a theoretically informed exploration of particular strategies for women's public embodiment—with emphasis on discursive strategies—and of the consequences of these strategies. This study is historically grounded but propelled by particular readings and by the theory produced through those readings. What is at stake here is not a set of historical "facts" as much as the meaning we construct around and from those "facts." Historical facticity, indeed, is frequently in question; it is often the very construction of that facticity that *Out in Public* examines.

Each chapter of this book addresses a different woman, analyzing her public self-construction. Because of scholarship that has unearthed the work of women outside the private sphere, critics now have access to a great many public women whose lives and writings merit study; however, this study examines not simply women in public but women's *embodiment*. The women featured here demonstrate bodily configurations which are significant and varying, engaging and intersecting with a number of key cultural discourses, from religion to law. These women enact different forms of public embodiment and thereby shape not only their corporeal identities but also the available options for women and the larger public culture. Their engagement with discourses and activities not always associated with women indicates the need for critical reconsideration of nineteenth-century gendered behavior. Further, these women all make use of contending discourses to construct their own embodiment, and all strive for public acceptance. They are connected, too, by the fact that all are forced to address the powerful ideologies of domesticity and sentimentality in order to distinguish their own ideologies from them. Viewed together, they represent a cross-section of the century's cultural development; each of these women had an impact on her society, either through popularity, controversy, authority, notoriety, or some combination of these. While one can imagine other women whose bodily constructions would fit within a study of this sort, *Out in Public* provides a model for a particular kind of interdisciplinary study rather than an exhaustive survey or catalog of such bodies.

The critical binarisms which have shaped scholars' view of the nineteenth century have had profound implications for the study of women writers; at this transitional moment in the process of rethinking the nineteenth century, scholars must continue the projects of feminist criticism and continue to assess and complicate our understanding of nineteenth-century womanhood through the exploration of new writers and the reassessment of familiar ones. *Out in*

Public, then, takes as its primary points of departure the writings of five women; each chapter analyzes a collection of related texts, interrogating a cultural-historical field not limited by gender. The book is arranged thematically rather than chronologically, examining particular strategies for publicizing womanhood rather than positing a historical development of these strategies. The analysis of each woman attends to her written document(s) in conjunction with salient historical referents; thus, while each chapter addresses one primary text or set of texts, each brings with it the larger history that makes it intelligible.

This study begins with Anna Cora Mowatt, a popular stage actress from 1845 to 1853. Her *Autobiography of an Actress* (1853) maps out a spectrum of available forms of female embodiment. She describes traveling bodies, athletic bodies, and sick bodies which maintain respectability through their ties to middle-class domesticity but which also extend beyond the home to intervene in public spaces and discourses; in addition, her autobiography features violated and freakish bodies which threaten stable boundaries and emphasize the extent to which the body is discursively constructed. Because Mowatt's text is probably the least familiar of the works analyzed here, the models of embodiment presented there are those least entangled in critical assumption, and they work to decenter the more familiar texts of Eddy, Truth, Wells, and Hale. Thus Mowatt, a woman little known today, serves as a gateway for the other women whose work is analyzed here. Her writing, which has received very little critical attention within the recent reconsiderations of the nineteenth-century womanhood, is crucial to this study because of its intervention in multiple cultural discourses central to women's embodiment. Mowatt's autobiography marshals crucial models of female public embodiment, and her writing thus provides an introduction to the issues which the subsequent chapters investigate.

The book begins with Mowatt's autobiography, a text which simultaneously reflects upon and constructs her life on stage. This chapter analyzes the ways in which Mowatt strategically combines sentimental and sensational discourses to create a public embodiment characterized by mobility, the endurance of violence and illness, and borderline freakishness. Her autobiography describes her as a woman both respectable and sensational; she veils herself in sentimentalism but continually reveals the eroticized, dramatic figure at the heart of her self-representation. Remarkably, her strategic manipulation of discourses allows her to describe sensational behaviors while still maintaining her respectable middle-class status.

While Mowatt suggests the costs and benefits of illness for the nineteenth-century woman, Mary Baker Eddy proposes an alternative envisioning of women's corporeality, one which eliminates the dangers of illness. Eddy's assertion in *Science and Health* (1875) that the body is an illusion is her response to a host of competing medical, scientific, and sentimental discourses that sought to tie women completely to a weak, passive physicality. Eddy inserts herself into these discourses as well as into the realm of religious iconography by founding her own religion, making herself an emphatically public figure and in the process creating a new version of the body. By articulating the body as an immaterial construct, Eddy brings women's subjectivity under the jurisdiction of the mind and thus counters the male medical discourses, which saw women as the victims of their corporeality. She thus eliminates the embodied woman and dislodges gender-based rhetoric and ideology, bringing women and men to a literal equality.

Sojourner Truth, a well-known advocate and activist for women's rights and abolition, stands at the nexus of a very different set of discourses. Truth configures a public body which is heroic and powerful in her *Narrative of Sojourner Truth* (1878), her speeches, and documents written about her by others. In her most famous speech, often called "Ain't I a Woman" or "Ar'n't I a Woman," given at the Akron Woman Rights Convention in 1851, Truth defines her body as that of a tall-tale character. Truth, like Mowatt, exists on the borders of freakishness; by enacting public behaviors in direct conflict with sentimentality or domesticity—emphasizing her own physical power as key to her public presence—she risks definition in unflattering and damaging terms. Her body is literally on display as she speaks before diverse audiences, and she utilizes the rhetoric of the tall tale to shape the way in which her body is interpreted, disrupting the potential narrative of freakishness by making herself into a heroic, powerful figure. Truth and Eddy represent contrasting models of female embodiment because each woman, addressing the culture's constraints of her physical expressiveness, utilizes a very different set of public discourses to move beyond those constraints. Seen in conjunction, these two models of embodiment—one immaterial, one grounded in bodily power—demonstrate the breadth of available public enactments of the female body.

Like Truth, the antilynching journalist and activist Ida B. Wells articulates a black female embodiment that is empowered and emphatically public. In her pamphlets *Southern Horrors* (1892), *The Reason Why the Colored American Is Not in the World's Columbian Exposition* (1893), and *A Red Record* (1895), Wells identifies the public rhetoric surrounding the many lynchings of the late nineteenth century as a means by which the dominant culture constructs white male citizenship and excludes black bodies from full belonging in the nation. She intervenes in the lynch narrative, dismantling the configurations of white male, white female, and black male corporeality which the narrative mobilizes. Like Mowatt, she makes use of sensational discourses, often reprinting graphic and melodramatic white accounts of lynchings, but in so doing she capitalizes on the slippages within these accounts, publicizing the white press's inability to maintain the bodily configurations within the lynch narrative. These slippages allow Wells to reclaim the body of the black woman, excluded from the discourse surrounding lynching, and propose a model of the black woman as the fully embodied, civilized citizen.

Finally, Sarah Josepha Hale, editor of *Godey's Lady's Book*, culminates the study because her engagement with the material grounding of print culture provides a larger model of women's embodiment through text. Hale is thoroughly enmeshed in the print culture of the mid century. While each of the women analyzed here defines her body through words and printed texts, Hale takes this rhetorical self-fashioning to its logical extreme, defining her body *as* a printed text. By identifying her corporeal self with the magazine she edits, Hale shows print culture to be a site which offers not erasure of the body but a complicated public embodiment for the women who exist there. Her work has important bearings on the work of all the women studied here because she demonstrates how women can utilize the material world of the printed page and the publishing marketplace to stand for—and to travel for and speak for—their bodies. She thus helps to provide a vocabulary for all these women's discursive constructions of their own bodies. In linking the body and the word, Hale prefigures the poststructuralist body theorists, who argue for the primacy of language, and provides a template for the discursive construction of the body in the nineteenth century.

The volume is interspersed with images of women's athleticism from the 1830s through the 1900s. These images—from popular magazines, advertising posters, lithographs, college yearbooks, and comic almanacs—supplement the bodily configurations developed by Mowatt, Eddy, Truth, Wells, and Hale, offering visual representations of different models of embodiment. These images echo the tensions reflected in the writings of Mowatt and her cohort, such as the tension between the sentimental and sensational, and between the domestic and public. The women pictured range from the appropriately feminine women demonstrating exercises within *Godey's Lady's Book* to the sensational Annie Oakley, to the freakish women from comic almanacs. Slim, modestly dressed white women riding bicycles, practicing archery, or advertising clothing while on horseback—without visible musculature—contrast with scantily clad ballet girls and comically grotesque tall-tale women; these images represent a continuum of active, physically exertive women and provide a corrective to the omnipresent hoop-skirted, corseted women of nineteenth-century stereotype and fashion plates. These are unfamiliar images; indeed, critical commentary on nineteenth-century womanhood does not document the extent to which women's athleticism was present in nineteenth-century America. While recent books have examined the history of women's involvement in sports, actual images of athletic women's bodies in the nineteenth century have rarely been assembled.[30] The images collected and presented here offer new ways of conceiving of nineteenth-century female corporeality. For instance, Mowatt's discussions of her physical training as an actress seem more familiar and less strange when juxtaposed to images of women exercising or participating in sports.

One insight that my analysis reveals is that locations in the public sphere which may seem to have been entirely populated by men in the nineteenth century—trains, stagecoaches, tall tales, lynch mobs, foundational religious documents, the publishing marketplace—were also always inhabited by women. While the male figures associated with such spaces have become central to the iconography of nineteenth-century America, from Whitman's train to Crockett's tall tales, from Poe's magazine to Barnum's stage, this book provides an alternative iconography, a landscape populated by female bodies. At their most basic level, these chapters demonstrate that women in the nineteenth century cannot be understood strictly in terms of privacy or victimization; women's constructions of their corporeality demonstrate the much more complex interpenetration of categories of society and identity.

I The Most Thrilling Sensations

Anna Cora Mowatt and Sensational Womanhood

> *The actor sways the multitude even as the preacher and the orator, often more powerfully than either. He arouses their slumbering energies; elevates their minds; calls forth their loftiest aspirations; excites their purest emotions; or, if he be false to his trust, a perverted instrument, he may minister to vitiated tastes, and help to corrupt, to enervate, to debase.*
>
> —Anna Cora Mowatt, *Autobiography of an Actress; or, Eight Years on the Stage*, 1853

At the midpoint of actress and author Anna Cora Mowatt's (1819–71) *Autobiography of an Actress; or, Eight Years on the Stage* (1853), Mowatt relates a horrific incident occurring backstage in a London theater:

> [A] shriek, wild and ear-piercing, broke upon the startled crowd. A flying figure, enveloped in flames, was seen rushing up the stage. One of the young ballet girls had stood too near the footlights; her ball dress . . . had taken fire. Screaming frantically, she darted from side to side, fanning by her flight the devouring element, from which, in mad bewilderment, she thought to escape. She looked like a cloud of fire as she flew. Her white arms, tossed wildly above her head, were all of human form that was visible through the flames.[1]

This is a stunning moment in the text. Mowatt's description is chilling. The girl, dehumanized and victimized—pure physicality on exhibit—is a casualty of this dangerous profession, the theater. The girl's body is on display, and through its violent description it becomes an almost erotic object. The girl is devoured by fire, the verb "devour" suggesting that her body is sexual, edible. She does not die, but her body is utterly destroyed. She is a vividly sensational figure.

The ballet girl is a stock character in nineteenth-century literature about the theater. Representative of the sexuality and immorality thought to be synonymous with theaters, the ballet girls, with their knee-length skirts and exposed legs, seemed to signify a pure, unbridled, uncontained physicality, an image of embodiment unmediated by the moral or spiritual. Their flammable dresses did occasionally brush against the gas stage lights, and what resulted was often a horrible, painful death—an event generally reported in graphic detail in local papers and occasionally becoming the topic of titillating literature. John Elsom explains that techniques were available for preventing these accidents, but that they were rarely utilized; more prominent actresses, for instance, rarely if ever perished by fire. The ballet girls, at the lowest end of the spectrum of theatrical respectability, were the only victims. He explains, "It is hard to resist the conclusion that burning ballet girls were good for trade and that the obvious danger added an extra spice to the entertainment."[2] Tracy Davis notes that ballet girls were common characters in erotica, and Kelly Taylor argues that their death by fire seemed to deliver a sexual thrill to readers.[3] The cover of an 1849 edition of *Turner's Comic Almanac* features a very buxom ballet girl with her legs spread in a pose which is both suggestive of the classical ballet and overtly sexual. The erotic characteristics are exaggerated; as she balances on one rather large toe, she has her head thrown back to look at her viewers and smile suggestively. Her legs are visible from the knee down, and her low-cut bodice reveals her cleavage. This image required no caption at the time of its publication; readers of the magazine would have recognized this character and her erotic significance. Through her graphic description of a ballet girl's immolation, Mowatt is participating in a sensational discourse that would have been familiar to her readers.

By sacrificing this ballet girl in her text, Mowatt enacts an almost ritual purification of the theater, killing off this element "known" to be bad. Given what follows this description in the text, it seems especially true that the ballet girl's destruction is intended to purify the theater: immediately after and in conjunction with this anecdote, Mowatt makes a sustained argument against the supposition that women in the theater are morally depraved. She argues, "The woman who, on the stage, is in danger of losing the highest attribute of her womanhood—her priceless, native dower of chastity,—would be in peril of that loss in any situation of life where she was in some degree of freedom. . . . I make this assertion fearlessly, for I believe it firmly. There is nothing in the profession *necessarily* demoralizing or degrading, not even to the poor ballet girl."[4] She then tells the story of the utterly sentimental Georgina to prove this point, bringing the sensational and the sentimental into conversation.

Ballet girl, Turner's Comic Almanac*, 1849*
(Courtesy American Antiquarian Society)

Georgina is a ballet girl who dances in the theater to support her invalid parents. She is a classic sentimental figure; working every waking hour, she devotes her entire life to her parents' comfort. She is an embodiment of piety, purity, and submissiveness, and she only leaves the domestic realm because she must. Mowatt writes, "Her fragile form spoke of strength overtasked; it was more care-worn than her face. . . . She bore her deep sorrow with that lovely submission which elevates and purifies the spirit."[5] Thus it may seem that Mowatt forecloses the sensational narrative—and the ballet girl's sensational body—with the story of Georgina's sentimentality. However, though she asserts that ballet girls can be pure and gives us the example of Georgina to prove it, she still capitalizes on the image of the eroticized, violated, devoured body of the ballet girl. Rather than deny this image altogether, she sets it into circulation in her text and then provides an image to counteract it; but the counteracting image of Georgina's weary, sentimental body does not convey the rhetorical power of the flaming ballet girl. The flaming ballet girl is the image that lingers; it is the powerful image of the sensational body that Mowatt's text continually deploys and backs away from.

These two dramatic narratives demonstrate a primary technique at work in Mowatt's autobiography: the juxtaposition of sensation and sentiment, genres understood in the nineteenth century to be almost mutually exclusive, in order to contest their division.[6] She does this through her own self-representation; rather than define herself as sentimental or sensational, Mowatt does both. The two ballet girls, surrogates of Mowatt herself, represent the two types of narrative: the nameless girl in flames embodies the sensational narrative, while Georgina enacts the sentimental body. These two figures are interconnected; however, they are not equally weighted. While the sentimental gets a good deal of lip service in Mowatt's text, the text's energy hovers around the sensational images she presents. Mowatt's rhetoric changes, becomes more forceful and less sentimentally formulaic, when she describes sensational events and people. These moments are surprising and vivid. However, they are always accompanied by—framed by—the sentimental. Mowatt suggests that the two bodily models are necessarily interconnected; she presents sensational bodies, especially her own, loosely clothed in the sentimental.

Mowatt, a nineteenth-century actress who is little known today, provides a paradigm for understanding Mary Baker Eddy, Sojourner

Truth, Ida B. Wells, and Sarah Josepha Hale. Although each of these women is better known than Mowatt, she provides a gateway for understanding the others. It is Mowatt who, by framing the sensational female body in the rhetoric of the sentimental, shows the extraordinary public circulation of the embodied American woman and shows the uses of embodiment to decommission easy dichotomies. She provides the model for a revisionist understanding of a cohort of women, each of whose careers discloses the extent to which the female body of the nineteenth century was publicly enactive. Through her deployment of the concepts of travel, athleticism, illness, and transgressive physicality, Mowatt maps out a spectrum of potential bodily models. She defines public female embodiment in continual tension among constraint, empowerment, and the demands of materiality. Further, Mowatt's energy and pleasure, the obvious delight she infuses into her text through her descriptions of her travels and ordeals, give the lie to simplistic and binaric readings of nineteenth-century womanhood. Mowatt cannot be read within the critical categories of victim versus agent or public versus private; her text and her constructed sensational body disrupt these seemingly oppositional categories by existing in both simultaneously, while giving more rhetorical energy and emphasis to the one culturally constructed as least appropriate for nineteenth-century women.

Mowatt's autobiography has been widely understood as a respectable and thus sentimental document. Her contemporaries interpreted it as "charming" and educational, and they did not question its moral message or Mowatt's status as a respectable woman.[7] Critics today repeat this pattern, identifying Mowatt as the woman who made the theater respectable by her presence in it.[8] One recently asserted that Mowatt's autobiography "does not have the violent sensationalism that so typifies melodrama."[9] Thus the overwhelming critical assessment of Mowatt from her own time to today has emphasized her respectability and her status as a true woman. Certainly Mowatt's autobiography promotes this view of herself. She uses sentimental tropes throughout in discussing her life, her decisions, even her body. For instance, she frames her decision to begin a public speaking career and later an acting career in terms of the sentimental—her desire to help her husband who has suffered financial losses. As one critic of women's autobiographical writings argues, "the outspoken woman mutes the autonomy and agency inherent in her decision to engage in [public work] by sustaining the subject position of the true woman—sensitive to suffering, eager to sacrifice herself to others, willing to serve as the vessel for another's will."[10] Mowatt's muting of her autonomy is part of the sentimental agenda of her autobiography, an agenda most readers have recognized.

What is more interesting, however, and much less recognized is the extent to which Mowatt uses sensational tropes in defining herself and her life. While the body of Georgina may be easiest for critics to acknowledge and categorize, the body of the flaming ballet girl demands attention; it is this body, dramatically active in its *flight* across stage, vivid and deeply physical, vocal—"screaming frantically,"—uncontained and mobile, victimized and inscribed upon by the dangers of the theater, that most resembles, in extreme version, Mowatt's descriptions of herself. The flaming ballet girl provides the template for the sensational body Mowatt's autobiography utilizes. An examination of Mowatt's use of the sensational in describing and constructing her body in her autobiography reveals the alternative rhetorical structure Mowatt provides for women to write their own lives. The sensational body is powerful in its ability to move beyond the bounds of the home, is victimized by violence, and is always in danger of being defined as a freak. Crafting this sensational body allows Mowatt to move outside the narrative constraints of true womanhood and sentimental literature. While the sensational body as Mowatt describes it can remain respectable as it enacts extreme possibilities, the sensational body may come to resemble and thus become the body of the freak, and the freakish body cannot be respectable. Mowatt's autobiography describes a trajectory from the fully respectable sentimental body through the potentially dangerous liminal site of the sensational body to the transgressive, abject freakish body. Although the sensational body may represent a way to escape the bounds of the sentimental body, the freak's body represents the boundary of sensationalism, the point of no return.

Thus, as an author, Mowatt had to negotiate her bodily representation carefully. This task was made even more complex by her status as an actress. As an actress, Mowatt's body was on display not only literally but also metaphorically: acting and prostitution were often conflated in the public mind. As Faye Dudden explains, "the problem with the theatre for women is that their very presence makes their bodies available to men's eyes—'the eyes of the world'—eyes prepared to read them as sexual objects."[11] John Elsom puts it even more bluntly: "On reading memoirs of the period, playbills and contemporary reviews, one is struck by the sheer burden of sexual fantasy which . . . actresses were doomed to drag around."[12] Sexuality was always already part of the narration of Mowatt's life simply because she was an actress. Therefore, her autobiography was already invested in sensational narrative because of its subject matter. Mowatt had to negotiate this investment carefully. The sexual subtext of Mowatt's career was one way in which the stage was a site constitutive of sensational female embodiment; rather than deny this sensational embodiment, Mowatt capitalized on it, utilizing sexuality, violence, and other sensational elements to define a complex public life in print.

The *Autobiography* was widely read and reprinted during Mowatt's lifetime, selling more than 20,000 copies in its first year in print; however, the era of scholarship committed to an ethos of true womanhood and domesticity foreclosed full consideration of this text and texts like it.[13] Because Mowatt is strategic in her use of sentimental tropes, pairing them always with an underlying sensational message, her autobiography has been difficult to interpret through traditional models. This text challenges the conventional narrative models for describing women's lives. However, even as Mowatt challenges the rhetorical structures for defining women's lives, her construction of her own sensational body ultimately reinscribes the differences between sensation and sentiment and threatens to rehierarchize these two forms, identifying the sensational with the freakish and valuing the sentimental above the sensational.

Mowatt is not an unknown figure within nineteenth-century literary and historical studies. She is most often noted as an author; her first play, *Fashion; or, Life in New York* (1845), is regularly recognized as one of the foundational works of early American drama.[14] Mowatt herself appears in histories of American theater, particularly in texts which examine actresses.[15] Her *Autobiography* appears both as a reference work in studies of American theater and as an example of nineteenth-century women's autobiography.[16] She is not, therefore, a forgotten figure.

She is, however, a neglected one, particularly within literary criticism. Excluded from major literary studies of the nineteenth century and major feminist reclamations of nineteenth-century women's work, Mowatt surfaces as "an example of" a historical figure whose words and actions are used to substantiate theories about acting or women's autobiography. Mowatt is remembered as a playwright primarily and an actress only secondarily, and her memoir, which represents her acting as a central part of her identity, is rarely analyzed in terms of its construction of Mowatt as a bodily identity outside the realm of true womanhood.[17]

Mowatt's text is multiple, fragmented, and layered, including letters from family and friends, reviews of her performances, and poems written to and about her along with her own narrative of her experiences. While some critics may read the autobiography's polyvocality as simply poor writing—Estelle Jelinek, for instance, says the text is "not a commendable literary work" and is "burdened by excessive detail"—these shifts and changes are evidence of the cultural work Mowatt's text attempts to do.[18] Jill Ker Conway writes, "Memoirs full of abrupt transitions and shifting narrative styles are sure signs that their authors are struggling to overcome the cultural taboos that define these women as witnesses rather than actors in life's events."[19] This is an accurate assessment of Mowatt's text. Mowatt is clearly an actor, in many senses of the word, and her different narrative approaches allow her to represent herself as an active agent in her life. Mowatt's multiple narrative approaches and voices also provide a critical model for understanding the other women studied here. Polyvocal writing is one way that these women negotiated their existence on competing ends of impossible dichotomies. Mowatt's autobiography is a heteroglossic text; however, rather than simply using multiple techniques, Mowatt's heteroglossia takes the form of embedded narrative voices, with the sensational narrative embedded within an outer shell of sentimentality.

Mowatt's life provided many opportunities for her to act. Born Anna Cora Ogden, she was the child of a wealthy and socially prominent family. She spent the first years of her life in France and then returned to America. She spent her childhood and early adulthood performing plays at home for her family and friends; she took part in her first play when she was four, and as she grew older she often wrote the plays she and her siblings performed. At age fifteen she married lawyer James Mowatt; in 1841 when James lost their fortune in stocks and real estate, she began a series of public readings of popular poems and stories, becoming the first woman public reader and the first American to embark on a series of public readings (a distinct genre from public *speaking*).[20] When health prevented her from continuing her readings, she wrote moderately popular novels and then the very successful play *Fashion; or, Life in New York* (1845), which Edgar Allan Poe claimed was "superior to any American play."[21] *Fashion* initiated Mowatt's involvement with the professional theater, and, with the approval of her family, particularly her father, she began an acting career that lasted from 1845 until 1853, when she retired from the stage, partially because of her health. Her first endeavor after her retirement was to write her autobiography, an autobiography which presents Mowatt's sensational womanhood.

While Mowatt's autobiography constructs a textual, sensational body, her emphasis on the body does not preclude a discussion of her mental life: in her extensive narration of her own acting career, Mowatt emphasizes the kinds of mental as well as physical demands placed on actors and actresses. The mental demands were many. One was the extensive and rapid memorization of many plays; since actors had to be prepared to perform in a different play every night with very little rehearsal even for new plays, they had to know many plays and be able to learn new ones in a matter of days. Mowatt explains, "Often after a protracted rehearsal in the morning, and an arduous performance at night, I returned home from the theatre wearied out in mind and body; yet I dared not rest. The character to be represented on the succeeding night still required several hours of reflection and application."[22] The actors also had to face company bickering, and stars particularly had to deal with jealousy from their fellow actors.

Mowatt discusses the mental strains of theater life, but these strains are continually interconnected with the physical challenges she faced. Mowatt carefully discusses her body; this is a topic which requires much strategy. Bodily identification could both empower and disempower women. Women were empowered—legitimated, accepted—through proper bodily identification; Georgina, enacting a true womanly, exhausted body, was a moral figure. On the other hand, women whose bodies were interpreted as transgressive or improper were silenced by their bodily identification; the flaming ballet girl, representative of the theater's sexuality, could scream, but she spoke no words, and her body was destroyed in the text. Prostitutes and freaks—both of which the flaming ballet girl resembles through her erotic and distorted body—were placed in this category, and any professional woman could potentially be perceived as transgressive and described, as orators Sarah and Angelina Grimké were, as "old maids anxious to attract men, abnormal creatures lusting for the degenerate pleasures of 'amalgamation,' embittered spinsters venting their frustrated emotions by public attacks on the sacred and time-honored institutions of society or, simply and most frequently, as cranks."[23] Thus, Mowatt's use of sensational discourses to define her body was both responsive to the physical challenges she faced and potentially challenging to her respectable status.

Mowatt was not the only woman writer invested in the sensational. A tradition of sensational autobiographies by women existed in the early and mid-nineteenth century; "domestic thrillers" were a common format for women's autobiographies. These texts, virtually unknown today but very popular at the time, feature female authors who are in jail or institutions, who have lived wild lives, and who have in various ways defied their traditional roles.[24] These "thrillers" would probably have been familiar to Mowatt, who read widely, and would have provided potential models for her own writing. Fully identifying her autobiography with this sensational tradition, however, would have invalidated her own respectability; the women who wrote them, after all, were on the margins of society. On the other hand, denying the sensational altogether would have severely limited her ability to discuss her career which was, as I have noted, already sensational. Mowatt responded to this dilemma by allying her narrative with certain elements of sensation and constructing a sensational body, a body characterized by mobility and an ability to endure violence. Perhaps most importantly, the sensational body Mowatt constructs does not entirely deny the erotic stigma attached to actresses; she partakes of the physicality associated with sensation while deflecting the eroticism onto other bodies or transforming it into violence. Mowatt's descriptions of sensational womanhood progress from those characteristics that offer the least threat to the sentimental ideal—the body's mobility and athletic strength—to those characteristics which dramatically differentiate the sensational body from models of respectable womanhood, including the body's endurance of violence and its potential to enact freakishness.

THE MOBILE BODY

The sensational female body's mobility is a characteristic which bridges the worlds of the sentimental and the sensational. Although mobility is not an overtly sensational characteristic in the way that violence is, a woman's mobility in the nineteenth century did present potentially transgressive associations, removing her from home and placing her in potentially dangerous situations. Mowatt embodies sensational womanhood through her travels. The sensational body does not stay in one place; travel can enable a body to become sensational by removing it from the moorings of its traditional definitions and routines and can also force a body to take on sensational characteristics in order to survive. Ultimately, *Autobiography of an Actress* challenges and confounds simplistic critical approaches which would consign nineteenth-century women eternally to the "private sphere"; Mowatt's careful negotiations allow her to occupy the space of sentimental womanhood while spending very little time in the literal domestic space. Her narrative also describes how travel provides an alternative space where the female body can escape the frame of true womanhood and become sensational.

Because Mowatt's career was extremely successful, and because of the nineteenth-century star system which was in place at the time of Mowatt's fame, she spent a great deal of time traveling. The star system was an arrangement common in the nineteenth-century theater which involved stock casts in place at various theaters around the country; these casts were then joined by traveling stars, who assumed leading roles in various plays which the company would produce. Star actors and the companies all knew the most popular plays of the time and would rehearse together very little, if at all, before performances. As one theater historian explains, "Up until about 1860, the only actor who traveled was the star. He [*sic*] journeyed from town to town acting with one of the resident companies in each city. He chose the plays he wished to give and the resident company provided the complete supporting cast as well as all the other elements of the production."[25] Thus Mowatt's career required her to travel; since she began her career as a star, travel was crucial from the very beginning of her professional life.[26]

She reports in her autobiography that in her first year on the stage, she spent two hundred nights performing at theaters across the country. In her second year she traveled to England and Ireland to perform. She provides detailed accounts of her travels in the *Autobiography*, describing how she survived shipwrecks, frozen riverboats, and overturned stagecoaches. Mowatt strategically juxtaposes her descriptions of her mobile, sensational body with descriptions of her childhood home, her home with her husband, and her sisters' homes. Her celebration of "home" aligns her with sentimental, domestic womanhood and provides her with a backdrop of respectability which enables her to describe her adventurous travels without threatening her respectable (true) womanhood. Just as with her descriptions of the two ballet girls, Mowatt pairs the sensational body with a sentimental counternarrative.

Travel for women had been dangerous throughout early American history.[27] As Frances Smith Foster explains, "Early nineteenth-century roads, transportation, the semi-wilderness condition of rural areas, the distances between settlements, and hostile weather made travel difficult and dangerous for anyone, but especially for women."[28] Not only did women face the dangers inherent in travel itself, but they also faced threats from those traveling with them: the vehicles in which travel took place—steamboats, stagecoaches, or trains—were public conveyances and regularly put women into contact with men who could watch them, speak to them, or make advances that would not have been possible or acceptable under normal circumstances.[29] Vehicles like stagecoaches were simultaneously private and public; while confining passengers within a closed space which might simulate a home—enclosed from the outside world, keeping passengers from being on the patently public space of the street—they were still public to the extent that they housed a diverse lot of people who were forced into contact with one another. A woman traveling could not control who would be on the coach or train with her. Thus travel, especially travel without a male escort, was risky business for nineteenth-century women, but the liminal, potentially dangerous space of travel allowed women the possibility of slipping free from the coverings of true womanhood.

By the 1830s, women were facing the dangers of travel in greater and greater numbers. Historians have documented a "transportation revolution" in the early nineteenth century; advances in the technology of travel, including the proliferation of steamboats, trains, and stagecoach roads, and increasingly comfortable accommodations made travel easier for women. Women therefore took to the roads in greater numbers than ever before.[30] While traveling for women was becoming more common, extensive travel was still not commonplace; as nineteenth-century travel narratives like the journal of Sarah Kemble Knight (written in 1704–1705 but not published until 1825) and Margaret Fuller's *Summer on the Lakes* (1843) demonstrate, travel was still unusual enough to provide an occasion for book writing. In fact, many nineteenth-century moral reformers felt that the dangers inherent in travel increased as traveling became more common, because more women were at the mercy of men on the roadways and rivers.[31]

Aside from the dangers and uncertainties accompanying it, traveling, of course, was a potentially transgressive act for a white, middle-class woman to undertake because it took her away from home. It is clear from novels, conduct manuals, and other literature marketed to women that the cultural *expectation* was that women be domestic beings whose lives centered around the home—first their father's, then their husband's. As Schriber explains, "Limited by perceived divine design to the contingencies of her biological being, defined by her ability to bear children, and assigned to the domestic sphere, the 'frail vessel' that was Woman was expected to remain close to her own front door."[32] Women's travel challenged that model of womanhood because "if the home is decommissioned, then the doctrine of separate spheres loses its topographical anchorage."[33] This challenge to the constraints of compulsory domesticity was freeing for many women travelers. As Cohen explains, "The possibility of movement, both rapid and far from home, untied people from obligations, restrictions and expectations. For some, it led to experimentation with different styles of behaviour."[34] Schriber describes white women's accounts of their travels as demonstrating "a sense of freedom and adventure"; in other words, the act of traveling allowed these women to experience their bodies differently.[35] They were the bodies of free people and adventurers—they were sensational.

Women's travel in the 1840s and 1850s existed on a borderline; increasingly accepted, yet still somewhat dangerous and therefore adventurous, travel—and the narratives that arose from it—could either help a woman solidify middle-class true womanly identity or allow a woman a forum for a more sensational identity. Mowatt's description of her travels traverse both sides of this border, but as with much of her autobiography, her sensational descriptions overpower or overwhelm the sentimental. She describes the dangers inherent in the travel she has experienced, and at the same time she reveals a sense of freedom and power in her traveling and discusses the excitement and joy traveling could incite. Her travels allow her to experience other cultures and to experience different kinds of behavior; they allow her to describe her body using different terms—terms consistent with heroism, adventure, and endurance, and her descriptions document the pleasures of this body. Mowatt's representations of her own traveling help to define the sensational womanhood central to her narrative: the sensational body is mobile, and that mobility allows for more overt expression and experience of other aspects of the sensational body.

Mowatt's traveling stories range from the shipwreck her family endured in its voyage from France to America—a wreck in which one of the Ogden sons died—to her comfortable travels through Europe with her older sister, when Mowatt was suffering from a bout of tuberculosis. Most of her early travels enabled her to define herself once again as a proper woman but also as a literary or cultured one; for instance, when she traveled to Europe with her sister, they engaged in genteel sightseeing and attended elite social gatherings, but in addition to enjoying these events, Mowatt wrote essays about them which were published in such magazines as *Ladies Companion*.

Late in her narrative, Mowatt describes a journey which demonstrates the ways in which travel allows the female body to become sensational—heroic, adventurous, and enduring. This one voyage captures many of the significant elements from the many travel narratives in Mowatt's autobiography. Mowatt devotes an entire chapter to her attempt to get from St. Louis to Philadelphia; as she explains, "I had promised to return to Philadelphia by Christmas. My father and all the members of our home circle within reach were to assemble beneath the roof of our brother-in-law, Mr. M—e," so that the children could enact *Gulzara, or the Persian Slave*."[36] Mowatt had agreed to be the stage manager, and she was determined to be at this family reunion; however, for the weeks preceding Christmas, she was engaged for performances which took her from Providence to St. Louis. Getting home was clearly important to her; she reports that she turned down the request for a complimentary benefit offered by the mayor of St. Louis so that she would not be late arriving in Philadelphia. The focus of this narrative of her travels, therefore, is her determination to arrive at the home where her family is awaiting her. She writes, "What would the expectant ones in Philadelphia do without their stage manager and costumer?"[37] This story is framed within a sentimental narrative structure which identifies Mowatt as a respectable woman: she is striving to reach her home and family.

The story itself, however, takes a different inflection than the framing narrative. Once Mowatt has established a structure of respectability on which to build her narrative, she then turns to a very different kind of discourse, that of adventure and heroism. Her story becomes an adventurous travel narrative in which Mowatt faces seemingly insurmountable obstacles to her desire to return home but continually overcomes these obstacles. Her body shifts from the sentimental body of the woman longing to be at home to the sensational body of the adventurer. The trouble begins when Mowatt, who is traveling without a male escort, informs her readers that "the season was the most severely cold that had been known for many years."[38] She boards a steamboat in St. Louis and travels comfortably for two days, but on the third the river freezes. On the fourth day the ice is so solid that the boat can no longer plow through it.

Mowatt questions the pilot, who estimates that they will be frozen in for three weeks or possibly a month. When she asks about the possibility of hiring a stage from the small town on the shoreline, the pilot responds, "'Stages! I don't believe they've got any thing better than a cart in the whole place. This is Indiana State. . . . But stages would be no good for the likes of you. You couldn't travel over these backwoods roads in stages—and at this time of year! Why, no woman could do it, unless it was an Indian squaw. . . . You don't know what's to be gone through; never think of trusting yourself in them stages, if you know when you are well off.'"[39] When Mowatt asks if anyone will leave the boat, the pilot replies that some of the men will: "'If they have to walk for it, they'll get on.'" Mowatt writes, "Then I'll *'get on'* too, I thought to myself."[40] In this significant passage, Mowatt establishes the terms of the rest of this particular story. The pilot is the voice of convention, marking out the dangers attendant on this kind of winter, backwoods travel and denying to any white woman the ability to endure the trip. His warnings prepare the reader for the adventure that is to come and inform the reader, without Mowatt herself having to do so, of the risks Mowatt faces in order to achieve her goal. Her insistence that she will "get on" just as if she were a man aligns her with a kind of frontier heroism and aligns her body with a masculine heroic body; undaunted by natural forces, Mowatt presents herself as physically powerful and courageous enough to keep moving in the face of obstacles.[41]

At one point in her description of this trip, Mowatt describes the men with whom she is traveling having to leave the stagecoach and physically lift it out of a ditch. She explains, "Major R—— made a good joke on the occasion. He had been in the habit of writing articles on the theatre—its uses, abuses, &c.; and turning to me, he remarked, 'I have been trying for years past to *elevate the stage*; and I have just succeeded, *with you upon it*!'"[42] In this way, Mowatt makes explicit a latent and significant pun at work throughout her discussion of her travels: the stage(coach) and the stage. A well-known actress, Mowatt demands that a stage(coach) be found for her; she refers to the difficult time she had to spend on the stage(coach); and she defies the riverboat pilot who says, "stages would be no good for the likes of you": she deliberately allows for slippage between the two meanings of the term. The significance of this slippage lies in its implications. Mowatt is on the stage—a performative space—when she is on the stage(coach). The performative space of the stage is a site which helps to construct the sensational body, and this space is not limited to the literal stage on which theatrical performances take place. Her travels provide a public venue which becomes a performative space and thus a site constitutive of the sensational female body; in this way Mowatt's work prefigures a kind of poststructuralist notion of the body itself as a site created by performance.

Her trip proves to be as difficult and dangerous as the riverboat pilot predicted. At many points Mowatt's narrative reads like a catalog of the difficulties inherent in nineteenth-century travel, from her description of riding in a farmer's ox cart, to her complaints about the quality of food and lodging available during the journey. They suffer through bitter cold, which Mowatt describes as "so intense that my breath froze upon the handkerchief which I held to my lips, and rendered it perfectly stiff"; this image of Mowatt holding a hardened handkerchief to her face suggests the changes travel can enact on the female body.[43] The true woman holds a soft, delicate handkerchief, representative of her true womanly body, but Mowatt's true womanly accessory has been altered by the circumstances of her travel; it has become hard and solid, suggestive of possible formulations of the physically powerful, endurant sensational body. Mowatt's description of the stagecoach travel, too, maps out the way that travel precludes the sentimentally defined female body:

> The roads were so rough that they seemed to be composed of huge logs placed a couple of feet apart; and our mode of progression was a sudden rising up of the stage, pitching every one backward; then a sudden ducking down of the wheels, throwing the passengers forwards, after having sent them up until many a head made the acquaintance of the roof of the vehicle. Then the coach would sway from side to side, until it appeared impossible that it should not upset, unless it had the faculty of maintaining its equilibrium belonging to an acrobat. Then it would drop down into a deep rut and be fastened there for some minutes. After much fierce struggling of the horses it jolted out again, tossing about every thing and every body inside as though we had been a set of jackstraws in a child's hand.[44]

"Every *body*" in the stagecoach, which is itself "an acrobat," is thrown about with abandon, like children's toys. The suggestion of acrobatics in conjunction with the imagery of bodies rising and falling chaotically in the coach does much to configure traveling bodies as sensational. Mowatt's language is descriptive: noting the "sudden ducking down," the "pitching," "swaying," and "dropping" of the coach and the "fierce struggling" of the horses, she represents the journey as a vividly—and perhaps painfully—physical experience. The road offers no accommodations for delicacy, fear, or weakness in the passengers. This trip not only allows Mowatt to enact a sensational body but forces her to.

Mowatt also notes the beauty of the situation; her journey is not only an adventure for her to relate but an opportunity for her to experience more of the world. She writes of their barely successful attempt to cross the frozen White River by foot: "The stars looked down from their azure thrones through a tissue of silver mist that spread itself over the heavens. Not a sound broke the deep silence, and we all stood gazing with hushed voices. I would have taken our perilous journey—thus far—merely to have beheld that awe-inspiring, winter picture."[45] Later she writes of a train ride approaching Philadelphia: "The sun was setting gloriously as we started, and rendered those Alleghany [*sic*] Mountains, in their glittering snow garments, almost as grandly beautiful as in their lovely spring or gorgeous autumn vesture."[46] Here Mowatt demonstrates the exhilaration at the ability to travel that critics such as Cohen and Schriber identify in many nineteenth-century women's travel narratives. Mowatt conveys to her readers the pleasures of traveling as well as the difficulties. Pleasure is an embodied experience that offers the body a kind of agency; pleasure registers in the body and heightens its energy. For Mowatt, the sense of pleasure is present even when she describes ordeals; the energy of adventure is linked to pleasure—to bodily engagement and vivacity—even when the specific moment being described may not be overtly pleasant. This bodily engagement—linked, in Mowatt's case, to the sensational rather than the sentimentally configured body—allows Mowatt another means to disrupt the script of domesticated womanhood. The difficulties of travel enable her to experience these noteworthy and beautiful events that are forbidden to the true woman at home. This is one benefit of the sensational female body.

At the end of this story, Mowatt returns to her emphasis on home and family and returns as well to the sentimental tone which enables the narrative. Home becomes an almost otherworldly edifice in Mowatt's description, as spiritualized as the true women housed there: "At last the hospitable mansion, which had shone in my mind like a far-off beacon through the long journey, and had been seen in every dream that visited my rare slumbers, was in sight!"[47] It bears mentioning that Mowatt prefaces this encomium to home with a description of how she arrived at her Grail-like destination: she walked a mile through the snow wearing wool socks over her shoes for traction; sensation again gleams through the sentiment.

THE ATHLETIC BODY

Another sensational characteristic which, like mobility, bridges the traditional womanly models of behavior and sensational models is athleticism. Mowatt defines her sensational womanhood and the sensational body through her descriptions of exercise and the unglamorous physical *work* involved in becoming a public performer. The sensational body is powerful and assertive, and it becomes this through exercise. In distinction to the submissive true womanly body, the sensational female body must be athletic in order to be able to endure the kinds of demands placed on it, from dangerous travel to violent attacks. Mowatt describes the work she does to transform herself from a weak body to a physically forceful woman.

When she first decides to begin public readings, she starts vocal exercises, "strengthening my voice by reading aloud for a couple of hours each day in the open air."[48] The image of Mowatt standing outside for hours at a time, attempting to make herself heard above the wind, birds, or other outdoor noises, is an image of the sensational female body in training. This image contradicts key tenets of true womanhood and establishes Mowatt as an active figure set on improving her body. The voice was a crucial component of nineteenth-century public performance, both oratorical and theatrical; in the early and mid-nineteenth century, actresses were appreciated as much for their elocution as for their physical appearance.[49] Performers carefully cultivated certain popular vocal qualities: "Antebellum orators [and actors] strove for a cadenced flow of sound, punctuated occasionally by broad gestures and building majestically toward a climactic conclusion"; the sound and rhythm of a voice were often more important than the content of the speech.[50] Mowatt's readers would have been familiar with these expectations of the performer; Mowatt is careful to explain to them the efforts that go into securing that type of performance quality: it is a demanding athletic endeavor involving disciplined exercise. This exercise also has symbolic importance: Mowatt is defining herself as a woman with a voice, a literally and figuratively powerful voice. She trains herself outdoors so that she learns to make her voice heard in venues other than the enclosed domestic space.

Later, when she decides to become an actress, she undertakes a more rigorous exercise method. Again, she wants to show her readers the physical efforts that go into producing a high-quality performance. She explains her routine: "I had three weeks only for preparation. Incessant study, training,—discipline of a kind which the actor-student alone can appreciate,—were indispensable to perfect success. I took fencing lessons, to gain firmness of position and freedom of limb. I used dumb bells, to overcome the constitutional weakness of my arms and chest. I exercised my voice during four hours every day, to increase its power. I wore a voluminous train for as many hours daily, to learn the graceful management of queenly or classic robes."[51] Mowatt becomes an athlete in this passage. She represents herself not as a true woman, whose body is encased in the rhetoric of purity and submission, but as a self-possessed agent, disciplined and willful. She is an athlete, using available techniques to prepare her for her career. She identifies the weak parts of her body—her arms and chest, her range of movement—and devises a routine to address these issues.[52] Her body thus becomes a material construct which she can improve just as true women like *The Wide, Wide World*'s Ellen Montgomery strive to improve their spiritual and moral beings. Her body is pliable, susceptible to her own agency. Significantly, the whole passage is written in active voice, with an emphasis on the *I* who chooses to undertake these actions: "*I* took fencing lessons. . . . *I* used dumb bells"; she is an actor, not a passive object acted upon, and she acts to make herself physically strong and vigorous. Mowatt uses this representation of her own strength as a way to counteract typical representations of the sentimental woman's body.[53] Here as elsewhere, however, Mowatt does not abandon the sentimental body; the ideals of domestic womanhood affect her training, as she includes in her exercise regimen the wearing of heavy women's clothing. She suggests here, in fact, that perhaps a certain degree of athleticism is required of the proper woman, to be able to carry herself gracefully. Mowatt does not eradicate the sentimental/sensational dichotomy but instead alters the use of the terms, showing them not to be dichotomous but interlocking or embedded within one another.

Continuing her emphasis on her body as susceptible to and worthy of improvement, Mowatt represents acting and the exercise that accompanied it as a way to escape illnesses. She writes of her first year in the theater, "Strange to say, my health, instead of failing entirely, as was predicted, visibly improved. The deleterious effects of late hours were counteracted by constant exercise, and animating, exhilarating pursuit, and the all-potent *nepenthe* of inner peace. I gained new vigor and elasticity. With the additional burden came the added strength whereby it could be borne."[54] She describes here the pleasures associated with the athletic body: strength is animating, exhilarating, and brings vigor. Importantly, this strength is a necessary component of many of the other demands placed on the sensational body: without the physical strength she developed through her exercise regimen, Mowatt would not have been strong enough to persist through the difficulties that confronted her in her travels or to endure the kinds of violence she describes throughout her autobiography.

In describing the benefits of exercise and an athletic female body, Mowatt is responding to and aligning herself with a midcentury trend in women's health that demanded exertion rather than inaction. Catharine Beecher, one of the main proponents of this system, which was later called "Real Womanhood" by critic Frances Cogan,[55] recommended domestic activity as a means of exercise, explaining that when a young lady makes her bed and cleans her room, "almost every muscle in the body will be called into vigorous activity; and this kind of exercise should be continued two or three hours." She also suggested that in schools "such accommodations should be secured, that, at all seasons, and in all weathers, the teacher can send out a portion of her school, every half hour, for sports."[56] Sarah Hale, too, promoted the benefits of domestic activity to provide women with exercise and health. In an 1859 edition of *Godey's Lady's Book,* she writes, "If young ladies would sweep the house, dust the furniture, work in the garden, spin, weave, and do many other things pertaining to good housewifery, they would lose nothing in true dignity, while they would greatly promote health."[57] It is possible to read such advice as an attempt to make virtue of necessity; since women were typically responsible for the many arduous duties that kept a middle-class household respectably outfitted and cleaned, they would often be performing the kinds of tasks Hale and Beecher describe simply out of duty rather than out of an attempt to strengthen their bodies. However, Beecher, Hale, and health reformers like them were presenting an alternative view of housekeeping; rather than being a thankless duty, housekeeping could help a woman to improve both her strength and her health. In addition, the emphasis on strength and health meant that the focus of housework was not on its benefits to others but on its benefits and transformative potential for the woman herself.

Other health reformers demanded that women leave the home and take their exercise in the fresh air, as Mowatt did. In an 1847 magazine editorial, Hale argued, "females should be accustomed to exercise in the open air; playing abroad when children, and walking and riding in maturer years should be considered a duty as well as recreation."[58] Physician J. Stainback Wilson wrote in an 1859 edition of *Godey's Lady's Book* that fresh air was a necessity for women's good health. In a description that could have been inspired by Mowatt's own description of her exercises, Wilson argues that "*Singing and reading* aloud are excellent methods of cultivating the voice organs, and of expanding the chest, provided the lungs are supplied with an abundance of pure air."[59] Despite the differences that might have emerged from their specific strategies, what Beecher and Hale, along with health reformers like Abba Gould Woolson and Harriot Hunt, had in common was their argument that women's inactivity was a cause of disease, and their promotion of healthful activity for women. They envisioned and promoted a female body that was active, vigorous, and capable. Very often the attempt to construct this body involved the outdoors and fresh air; thus, health reformers promoted an embodiment characterized by a certain degree of freedom, movement, and independence.

The demand for health reform for women arose in many popular nineteenth-century magazines for women, including *Godey's Lady's Book* and *Harper's*. For instance, in 1847, *Godey's Lady's Book* began a monthly feature called "Health and Beauty" which focused on women's health and fashion reform. The column was initially written by Hale but was later taken over by several different medical doctors. Hale discussed the importance of exercise for women, offering her readers columns on such things as walking, exercises for flexibility, and a series of illustrations of exercises with a scepter. In the February 1849 column, Hale explained, "It would . . . be a prejudicial error to suppose that females should be subjected only to passive exercises. On the contrary, the sedentary occupations of women impose upon them, more than on men, the necessity of engaging in active exercises."[60] Exercise was so important that the *Lady's Book* provided illustrations and detailed descriptions of such activities as walking.

The stories published in magazines like the *Lady's Book* also often presented healthy, active heroines rather than heroines who would fit neatly within a model of true womanhood. According to the stories and columns in such magazines, young women around the middle of the nineteenth century were expected to be able to engage in such activities as walking several miles, bowling, and horseback riding. Women were also featured in such magazines fishing, hunting, shooting bows and arrows, rowing, and even jumping rope. In fact, in an 1847 story by Grace Greenwood called "My First Hunting and Fishing," the heroine compares catching her first fish to falling in love.[61] Magazines like the *Lady's Book* were read widely by nineteenth-century women, and they promoted an ideal of womanly health which contradicted the popular sentimental invalidism propounded in many novels.[62] Some doctors, too, promoted health reform; unlike the well-known S. Weir Mitchell with his rest cure, physicians like William Blaikie and Dio Lewis wrote advice manuals promoting women's athleticism—including calisthenics and lifting dumbbells—in the 1860s and 1870s.[63]

The popular emphasis on exercise and health, however, did not negate the demands on women to embody a certain kind of feminine beauty and grace. In her detailed description of how to walk, Hale emphasizes the importance of feminine grace, deriding women who do not enact this grace: "Nothing can be more ridiculous than a little woman who takes innumerable minute steps with great rapidity to get on with greater speed, except it be a tall woman who throws out long legs as though she would dispute the road with the horses."[64] Although a woman may be promoting her own health, she becomes a spectacle if she does not do so gracefully. In a later column, Hale repeats this point, arguing that the exercises her magazine promotes aim to improve women's deportment. This deportment, she argues, is a crucial element not only of a woman's physical appearance but of her class status; she argues, "A suitable deportment is the proof of good education and habitual sense of order; it heightens the value of intellectual attainments, as well as constitutes a finish to beauty."[65] In other words, exercise is not only valuable because it promotes health; it also allows a woman to enact more fully her middle-class standing. Thus the health reforms promoted by such women as Hale and Beecher touched on women's beauty and public performance of their class status. Although the athletic female body was promoted in mainstream publications, it was still not a fully normalized concept; it remained challenging enough that in order to be appropriate,

Women were involved in a wide variety of athletic activities throughout the nineteenth century. Individual athletic activities—including calisthenics, equestrianism, and archery—were promoted in such popular women's magazines as Harper's Weekly *and* Godey's Lady's Book. *Women's team sports were somewhat more controversial, but by the end of the century many women's colleges had baseball and basketball teams, and much of the stigma was gone.*

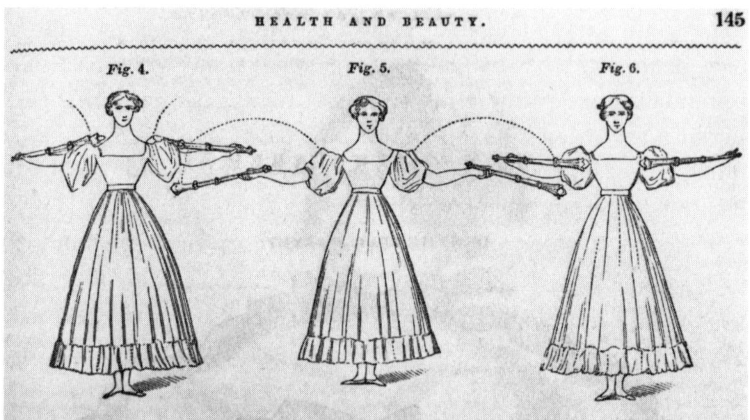

"Health and Beauty," Godey's Lady's Book, *1849*

"Hints on Equestrianism," Godey's Lady's Book, *1849*

Cover of Harper's Weekly, *1878*

The Resolutes, Vassar College's baseball team, ca. 1876 (Courtesy Vassar College Library, Special Collections)

"Practice," Scribner's Magazine*, 1898*

female athleticism had to be overtly connected to such sentimental markers as beauty and class standing. Health reformers such as Hale and Beecher framed their own discussions of women's health as somewhat resistant to dominant discourses, and Mowatt's exercises were unusual enough to warrant documentation in her autobiography. Women's athleticism, therefore, was on a spectrum of acceptable female embodiment, but it remained somewhat liminal —and thus sensational—throughout the nineteenth century. Mowatt's autobiography demonstrates the importance of this athletic movement. The movement provided a vocabulary and a set of techniques for women to understand their bodies differently than true womanly models allowed.

While health reform gave Mowatt a vocabulary, the theater gave Mowatt a *site* around which to structure her body differently from typical true womanly constructions. As Claudia Johnson explains, "The stage was Anna Cora's miracle: in the theater that fragile and sickly frame took on strength and endurance; the old nervous disorders gave way to a kind of grace."[66] Mowatt identifies exercise and athleticism, not the theater itself, as the cause of her improved health; she prefigures this athleticism earlier in her narrative, when she explains how in the early days of their marriage, her husband taught her to shoot a gun and to hunt in order to help build up her strength and prevent her from becoming ill. However, the stage was the location which gave her health meaning. Mowatt also associates her overcoming of illness and gaining of physical strength with her increased acceptance as an actress: she says of her second year in the theater, "I had gained mental and physical strength; improved in health; become inured to the thousand *desagremens*, the discomforts, the endless vexations, and unavoidable fatigues of the profession; and I had watched the frown of disapproval slowly melting away from faces that I loved, and the benignest of smiles dawning in its place."[67] While the exercise associated with the theater helped her gain health, her health helped her to increase her status in the theater.

The athletic female body was, like the mobile body, a sensational form of embodiment. Allowing women like Mowatt to develop strength, power, and endurance—qualities not associated with true womanly embodiment—the nineteenth-century discourse of health and exercise presented an alternative model of respectable corporeality on which Mowatt capitalized. The athletic body, however, was not entirely "safe"; indeed, as we will see, too much athleticism—

excessive strength, agility, or physical size—could move a woman's body out of the interpretive frame of middle-class respectability that Hale and Beecher outlined and into the realm of the freakish. In her descriptions of her athleticism, Mowatt emphasized the approval of those she loved, in this way carefully differentiating herself from the ballet girl, whose flight across stage and violent flailing could be read as a parody of the exercises Hale and Beecher recommended.

THE SICK BODY

Illness performs an important rhetorical and cultural role, designating Mowatt as a domesticated body. She utilizes her descriptions of her illnesses to act as a sentimental mask which conceals her sensational body. Her depictions of her illnesses counterbalance her depictions of the kinds of violence her body suffers; as a later section discusses, Mowatt's descriptions of violence align her most closely with the body of the freak. At the same time that her illnesses define her as sentimental, however, her descriptions of her ill body prefigure the almost freakishly violated female body her narrative also deploys. Medical anthropologists note that illnesses or other bodily problems can cause the body to assume a more vivid and central presence.[68] By explaining to her readers the illnesses she has suffered and the time she has spent as an invalid, Mowatt inscribes her body within the realm of the sentimental but also suggests the sensational body which can endure acts of violence.

Throughout her life Mowatt alternated between periods of great strength and periods of devastating illness; as a child she was sickly and weak, and into her adulthood she had recurrent tuberculosis and was occasionally incapable of working for months at a time. Mowatt's descriptions establish her illnesses as a recurrent theme in her autobiography. Women's illness in the nineteenth century had a range of symbolic meanings as well as literal referents; it is therefore important to analyze Mowatt's representations of her diseased body as a way of clothing the sensational body with sentimental imagery.

Illness in the nineteenth century often had positive connotations; a sick woman, specifically if she were white and middle-class, could be interpreted as more spiritualized and better fitting the model of true womanhood than a healthy woman, as seen in such literary figures as Warner's Alice, Stowe's Eva, and Alcott's Beth.[69] Therefore Mowatt's representation of her own illness could fortify her description of herself as a respectable woman. Her representation of her illnesses offers a different view of her physical body than many of

Riflery was not a common sport for women, although it became a popular image in the late nineteenth century. The adventurous and somewhat gothic scene of a respectable woman defending herself with a gun ("Delicia"), along with the images of Annie Oakley, show sensational and yet still respectable female bodies. Annie Oakley, who might well be compared to Mowatt in her celebrity, was not only an excellent shot but also, according to Scott Crawford ("Oakley, Annie," 815), "the first female athlete to achieve worldwide superstar status." The image of Madam Yucca highlights women's strength, but in such a way that the strong woman becomes a freak.

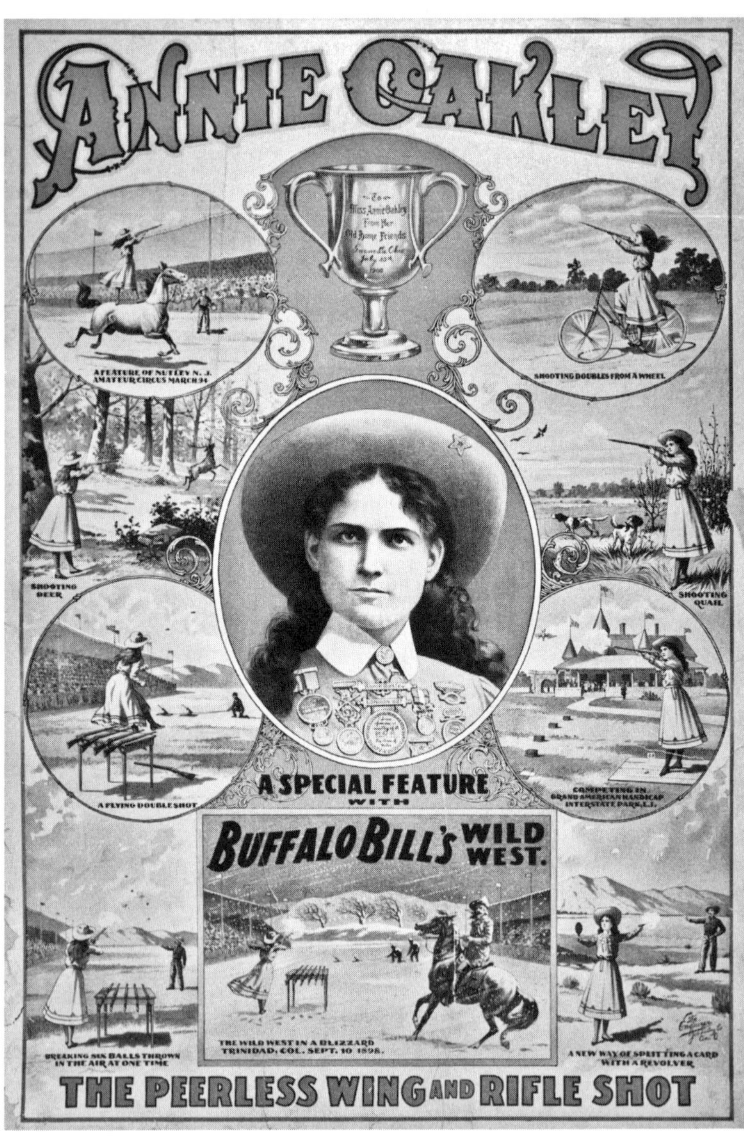

"Annie Oakley, the Peerless Wing and Rifle Shot," ca. 1900 (Courtesy Circus World Museum, Baraboo, Wisconsin)

Image accompanying story "Delicia," Frank Leslie's Popular Monthly, *1883*

"Madam Yucca, the Champion American Female Hercules," 1892 (Courtesy Circus World Museum, with permission from Ringling Bros. and Barnum and Bailey Circus/ The Greatest Show on Earth)

her other representations of herself. Rather than being an agent—in control of her travels, adventuring—she is a victim of her diseases: "I was attacked with fever and hemorrhages of the lungs. For several months I was considered by my physician, Dr. C—g, in a state which rendered recovery very improbable."[70] She is here acted upon rather than acting, and her body as she represents it in sickness moves away from sensational womanhood.

Mowatt describes her attempts to overcome her illnesses as a domesticating activity. Like many nineteenth-century sufferers, she relied on mesmerism as part of her medical treatment. A friend wrote of Mowatt's behavior when in a mesmeric trance, "It was remarked by all that your voice was much more soft and childlike than usual. Indeed, your whole manner would be changed, as if you had become once more as a little child."[71] Similarly, the friend wrote, "while somnambulic you were far more manageable and reliable in observing all necessary precautions," and her powers of sympathy were greatly enhanced, allowing her to feel compassion "toward the brute creation, especially the more despised, such as insects, spiders, snakes, &c."[72] In other words, Mowatt's friend describes her mesmerized behavior as more fully aligned with expectations for a domesticated woman: she was passive, childlike, willing to follow instructions ("manageable"), and more fully compassionate.[73]

Again, at the end of her text, Mowatt describes her diseased body: "I had lost all power of locomotion, and was thoroughly helpless."[74] This image of Mowatt, lying in her childhood bedroom at her father's house, unable to care for herself, is a portrayal of Mowatt as a conventional true woman. Through illness Mowatt offers her readers a sentimentalized image of herself, an image of a woman victimized and dependent on others. Discussions of her illness are interspersed throughout the text, presenting a fairly conventional sentimental female body. Illness inscribes Mowatt within the model of the appropriately domesticated female body. However, nestled within her representations of her illnesses are suggestions of illness as violence enacted on the body. The illnesses Mowatt describes are violence at its least visible, least erotic, and most true womanly, acting on Mowatt internally and causing her to behave in a more passive manner; these illnesses, however, provide a bridge to the more overt violence she also discusses in her autobiography. Mowatt's internalized violence of illness and externalized violence are juxtaposed.

Mowatt's use of illness as a sentimental mask for her sensational body is perhaps most evident in her discussions of stage fright. Mowatt describes stage fright in terms which characterize it as a devastating disease, noting its debilitating effect on the body of the actor experiencing it and the actor's powerlessness to stop it. In discussing her own experiences with it, she describes it as a force which completely separates her from her body: "I could not force my quivering lips into a smile; when I spoke, I could not hear the sound of my own voice; floating mists were dancing before my eyes. . . . What was the matter with my feet? . . . And my limbs—why could not the most resolute effort prevent their tremulous motion? My very hair, as it touched my shoulders, seemed to have a clammy, Medusa-like coil."[75] Significantly, stage fright undermines Mowatt's control over her body, which has been a dominant characteristic of her sensational womanhood throughout her autobiography. Not only is her body completely unfamiliar, but she cannot move it, cannot act, cannot speak. Her imagery suggests that she is not only estranged from her body but that she is simultaneously trapped within it; her body becomes a kind of enclosure which she cannot escape. Like a gothic heroine trapped in a haunted house, Mowatt's consciousness is trapped within her unresponsive body.

According to Mowatt, stage fright is her body's rejection of its position of visibility and publicity. Elaine Scarry discusses embodiment as "the *consent* to be perceived and . . . to be described," but the suggestion of consent implies the potential to refuse this consent.[76] What Mowatt demonstrates is what happens to the body that refuses this perception and description: the body becomes monstrous and begins turning on itself. Stage fright is a physical manifestation of her culture's proscriptions against women in the theater. Her body is acting out her culture's demands that she not be embodied; her body refuses to be on display and thus becomes monstrous. Her reference to Medusa suggests a connection to a tradition of monstrous, assertive, and unruly women. At once Medusa and a victim of Medusa's stare, Mowatt is turned to stone, into a pure object on display like the statues which traveled the country in the mid century.[77] The audience's observation freezes her, so the audience becomes a Medusa and thus also monstrous and powerful.[78]

Angelina Grimké's expression of her feelings before a particular speech reveals the significant public demand women faced not to perform publicly: "I never was so near fainting under the tremendous pressure of feeling. My heart almost died within me."[79] The world of women's public performance was an unfriendly one. Mowatt, too, felt the "tremendous pressure of feeling" Angelina

Grimké described; before her first reading, as she attempts to practice in the Boston Masonic Temple where she will appear, she explains, "I made effort after effort to recite, but my voice was choked —I could scarcely utter a word."[80] The public pressure on women not to speak is here enacted at the level of Mowatt's body; her fear makes her literally unable to vocalize. Her body temporarily internalizes her culture's proscription against women's public orations. Stage fright is a manifestation of violence enacted at the mental level on female bodies in public. By internalizing her culture's proscriptions against women's public speaking and public performance, Mowatt victimizes herself, inflicting violence on her body from within by visualizing her body as entrapping and monstrous. Like illness, which makes women more properly submissive and immobile, stage fright acts at the level of the body to force women to follow cultural mandates for their behavior.[81]

Even as she victimized her own body, however, Mowatt was utilizing stage fright for a rhetorical purpose in her autobiography. Showing her body suffering and immobilized allows her to align herself with the submissiveness and docility characteristic of true womanhood, muting the effect of her acting and legitimating her body as properly sentimental and domesticated. At the same time, the stage fright communicates another message. Her descriptions of stage fright are graphic; at one point she represents it in another actor as a kind of fit, saying, "I have seen them seized with a sudden tremor—their utterance choked—their eyes rolling around, or fixed on vacancy—their limbs shaking, and every faculty paralyzed."[82] These graphic descriptions evoke the kinds of sensational violence which are crucial to her descriptions of life in the theater. Thus even as Mowatt describes herself as a victim, she is in fact an actor, creating a nuanced textual self-portrait which balances the sentimental and the sensational.

Mowatt's most internalized, most sentimental depiction of violence comes through her descriptions of her illnesses. In this aspect of Mowatt's autobiography, the parallel to the two ballet girls is clearest. While Mowatt offers her readers a version of herself as a sickly, true womanly body aligned with the "overtasked" body of Georgina, the image which is most vivid and compelling stands in distinct contrast: the survivor of external, penetrative violence through collisions, cuts, and other theatrical accidents. Mowatt represents her body as one which can endure dangers and injury, making it into a kind of heroic body.[83] She also describes it as unruly, with permeable boundaries between "inside" and "outside."

THE FREAKISH BODY

Mowatt's depiction of sensational womanhood is most easily identifiable in her descriptions of violence inflicted on the female body. Violence is a continual subtext in the autobiography; brief but vivid segments of Mowatt's narrative are concerned with external, invasive, and visible acts of violence constantly threatening those who work in theaters. Mowatt's depictions of the violence inflicted on her body and on the bodies of fellow performers most fully configure the sensational body as distinct from sentimental bodies. Through her images of violence, she alludes to sexuality without addressing it directly. Her most erotic descriptions of violence are deflected onto the surrogate bodies of other characters. Mowatt's descriptions of violence present a female body with permeable boundaries, a body on the borders of the freakish. Her descriptions of violence are as close as Mowatt will come to comparing her body to the body of the freak.

The combination and balance of the sentimental and the sensational which Mowatt enacts throughout her narrative is crucial for the sensational woman, because freakishness is a point of no return. This is the boundary that marks the outer reaches of sensational womanhood as Mowatt defines it. All the characteristics of the sensational female body can become freakish if taken too far; travel, for instance, can become an inappropriate rootlessness, athleticism can become excessive strength, and illness can become disfiguring disease. The violence Mowatt describes can also blur into freakishness. Freakishness is a marketable commodity which offers its own benefits, but the drawbacks are severe. Mowatt makes use of the benefits in her writing, but she is especially careful to avoid the drawbacks.

Nineteenth-century freaks were always on display, and their display defined them as forever other, forever abject. Freaks existed at the borders of humanity; their status was perpetually liminal. They were looked at in amazement and disgust, their bodies seen as objects, their human identity erased. As Elizabeth Grosz argues, the freak "is not an object of *simple* admiration or pity, but is a being who is considered simultaneously and compulsively fascinating and repulsive, enticing and sickening."[84] Once someone was defined as a freak, the person could never again remove that classification. As

Andrea Dennett explains, "Once their freakishness was discovered and labeled, it was inescapable. They would always be branded the legless wonder, the bearded lady, or the What Is It?"[85] The objectification associated with freakishness is evident in Dennett's quote; a freak is an object, "*the* legless wonder," rather than a person.

Mowatt could not risk allowing her own self-representation to slip into the freakish because then she would lose absolutely her middle-class status and her respectability. This concern is especially valid considering the fact that the bodies of freaks were created discursively. Freaks were created by the flyers and banners advertising them, the barkers who attempted to draw customers in, and the brief and often false biographies freaks sold to supplement their incomes. For instance, a young girl with excess hair covering her body could become, through the power of the rhetoric surrounding her, "Krao, the Ape Girl." As Rosemarie Garland Thomson explains, "An interlocking set of stylized, highly embellished narratives fashioned unusual bodies into freaks."[86] Freaks are a clear example of how language can actually create particular bodies. Even though Mowatt's body was not disfigured, an autobiographical narrative which described her in freakish terms could make her into a freak.

Freak shows were extremely popular throughout most of the nineteenth century; the heyday of freak show popularity stretched from the 1840s well into the early decades of the twentieth century, although individual freaks were on display at taverns and festivals in America from the earliest days of the colonies. Thomson describes freak shows as a widespread cultural phenomenon in the nineteenth century: "Especially in Victorian America, the exhibition of freaks exploded into a public ritual that bonded a sundering polity together in the collective act of looking. . . . From the Jacksonian to the Progressive eras, Americans flocked to freak shows."[87] Not only were freak shows wildly popular, but the freaks themselves were often well paid for their performances; although they worked grueling schedules, freaks often made more money than actors.[88]

The popularity of freak shows is evident in the career of P. T. Barnum, a public figure whose three widely studied autobiographies might have provided a model for Mowatt's own autobiography. Barnum's American Museum opened in New York City 1841 and was very successful until it burned down in 1863. It featured a congeries of exhibits ranging from the scientific to the spectacular; freak shows were a crucial element of the museum's popularity. Barnum's career often involved freaks, from his earliest exhibit, Joice Heth, an African American woman who claimed to have been George Washington's mammy, to his most famous, General Tom Thumb.

Barnum's museum featured every kind of real and imagined human oddity he could display, from conjoined twins like Chang and Eng, to hirsute people like Jo-Jo the Dogfaced Boy, to fraudulent exhibits like the 1843 Fejee Mermaid. Barnum's freak shows often set the standard for other shows like them. Audiences would come to the museum in order to see the freaks and believe them, and they would often return because Barnum's publicity had led them to believe the freak a fake, and they would want to try to see through the act.[89] In fact, although Barnum did make use of hoaxes like the Fejee Mermaid and Joice Heth herself, and although he certainly made use of embellishing narratives to increase the marketability of his freaks, Barnum did display many people with real, often striking, physical abnormalities. Barnum became wealthy through his display of freaks; his career both flourished and profited from the public demand for freak shows which persisted throughout the century. As one Barnum biographer explains, "The spectacular and the bizarre captured the imaginations of . . . nineteenth-century Americans."[90]

However, for all the popularity and financial reward that accrued around freak shows, being a freak had many serious drawbacks. Freaks were often exploited and taken advantage of: many so-called Aztecs, Pinheads, and What Is Its? in nineteenth-century freak shows were actually mentally disabled people dressed in wild costumes and forced to perform.[91] Thus freakishness often implied loss of control over one's self and one's destiny. These were issues Mowatt had to address in crafting narrative bodies which in their sensationalism often bordered on the freakish.

Mowatt's depictions of the violence inflicted on her body and the bodies of other actors demonstrate her negotiation of this border. For instance, during a performance in Buffalo in her second year of acting, Mowatt collided with another actor backstage and then found that she could hardly speak her lines. She explains, "A blood vessel had been ruptured, and I was nearly suffocated with the sanguineous stream than poured from my lips."[92] This is a surprising image of the body opened, the inner material rushing out. While the sentimental body is contained, presenting clear boundaries between internal and external, the sensational body Mowatt describes has permeable boundaries. The image of Mowatt choking as blood pours from her mouth is almost as startling as the image of the flaming ballet girl; both these events disrupt the body's boundaries.

Similarly, during a performance in London, Mowatt fell and cut her head; although she was bleeding, she continued with her performance, with "crimson drops that still trickled amongst (my) hair," and performed the next night "in spite of an unbecoming wound, that could not be concealed by the most ingenious arrangement of curls."[93] This description again demonstrates the sensational body's permeable boundaries. Not only can what is supposed to be inside emerge, as with the blood pouring from her mouth, but what is outside can penetrate the sensational body.[94] This description is significant, pointing to a key characteristic of the sensational body—its permeability—which makes the sensational body simultaneously vulnerable and threatening. While the sensational body can exceed its boundaries and thus threaten stable categorization and bodily identity, this body is also susceptible to violence because of its public presence and its mobility. These two characteristics—the threatening and the vulnerable—seem inseparable in nineteenth-century depictions.[95]

The true woman's body is never penetrated since violence emerges from within in illness; this fully enclosed body is not vulnerable to external attack, and it is not threatening because its boundaries are clearly defined. The sensational body, however, may spill beyond the conventional bodily boundaries. The permeability of bodily boundaries is a visible manifestation of the sensational body's challenge to simplistic—dualistic—categories such as "in" and "out" or, indeed, "self" and "other." Mowatt's body resists description within the bifurcated rhetoric of nineteenth-century womanhood, and by exceeding its boundaries, her body challenges the validity of the categories themselves. Just as her polyvocality demonstrates her textual resistance to impossible dichotomies, so, too, does her description of her bodily permeability. Grosz notes that the permeability of the body often has larger meanings: the body's "orifices and surfaces can represent the sites of cultural marginality, places of social entry and exit, regions of confrontation or compromise."[96] In this way, too, the sensational body is linked to the body of the freak. As Leslie Fiedler says of freaks, "Only the true Freak challenges the conventional boundaries between male and female, sexed and sexless, animal and human, large and small, self and other, and consequently between reality and illusion, experience and fantasy, fact and myth."[97] Thus the transgression of bodily boundaries in Mowatt's text may run the risk of transforming the sensational bodies she describes into freakish bodies. While Mowatt employs a light tone, the tone does not negate the violence she has described or the dangerous borders she traverses; the "ingenious arrangement of curls" cannot hide the gashed forehead; drops of blood still linger in her hair; the freakish body peers out from the wounded female body on display.

Mowatt accentuates the danger associated with the theater when she explains "there are instances of men's continuing in a performance upon the stage after they have had a finger or thumb accidentally shot off. The putting out of an eye, or the breaking of a limb, might possibly be considered disabling; but minor calamities would be looked upon as too trivial to frustrate the enjoyment of a despotic audience."[98] To counteract this somewhat graphic description of potentially dismembered bodies and thus potentially freakish ones, Mowatt provides her readers with a template for understanding the acts of violence she describes. She describes herself in rhetoric aligned not with the freak but with a *heroic* body, able to endure violent attacks in order to fulfill her duty to please the audience. Her tone is light and confident; she and the other actors scorn "minor calamities," acts of violence which she attempts to construct in terms of an adventure rather than a tragedy. Yet even as she attempts to differentiate her body and those of the other actors from the horrifically wounded body of the ballet girl in flames, that body is always present, hovering at the borders of her narrative. Each actor onstage is a potential freak.

These descriptions of violence are the most erotic moments in Mowatt's autobiography. In sensational literature of the nineteenth century, sex and violence were interconnected.[99] As Tracy Davis notes, the nineteenth-century theater was infused with sexual references available to those viewers who were familiar with the erotica surrounding the theater. Flowing hair, for instance, appears in nineteenth-century pornography as a particularly erotic image; perhaps the readers of Mowatt's autobiography would take special notice of the drops of blood trickling through her curls. The freakish body, too, contains elements of the erotic. Fiedler refers to "the sense of the pornographic implicit in all Freak shows."[100] Andrea Dennett explains this sexual element more fully: "Sex, in fact, was a powerful component of the performative text of the freak show; spectators imagined sexual intercourse between incongruous partners. . . . Sometimes patrons were allowed to touch the limbs of fat ladies or pull on the whiskers of bearded ladies. . . . A wondrously titillating dialectic emerged, in which performers were alluring as well as repulsive."[101] By offering recurrent images of violence and potential freakishness, Mowatt offers a tangentially erotic sensational body to her readers. However, the ultimate and most extreme image of violence against a body remains the flaming ballet girl. This image, the most erotic and the most violent—perhaps the most erotic *because* the most violent—capitalizes on the already sexualized figure of the ballet girl; through her brutally physical suffering, the literal consumption of her body, and her transformation into a kind of freak, the ballet girl becomes a scapegoat for the erotic baggage accompanying sensational womanhood.

Mowatt's text reveals that for all the freedom accorded to the sensational female body, that body's vulnerability to violent penetration could permanently identify it as sensational. The violent acts Mowatt describes in her autobiography inscribe the sensational on her body, like a tattoo. When her body is wounded and penetrated, it is written on in a language of scars and blood. These inscriptions make her identifiable and ultimately not a threat. As she notes, her wound "could not be concealed by the most ingenious arrangement of curls." The significance of this trope in terms of Mowatt's autobiography is that the inscriptions on her body limit sensational womanhood as a rhetorical strategy by marking the sensational body and thus differentiating it indelibly from the sentimental, domesticated body.

These bodily inscriptions not only indelibly mark Mowatt's body as sensational but could align her with a particular kind of freak popular in American freak shows as early as the 1830s: the tattooed man (and then, after the Civil War, the tattooed woman as well). These men were initially sailors, and the biographies for sale at the shows and called out by barkers and announcers described the men's forcible tattooing at the hands of savage island natives. As one critic notes, these stories "portrayed the tattooed freak as someone without will, as one who had been unable to prevent his body—his most personal space—from becoming indelibly marked. Tattooing thus stands as an immediately visible reminder of a failure of will. Ironically, tattooing was actually one of the few ways that an able-bodied person could voluntarily become a freak, yet the conventional exhibition of such people invariably made the decision appear involuntary."[102] When tattooed women appeared in freak shows, their biographies even more clearly articulated the powerlessness and also eroticism invested in tattooed bodies; their forcible tattooing at the hands of native people was characterized as "tattoo rape."[103] While

Mowatt is not actually tattooed, the scars on her body forever identify her as a sensational woman. These permanent inscriptions also blur the line separating the sensational body from the freak. Freakishness is a physical categorization that functions as a permanent inscription of liminality and abjection, and the inscription "freak" is one which Mowatt avoids carefully.

Because Mowatt was writing a text which purported to define and describe her own existence, she treaded this border very carefully. The most freakish bodies in Mowatt's text are those of others—the men disfigured by losing fingers or limbs backstage, and the flaming ballet girl who becomes a freakish spectacle during her immolation and then continues to be a freak afterward, because of her deeply scarred body. Rather than identify her body with the permanent objectification inherent in the freak's body, Mowatt amplifies her own separation from the freakish body on several occasions, as, for instance, when she describes two mentally ill women on the frozen steamboat during her trip to Philadelphia. She writes, "Among the passengers there were two young lunatic sisters. One of them talked, shrieked, or sang from morning until night, and almost infected those around her with frenzy. . . . Remain on board with these sounds in our ears—this mournful sight daily before our eyes for weeks! The prospect seemed unendurable."[104] Her description of her desire to separate herself from this woman signifies her desire to separate her body from the freakish female body in her narrative. Being around these women is "unendurable," and she suggests that their insanity may be contagious to those who spend too much time with them. It may be especially important for Mowatt to demonstrate her separation from the lunatic sisters because the description she gives of the vocal sister—who "talked, shrieked, or sang from morning until night" resembles the description one might give of an actress, constantly vocal, constantly performing. By removing her textual body from the freakish body, Mowatt clarifies her own separation from the world of the freak.

Mowatt is careful to describe herself in terms which balance the sentimental and the sensational. She reprints reviews of her performances which describe her in traditionally sentimental terms. For instance, she reprints a poem about her by Frances Sargent Osgood; the poem refers to Mowatt as "a being young and fair / In purest white arrayed" and describes her "timid grace."[105] Similarly, a review Mowatt reprints from the *Sun* describes her as "the most ladylike of genteel comedians."[106] These reports highlight Mowatt's moral purity and her traditional beauty. These womanly characteristics take on increased importance when viewed in light of the fact that the kinds of women displayed in freak shows were often those who did not embody the accepted forms of true womanly beauty, including white skin, dainty hands and feet, and slender figures. For instance, throughout the 1850s, a dark-skinned, hirsute Mexican Indian woman named Julia Pastrana was exhibited in America and Europe as "The Ugliest Woman in the World" and "The Girl with the Ape Face." Her body was so completely objectified that after she died in 1860, her body was embalmed and continued to be displayed in freak shows for several decades. Similarly, Sartje Baartman, an African woman with enlarged buttocks, was presented as "The Hottentot Venus" and toured Europe in the early years of the nineteenth century; for an extra payment, select visitors could examine not only her buttocks but her genitals, which were touted as similarly enlarged. The careers of these women demonstrate the ways women's bodies could be read and presented if they deviated from the true womanly norm. As Thomson argues, "Exhibition framed these women's bodies as grotesque icons of deviant womanhood that confirmed the West's version of femininity."[107]

Mowatt's autobiography, then, defines a trajectory of female embodiment, moving from the most respectable sentimental body, through progressively more transgressive bodily configurations of mobility and travel, to the violated female body, which is always in danger of becoming read as the body of a freak. Her body and the other bodies represented in her autobiography explore the boundary dividing the sensational body from the freak. The alternative formulations of womanhood and of the female body articulated in Mowatt's writings provide a tool for complicating the separate spheres model of gendered behavior. Mowatt's writings demonstrate the fluidity of embodiment possible for a woman who skillfully negotiated competing discourses of womanhood. This trajectory of sensational female embodiment dislodges simplistic dichotomies that define nineteenth-century womanhood.

Although the discourses of the sensational allow Mowatt to escape from the confines of the sentimental and to define her body in terms often more expansive and empowered than those provided in sentimental discourses, the sensational body had its cost. At the end of her autobiography, Mowatt describes herself—widowed, invalid, her retirement from her acting career imminent—lying in bed in her father's house, her body passive. She seems to have paid for her sensational embodiment with her independence, her health, and her livelihood, and to have been forcibly reintegrated into a sentimental narrative mode. However, even as she describes her sentimental surroundings, Mowatt acknowledges the pleasures of the sensational body, writing, "I have received intense delight from the personation of some characters. The power of swaying the emotions of a crowd is one of the most thrilling sensations that I ever experienced."[108] She not only emphasizes the command acting gave her over others' emotions but the "thrill" that this gave her. As is the case so often in her autobiography, Mowatt provides a loose sentimental covering but allows the sensational body to gleam through.

2 Woman Goes Forth to Battle with Goliath

Mary Baker Eddy, Medical Science, and Sentimental Invalidism

With the wreck of her frail body, Beth's soul grew strong; and, though she said little, those about her felt that she was ready, saw that the first pilgrim called was likewise the fittest.
—Louisa May Alcott, *Little Women*, 1868

Throughout her early life, Mary Baker Eddy suffered from recurrent illnesses. In an 1837 letter, her sister wrote of her, "In addition to her former diseases her stomach became most shockingly cankered, and an ulcer collected on her lungs, causing the most severe distress you can conceive of; the physician with the family thought her cure impossible, but she has a good deal recovered for two weeks past, and this morning was carried out to ride."[1] Similarly, her sister-in-law wrote of her in 1852, "After so long and inconceivable suffering, though still living, and perhaps doomed to yet longer and greater affliction by an all-wise but inscrutable Providence . . . there is scarcely a ray of hope left of her recovery. Her strength gradually fails, and all the power of life seems yielding to the force of disease."[2]

Eddy suffered from all manner of illnesses, from indigestion and nervousness to spinal disorders and chronic "fits" resembling epileptic seizures.[3] The "severe distress" and "inconceivable suffering" her relatives describe seem to have been familiar features of her early life. Debilitating illnesses like the ones Eddy experienced were not uncommon for nineteenth-century women; Anna Cora Mowatt suffered from recurrent tuberculosis in addition to many other ailments. Her *Autobiography* details numerous occasions when Mowatt had to fight sickness or was incapacitated by it. She wrote her *Autobiography* while recovering from an extended illness.

Eddy, too, wrote a book due to the influences of her illnesses. *Science and Health* (1875), the founding document of the religion Christian Science was the text that emerged from Eddy's extended struggle with, and eventual victory over, her illnesses. While Mowatt used sickness rhetorically as a way to augment her status within middle-class models of womanly respectability and domesticity, Eddy responded differently to her illnesses. In *Science and Health*, Eddy describes a means for overcoming illness by erasing the material substance of the body. Combining and combating key nineteenth-century discourses, specifically medical science and sentimental invalidism, *Science and Health* presents illness as the catalyst for a new envisioning of the female body—a body that, because of its immateriality, decommissioned many of the dichotomies that limited women's roles and options.

Through its immateriality, Eddy's constructed version of the female body may appear more aligned with respectable models than Mowatt's, but this appearance is deceptive. Mowatt articulated the female body in such a way as to verify its materiality, emphasizing bodily difficulties and the appearance of the body. Although Mowatt often used illnesses to identify herself as a respectable woman, her descriptions of her illnesses were also part of her larger technique of highlighting the sensationalism of her life. For instance, Mowatt offers many anecdotes of actors fighting illnesses in order to perform, and often dying in the process. She describes her own experience of acting while "making a desperate struggle with indisposition," which she later characterizes as bronchitis and malaria. She explains, "As the curtain fell upon each act of Ingomar, I found it more and more difficult to proceed; but I knew from experience that a strongly concentrated will could master the infirmities of an exhausted *physique*. I invoked to my aid all the mental energy that could obey the summons, and ended the play successfully."[4] This anecdote, presented late in her autobiography, characterizes Mowatt's illnesses as a villainous force which she overcomes by force of will; by couching this story amid stories of actors literally dying in order to perform, Mowatt identifies herself not as a sentimental invalid but as a sensational body, embattled and bravely attempting to overcome obstacles to her duty. She thus utilizes illness both to sentimentalize and to sensationalize her body, and in both cases her descriptions of her illnesses serve to emphasize her body's materiality.

Eddy avoided the materiality of the body altogether; in this way she appears to be more aligned with nineteenth-century directives that women be moral, spiritual beings. However, Eddy is ultimately positing a more radical conception of the female body than one which is simply aligned with traditional expectations. Eddy is not merely avoiding the female body's materiality but erasing that materiality entirely; she articulates the dangers that accompany materiality, arguing in a reading of Genesis that "the serpent, material sense, will bite the heel of the woman" and that "corporeal sense is the serpent" toward which woman is biblically determined to have eternal enmity. Humans' belief in the material reality of their bodies is the original sin, according to Eddy, because all humans are ultimately Mind, which she characterizes as "infinite, not bounded by corporeality, not dependent upon the ear and eye for sound or sight nor upon muscles and bones for locomotion."[5] By dematerializing the body, Eddy constructs a version of womanhood which is freed from gendered expectations and is able to align with mind as well as spirit. Eddy addresses the problematics of women's public embodiment by eliminating the body.

Science and Health was one of a number of reformist medical and spiritual texts which began appearing in the mid-nineteenth century: Joel Shew's *The Hydropathic Family Physician* (1855) introduced hydropathy or water cures, David Campbell's *The Graham Journal of Health and Longevity* (1837–39) promoted Grahamist reforms based on vegetarian diets, and Catharine Beecher's *Letters to the People on Health and Happiness* (1856) encouraged women to improve their health by becoming active and abandoning restrictive clothing. *Science and Health,* part of the New Thought movement in the early Progressive era, advanced a new kind of reform in which existing movements and ideas were combined and synthesized. Although Eddy and *Science and Health* shared common features with other New Thought practitioners and practices, few of the other movements achieved the broad congeries of political, medical, and spiritual issues evident in *Science and Health,* and none have endured as Christian Science has. By addressing the problematic constructions of the female body posited in both medical science and in sentimental novels, *Science and Health* brought to light many of the tensions surrounding women's health and physicality in the nineteenth century and in so doing offered alternative constructions of womanhood.

Although not an overtly feminist text, *Science and Health* established a new ideology of womanhood through its negotiations of discourses that affected women's lives. Historians have pointed out that Eddy did not classify herself as a feminist and that she tried, ineffectually, to "prevent Christian Science from become a 'women's religion,' exhorting her female followers to bring their husbands."[6]

The philosophy she developed, however, and the organization she built around it clearly offered women a much greater role and a much more positive self-image than many other ideologies and institutions available at the time. *Science and Health* promotes not only women's health but also women's independence of the nineteenth century's various male-centered health institutions. Most importantly for this study, *Science and Health* constructs a dematerialized female body which allows women to be public figures on par with men by erasing any perceived physical differences between the sexes.

Science and Health combats a number of key nineteenth-century discourses which define and shape women's bodies. Throughout the document, Eddy refers to Mind, explaining, "Mind is the grand creator, and there can be no power except that which is derived from Mind."[7] By appropriating the mind, the masculine side of the nineteenth-century mind/body split, Eddy gained access to a range of traditional male-dominated discourses, including medicine and science. Rather than simply aligning herself with these sources of authority, Eddy asserted the importance of her womanhood in helping her to see the fallibility of the authorities. She took control of the mind from the subject-position of a woman and utilized this juxtaposition to construct a public, authoritative, spiritually attuned female identity.[8] Her writing of her own body and of bodies in general as noncorporeal entities makes public spaces equally available for men or women. Eddy thus disrupts gender norms. Just as Mowatt's descriptions of her bodily pleasure disrupt dichotomies that shape bodily existence, so does Eddy's dematerialization of the body. Pleasure operates to heighten corporeal energy in Mowatt's text, while Eddy's dematerializing rhetoric sends the body's energies elsewhere; but both strategies destabilize the private and public spheres and heighten women's agency.

As a religious text, *Science and Health* has been controversial from the nineteenth century through the twentieth, drawing passionate praise from adherents and attacks from contemporaries and from later scholars and historians.[9] Theologians and religious scholars have studied Christian Science, along with Seventh-Day Adventism and Mormonism, as an American religion. In addition, historians have examined Eddy as part of the New Thought movement in the late nineteenth century[10] and Christian Science as one of a variety of nineteenth-century alternative medicines,[11] most of which Eddy tried at one point or another.[12]

Eddy has received little attention from feminist scholars, who might be interested in a woman whose impact on her age was profound and whom Mark Twain, even as he criticized her, called "the most interesting woman that ever lived, and the most extraordinary."[13] Recent biographer Gillian Gill suggests that this neglect results from the fact that Eddy's life does not follow typical patterns for successful nineteenth-century womanhood. This is assuredly the case; Eddy, married three times, mother of a child who was taken from her, ultimately quite wealthy, and sometimes characterized in her later life as tyrannical, is a fascinating but not always a sympathetic figure. The conflicts surrounding Christian Science today, too, serve to make Eddy less a safely distant historical figure than one with current resonances that may make her an uncomfortable object of study. The Christian Science Church's control over the vast majority of material about Eddy's life and work also complicates possible research about her.[14]

In addition, *Science and Health* as a text has received little scholarly attention, even recently, in the fields of literary and cultural studies. Its tone draws heavily on biblical language and imagery—each chapter, for instance, being prefaced by verses from the Bible—although the biblical imagery is set side-by-side with medical, scientific, quasi-scientific, and sentimental discourses. Perhaps this overt juxtaposition of discourses, joined in a seemingly inchoate mélange, is one of the reasons the book has not received broader scholarly attention in literary studies. *Science and Health*, however, is engaging precisely because of the congeries of discourses at work in it. In order to understand *Science and Health* and its power in its cultural moment, we must examine this text, which "meant more to Mary Baker Eddy than any other thing or person she encountered during her lifetime,"[15] as a rewriting of the discourses of medicine, science, and sentimental invalidism as a means to rewrite the body. Eddy's use of a polyvocal approach—often pitting one discursive model against another, and aligning herself with them strategically—allowed her to undercut dominant discourses, particularly those governing women's bodies and women's access to public authority.

These discourses are, not surprisingly, autobiographically based. Because Mary Baker Eddy remains a relatively unfamiliar figure, a brief description of her life is in order. Eddy, born July 16, 1821 in Bow, New Hampshire, spent her early life with a strict disciplinarian father and a compassionate, loving mother.[16] Eddy's childhood and much of her adulthood were characterized by recurrent bouts of serious, debilitating illnesses. In attempting to overcome these illnesses, Eddy experimented with various alternative medicines; however, none of these alternative medicines was able to provide her with a lasting cure. Thus, Eddy defined the key moment in her life as the moment when she was able to cure herself in a way that was not only comprehensive but enduring.

This key moment—the Great Discovery—occurred in February 1866. On February 1, Eddy fell on ice and apparently suffered severe internal injuries. Her doctor, a homeopathic physician, was unable to help her, and those around her doubted whether she would live, much less walk, again. Eddy describes her condition as something "that neither medicine nor surgery could reach," and the local newspaper described her as "severely injured."[17] After reading her Bible, however, Eddy came to the realization, as one biographer puts it, "that her life was in God—that God was the only Life, the only I AM. At that moment she was healed."[18] Connecting this event both to the Christian creation story and to the mythical origins of Newtonian science, Eddy described her recovery as "the falling apple that led me to the discovery how to be well myself, and how to make others so."[19] She identified this moment as the birth of Christian Science. After withdrawing from society "to ponder my mission,"[20] Eddy began in 1870 to teach the first of many classes in Christian Science healing, and from 1872 until 1875, Eddy worked on her book, *Science and Health*, which was published in 1875 at her expense.

THE NEW IDEOLOGY OF WOMANHOOD

Significantly, the ways in which Eddy chose to negotiate the complicated issues surrounding women's bodily well-being offered a comprehensive and empowering view of women. *Science and Health* stands as an alternative both to the sentimental valorization and political limitations of the invalid woman and to the medical discourse which objectified women as essentially faulty, uterus-driven bodies. Eddy proposed the valorization of health and the valorization of women as spiritual, not biological, beings. By rewriting the discourses of sentimental invalidism and medicine, she brought herself forward as a major reformer and a major public voice, one who is remembered today much more widely than other health reformers like Harriot K. Hunt or religious reformers like Ann Lee. Eddy's revisioning of the female body in *Science and Health* both secured her fame and presented a complex and effective rewriting of dominant nineteenth-century discourses.

It is important to note that the female body Eddy and other New Thought reformers addressed was primarily white and middle-class. Indeed, the New Thought movement emerged in a national climate in which race, class, and gender questions were of heightened concern for the nation.[21] Many Social Darwinist physicians and commentators argued that exaggerated sex-role differences were a sign of white civilization and that middle-class white women's education and social advancement would lead to "race suicide" by blurring the differences between men and women and, further, by blurring the differences between middle-class white women and women of other races and classes.[22] Although Eddy does not address race or class directly in *Science and Health*, middle-class white women were her primary audience, and many of the discourses she dismantles in the text exerted their influence primarily over the lives and bodies of this particular population.

The philosophical foundation of Christian Science as expressed in *Science and Health*—the characteristic which distinguishes it from other New Thought systems or alternative medicines—is its insistence that the material world, including and especially the human body, does not exist. This is both a medical and a religious axiom for Christian Scientists. Eddy explains repeatedly throughout *Science and Health* that "matter and its claims of sin, sickness, and death are contrary to God, and cannot emanate from Him. There is no *material* truth."[23] Matter, the material world with its host of troubles, is not the true world, according to Eddy. While some critics, especially twentieth-century critics, have seen this belief as laughable,[24] it is a belief which is central to *Science and Health*'s revisioning of nineteenth-century womanhood.

One doctor summarized a key component of the nineteenth century's contradictory views of female bodies, writing, "Woman, with her exalted spiritualism, is more forcibly under the control of matter; her sensations are more vivid and acute, her sympathies more irresistible. She is less under the influence of the brain than the uterine system, the plexi of abdominal nerves, and irritation of the spinal cord."[25] While women were viewed as inherently spiritual creatures, they were simultaneously perceived to be under the control of their bodies. In a culture that viewed woman as "more spiritual than men, yet less intellectual, closer to the divine, yet prisoner of her most animal characteristics,"[26] *Science and Health* eliminated the category of the physical body altogether, freeing women from the "prison" of corporeal life. To the nineteenth-century assertion that woman was "peculiarly the creature of her internal organs, of tidal forces she could not consciously control,"[27] *Science and Health* said that the body and its effects were illusions.

Virtually every page in *Science and Health* features a repudiation of the material world. Eddy explains, "Christian Science reveals incontrovertibly that Mind is All-in-all, that the only realities are the divine Mind and idea." She argues that because God is incorporeal Mind, and because humans are created in the image of God, then we, too, are manifestations of Mind, not matter. She asserts that "there is no life, truth, intelligence, nor substance in matter. All is infinite Mind and its infinite manifestation, for God is All-in-all."[28] In other words, matter is nothing but an illusion created by our mortal minds; all that is, is God, and immaterial. Eddy's message of corporeal transcendence emphasized life and health for women rather than sickness and death. This central premise of *Science and Health* allowed Eddy to practice healing and undercut key aspects of nineteenth-century ideology of womanhood, particularly white, middle-class womanhood.

Eddy's invalidation of embodiment can be read as an assertion in favor of stereotypes of woman's Victorian spiritual superiority. The spiritualized body Eddy represents, however, is identified not with stereotypes of femininity but with insubstantiality as *Mind*. She conflates God, Spirit, Love, and Mind, creating a specified erasure of the body which empowers women on similar terms with men. She then exalts this concept of Mind: "Mind is the grand creator, and there can be no power except that which is derived from Mind. If Mind was first chronologically, is first potentially, and must be first eternally, then give to Mind the glory, honor, dominion, and power everlastingly due its holy name."[29] Not compassion, love, or stereotypically feminine qualities but *Mind* is central in Eddy's religious universe. Her repetition of the word Mind throughout *Science and Health* and her strong emphasis on the importance of Mind within Christian Science has significant implications for women, suggesting Eddy's refusal to capitulate to traditional configurations of womanhood.

Eddy's revision of women's embodiment dismantles dominant concepts of gendered physicality, and in so doing, it destabilizes the cultural dichotomies predicated on clear gender difference. Discourses of power, such as those surrounding gender difference in the nineteenth century, require a material substance to validate them. As Scarry asserts, for contested ideologies, "the sheer material factualness of the human body will be borrowed to lend that cultural construct the aura of 'realness' and 'certainty.'" She continues, "The body tends to be brought forward in its most extreme and absolute form only on behalf of a cultural artifact or a symbolic fragment or made thing (a sentence) that is without any other basis in material reality: that is, it is only brought forward when there is a crisis of substantiation."[30] In other words, immaterial ideas may gain materiality through strategic appropriation and use of the human body. Debates over men's and women's rights and roles in the late nineteenth century focused on biological, physiological differences between male and female bodies: female bodies were figured as weak and passive while male bodies were figured as rational and passionate. These biological differences were utilized as "analogical verification" to validate particular economic, political, and societal power structures.[31] By challenging the gendered body—indeed, the materiality of any body—Eddy undercuts the validity of the private and public sphere as well as the ideal of female weakness and passivity.

Eddy felt that she was called to write *Science and Health* and to receive the healing message because she was a woman; she wrote, "To one 'born of the flesh' . . . divine Science must be a discovery. Woman must give it birth . . . and none but the 'poor in spirit' could first state the Principle, could know yet more of the nothingness of matter and the allness of Spirit, could utilize Truth, and absolutely reduce the demonstration of being, in Science, to the apprehension of the age."[32] Similarly, in *Science and Health* she describes how "[i]n this revolutionary period, like the shepherd-boy with his sling, woman goes forth to battle with Goliath," Goliath representing the materialistic forces of medicine and science.[33] Eddy seems to suggest that, because she is a woman and therefore privy to a range of contradictory cultural imperatives relating to the body and the spirit, she is qualified to receive this message. Significantly, she configures her role within these contradictory cultural mandates as a battle—an emphatically public event—in which she as a woman is uniquely qualified, even called, to fight. This martial imagery further destabilizes dominant concepts of gendered physicality and gendered location, and figures the female invalid body as a warrior in this conflict.

Eddy continually experienced the conflict between the cultural imperatives for womanhood and her own strengths and needs. For nine years after the death of her first husband in 1844, Eddy was impoverished, ill, and utterly dependent on her relatives as she moved from home to home. She lost custody of her young son and experienced an unsuccessful second marriage. Her three marriages, strained mothering, and later financial success (she charged high fees to train others to enact Christian Science healings) made Eddy a controversial figure in her own time. These were factors that were controversial only, or primarily, because Eddy was a woman. As Gill explains, "Shallow, egotistic, incapable of love; painted, bedizened, affected; hysteric, paranoiac, mad; ambitious, mercenary, tyrannical; man-eater, drug addict, mesmerist; illiterate, illogical, uncultured, plagiarist: these are only a few of the accusations that were aimed at Mary Baker Eddy during her life and afterward."[34] The same intensity of denunciation has not been directed toward male religious leaders like the Mormons' Joseph Smith or other broadly successful public figures like P. T. Barnum. Although she was and is a somewhat anomalous figure as a female religious leader, Eddy argued that her existence as a woman was what allowed her to receive her divine calling.

Eddy argued that a woman, existing within a material culture that overemphasized the importance of her body—emphasizing the clothes she wore, her bodily deportment, and the influence her sexual organs exerted on her mental facilities—could best see through the assumptions and recognize that the body was a hurtful illusion. Denying the body, *Science and Health* made it possible to deny the whole array of assumptions about womanhood, womanly instinct, womanly weakness, and women's "place," and thus bring men and women to a level of relative equality. Famed physician S. Weir Mitchell, whose well-known rest treatment is condemned in Charlotte Perkins Gilman's "The Yellow Wallpaper," argued that for young women, "over-use, or even a very steady use, of the brain is dangerous to health and to every probability of future womanly usefulness"; to this Eddy could respond, "The elements and functions of the physical body and of the physical world will change as mortal mind changes its beliefs. What is now considered the best condition for organic and functional health in the human body may no longer be found indispensable to health."[35] She directly and indirectly combated medical and sentimental configurations of female embodiment.

Eddy undercuts the authority of these discourses not only by claiming for herself their cultural role as definer of corporeality but also by *removing* that corporeality. As did the larger discourse of gendered roles and spheres, nineteenth-century medical discourses utilized "analogical verification,"[36] defining the female body in terms of its materiality and using that materiality to assert the importance of professional medicine. Eddy interrupts this verification process by removing the substantive body, the material ground for her culture's defining of gender. When Eddy argues that "matter cannot be sick, and Mind is immortal,"[37] she is denying the facts on which medicine establishes its control over women's bodies.

Eddy also intervenes in religious discourses to redefine female embodiment. *Science and Health* formulates a God who encompasses male and female qualities. Eddy states that "Love, the divine Principle, is the Father and Mother of the universe, including man" and describes God as "the Father and Mother of all." She states, "In divine Science, we have not as much authority for considering God masculine, as we have for considering Him feminine."[38] By presenting God through masculine and feminine metaphors, Eddy undercuts the patriarchal biases of Protestant Christianity as it was practiced in the nineteenth century. She speaks of God in terms which are truly inviting to women as well as men, including women in the divinity, which suggests both that women contain divinity, being created in that image, and that women are or can be, like men, creators and rulers. Eddy frequently employs the language of sentiment to assert the womanhood of God, as when she asserts, "Father-Mother is the name for Deity, which indicates his tender relationship to His spiritual creation."[39] In this way, Eddy aligns her text with a sentimental emphasis on women's capacity for caring and moral strength and aligns this capacity with God. She thus rhetorically invests women in her text.

Eddy also influenced the worlds of women through the *practice* of Christian Science, which placed women in administrative and authoritative roles at every level. She recruited and trained women healers and constructed a church administration which was in great part female-run. Julia Bartlett, for instance, was the treasurer of the Church in the 1880s, and Emma Curtis Hopkins trained many of the New Thought leaders of the western United States. Women attended Christian Science classes and edited the *Christian Science Journal*. In 1888 the National Christian Science Association met in Chicago, and women delegates greatly outnumbered men.[40] Although many of Eddy's close personal and professional relationships throughout her life, particularly after the Great Discovery, were men, the religion she created was appealing to women. In fact, in its early years as a movement, Christian Science targeted obstetrics and gynecology as particular fields of its expertise, identifying itself as a movement which could attend to the medical needs of women. As one critic explains, "It is not an exaggeration to describe Christian Science in the early years as largely a religion in which women helped other women overcome suffering."[41] This female-centered structure through which Christian Science was practiced and promoted was further means by which Eddy reconfigured nineteenth-century womanhood.

In an era when, as Catharine Beecher laments, "American women every year become more and more nervous, sickly, and miserable, while they are bringing into existence a feeble, delicate, or deformed offspring," *Science and Health* praised the healthy woman and offered her a way to become healthy, even to enact her own healing.[42] *Science and Health*'s rewriting of major nineteenth-century discourses—science, sentimental invalidism, and medicine—represents a major rethinking of women's roles and rights. Just as invalidism represents the apex of nineteenth-century society's requirements for womanhood, *Science and Health* represents the apex of the century's attempts to reform the world of medicine and reformulate the picture of the woman's body and role.[43] Eddy's dramatic assertion that the body does not exist and that true health is within reach of anyone who is willing to try her program affected many women in the nineteenth century. Although today Eddy may be an anomalous figure for many historians and scholars, *Science and Health* demands attention from those concerned with how nineteenth-century discourses shaped women's lives.

SENTIMENTAL INVALIDISM

Science and Health by its very title invites examination within the context of nineteenth-century medicine and the scientific theories that authorized that medical practice. Health and medicine were popular and contested topics in the nineteenth century because middle-class women across America seemed to be sick. Many observers perceived a widespread and worsening state of poor health for women. For instance, in 1872 William Dean Howells said that American society "seems little better than a hospital for invalid women," and S. Weir Mitchell asserted that "[t]he man who does not know sick women does not know women."[44] Catharine Beecher explained in her *Letters to the People on Health and Happiness* that "the conviction was pressed on my attention that there was a terrible decay of female health all over the land, and that this evil was bringing with it an incredible extent of individual, domestic, and social suffering, that was increasing in a most alarming ratio." Similarly, Abba Gould Woolson wrote, "This invalidism of which we speak is apparent on every hand. One may have a wide acquaintance among women and yet know but one or two who have no physical ills to complain of. The majority everywhere are constantly ailing, and incapable of vigorous exertion."[45] While historians have suggested that the actual state of health in the country was probably not as dire as these commentaries suggest and that men were likely as healthy or unhealthy as women, clearly the public perception was otherwise.

In recent years, scholars of the nineteenth century have examined this widespread perception of women's invalidism; this work has been especially aided by the research of historians examining health texts.[46] This ideology of invalidism appeared in a variety of texts in the nineteenth century, including sentimental fiction, which greeted readers with a succession of representations of middle-class women's invalidism to which *Science and Health* responded. The ill woman as she is portrayed—and often glorified—in sentimental literature provides a useful starting point for an analysis of the available ideologies of womanhood. Diane Price Herndl explains, "The sickly woman emerged as a figure in American society just as the sickly woman became a predominant literary figure. There have, of course, always been ill, suffering, and dying characters in literature, and many of them have been women, but in the mid-nineteenth century, the female invalid became a standard feature of much American fiction."[47] Harriet Beecher Stowe's *Uncle Tom's Cabin*, Susan Warner's *Wide, Wide World*, Augusta Jane Evans's *Beulah*, and Louisa May Alcott's *Little Women* are some of the many nineteenth-century novels in which women's illness is highlighted.

These literary representations of sickness not only made sickness a visible public phenomenon, they also made sickness in some ways a fashionable state. As Ann Douglas Wood observes, "Heroines of the sentimental fiction so popular with the women in the middle ranks of society . . . were more often than not bearing up under a burden of sickness that would have incapacitated any less noble being. Indeed, as commentators on American society at the time emphasized, ill health in women had become positively fashionable and was exploited by its victims and practitioners as an advertisement of genteel sensibility and an escape from the too pressing demands of bedroom and kitchen."[48] Wood notes that illness in much sentimental literature was presented in a positive, even desirable, light. Although she is sarcastic in her reference to "any less noble being," careful reading of sentimental fiction suggests that this nobility was a prerequisite of illness.

Significantly, the sick woman in literature was often delicate, pale, and passive—characteristics valued for women in general—which suggests that poor health was not only widespread but could be, in some ways, a state to be desired. In *Uncle Tom's Cabin*, for instance, Eva's illness transforms her into "a wearied dove"—pale, delicate, and beautiful—and heightens her religious devotion, bringing about "a high and sublime expression,—the over-shadowing presence of spiritual natures, the dawning of immortal life."[49] Similarly, in Evans's *Beulah*, the wholly admirable, true womanly Clara Sanders falls ill with yellow fever, which, like Eva's illness, heightens her religious devotion and emotional sensitivity, and she describes herself somewhat cheerfully as "perfectly weak and helpless."[50] Promoting the nineteenth-century ideology that those too good for earth often die young, these works show illness as a virtuous, even beatific, state.

In Susan Warner's *Wide, Wide World*, for instance, the utterly virtuous Alice Humphreys—in some ways an adult precursor to Stowe's Eva—uses her illness to educate those around her to the goodness of God's love. As she grows weaker, she tells the protagonist, Ellen, "'Ellie, dear,—you must love [God] with all your heart, and live constantly in his presence. I know if you do he will make you happy, in any event. He can always give more than he takes away. O how good he is!'"[51] Even Louisa May Alcott's *Little Women*, the heroine of which is the indomitably healthy Jo, idolizes the sickly Beth for her true womanly virtues.[52] The epigraph to this chapter notes how Beth's virtue is enhanced by her illness so that her bodily debility made her "soul [grow] strong." The illness and Beth's virtue are interdependent, even indistinguishable, entities. The fictional representations of women's illnesses made these illnesses virtuous, almost laudable states of being which amplified true womanly qualities, bringing women closer to the ideal. Sickness in literature is both the cause of and the evidence for women characters' spiritual purity.

It is important to note that this appealing sentimental invalidism was a corporeal model available only for wealthy white women. The "pale" appearance of Eva and other noble invalids is not coincidental: black women and other women of color were not privy to this spiritualized illness, nor were poor women. An example of the way in which attractive, elegant sickness was a privilege reserved for the middle and upper classes can be found in Rebecca Harding

Davis's *Life in the Iron Mills*, a novel whose lower-class heroine, Deb, is described as a "weak, flaccid wretch" with "pale, watery eyes." Notably, Deb's eyes are pale, not her skin. Unlike Eva's comparison to a "wearied dove," Deb looks "like a limp, dirty rag . . . [a] wet, faded thing, half-covered with ashes."[53] Because of her lower class status, Deb's bodily pain and weakness—virtuous characteristics in sentimental, middle-class heroines—are not appealing. Her illness serves to lower her status rather than heighten her to a state of godly gentility. Thus only *certain* sick bodies were coded with virtue and spiritual sublimity. Only wealthy white women had the option of languishing under a burden of sickness; poor women, like Deb, had to continue to work.

Although not attuned to the race and class valences affiliated with illness,[54] contemporary health reformers condemned the fashionable nature of disease in the nineteenth century, what, in *Science and Health*, Eddy sarcastically referred to as "the refinement of inflamed bronchial tubes" and "selfishness, coddling, and sickly after-dinner talk."[55] Abba Woolson argued that the fashionable look and attitude were best achieved by a woman who was not healthy. She explained, "With us, to be ladylike is to be lifeless, inane, and dawdling. . . . Instead, therefore, of being ashamed of physical infirmities, our fine ladies aspire to be called *invalides*; and the long, French accent with which they roll off the last syllable of this word seems to give it a peculiar charm."[56] Similarly, nineteenth-century physician Mary Putnam Jacobi indicted the larger cultural message sent to women, which stressed that weak and sickly behavior was appropriate: "It is considered natural and almost laudable to break down under all conceivable varieties of strain—a winter dissipation, a houseful of servants, a quarrel with a female friend, not to speak of more legitimate reasons. . . . Constantly considering their nerves, urged to consider them by well-intentioned but short-sighted advisors, [women] pretty soon become nothing but a bundle of nerves."[57]

Thus, women were not inherently unhealthy, according to these commentators. It was not an inherent weakness of the female body which led to the many infirmities but a society which promoted, even praised, illness. As one twentieth-century critic explains, "Sickly women . . . were thought more aesthetically pleasing and interesting than healthy people."[58] Beecher intensified this analysis, suggesting that the nineteenth-century ideology of womanhood not only glorified illness but made women sick; she explained, "I think we can show . . . that if a plan for *destroying female health*, in all the ways in which it could be most effectively done, were drawn up, it would be exactly the course which is now pursued by a large portion of this nation."[59] Twentieth-century critics have noted that the pervasive cultural model of true womanhood placed great demands on women, particularly middle-class, white women, who were the women expected to enact this model. Being held to the model of true womanly virtue could make a woman sick; as Gilbert and Gubar explain, "It is debilitating to be *any* woman in a society where women are warned that if they do not behave like angels they must be monsters. . . . [P]atriarchal socialization literally makes women sick, both physically and mentally."[60] Sentimental texts suggest that true womanhood could be better achieved by a sick woman.

In addition to the demands of true womanhood coinciding with the characteristics of sickness, the cultural surroundings that accompanied a true womanly or sentimentally appropriate body could promote women's illness. Beecher's declamation on the nationwide "plan for destroying female health" referred to a number of different issues which she and many other health reformers identified as problematic, including fashionable clothing that constricted women's breathing and privileged women's neglect of regular physical activity. Sarah Hale wrote about these topics regularly in *Godey's Lady's Book*; during the winter months she often warned her female readers to wear warm clothing and waterproof boots rather than the thin slippers and gowns which were popular, explaining, "Pale consumption's in the sky."[61] Beecher, Hale, and other health reformers thus argued that the props that helped to construct the sentimental female body could cause illness; not just the moral expectations accompanying sentimentality but also the physical accessories necessary to inhabit a sentimental body could make women sick.

White, middle-class women's poor health was attractive, appealing, and evidence of refinement. Because of this, some twentieth-century critics suggest that illness could provide women with a voice to express transgressive desires, allowing them an outlet for their anxieties and a reprieve from household chores and sexual relations, which could lead to exhausting and life-threatening pregnancies.[62] In addition, illness could become a kind of persona for women, a persona which characterized the women as morally sensitive and economically privileged. If an individual woman could not achieve the otherworldly spiritual goodness of an Alice Humphreys or a Clara Saunders, she could at least approach this appearance through illness. Heightening many of the nineteenth century's most troubling demands for the true woman—submission, inactivity, docility—invalidism could provide middle-class women with a useful, although problematic, persona. The sentimental invalid was generally the most thoroughly domesticated female body visible in nineteenth-century literature—confined to the home, and often to the most private parts of the home, by her illness. In current critical discourses, she comes to represent the apex of female victimization and lack of agency. Although illness might have provided white, middle-class women with a certain degree of cultural capital because of their alliance with culturally appropriate models of womanhood, this persona was one target of Eddy's critique in *Science and Health*. Her dematerializing of the body contradicted the attractive sentimental invalid and undercut the domesticating and victimizing functions of the sick female body, offering virtue not through illness but through the spiritualized body.

THE SICK WOMAN AND MEDICAL SCIENCE

Any discussion of the body in the nineteenth century must draw on the discourses of medicine, and certainly the in-depth discussion of illness and healing that took place in *Science and Health* addressed the field of medicine, a field which had its own specific language and issues which *Science and Health* skillfully employed and dismantled. Without understanding the medical culture out of which *Science and Health* arose, one cannot fully understand the text itself. A document like this one, which may initially appear to be a compilation of unrelated discourses, demands a careful, culturally-aware reading.

Eddy herself had broad-based experience with many varieties of nineteenth-century medicine, and her work was clearly involved with medical discourse, challenging its basic assertions and, more importantly, the implications of nineteenth-century medical theories of the female body, both as the body was ideologically viewed and as it was physically treated. In a sense, Eddy functioned as a channel for the congeries of medical discourses available in the nineteenth century, and what resulted from this channeling was *Science and Health*.

Medicine was a growing and heterogeneous field in the nineteenth century. While this growth was at least partially in response to the increasing demand for medical attention springing from the increase in illness, some critics suggest that the medical field itself contributed to the rise in illnesses in the mid- to late nineteenth century. As many medical historians explain, health care before the middle of the nineteenth century had been predominantly the precinct of women, working within the home to care for their families. With the growth of medicine as a profession throughout the nineteenth century, physicians had to bring health care into their own hands. Thus, they had to invalidate women's health care techniques and promote their own, both convincing women of the necessity of bringing their families to professional physicians and emphasizing the biological origins of many discomforts and anxieties.[63] As Herndl points out, these physicians "had a vested interest in maintaining the doctrine of women's innate physical inferiority" because women's weaknesses made professional (male) medical treatment necessary.[64]

Eddy intensified this criticism, arguing that doctors could cause illness because of their focus on and intensive belief in the reality of sickness. *Science and Health* explains, "The hosts of Aesculapius are flooding the world with diseases, because they are ignorant that the human mind and body are myths."[65] While *Science and Health* stresses Eddy's sympathy for the good intentions with which physicians treat sick patients, the text portrays this burgeoning field of professionals as ignorant bumblers, exacerbating illnesses as they plunge in with their specious expertise. *Science and Health* explains, "When there are fewer prescriptions, and less thought is given to sanitary subjects, there will be better constitutions and less disease." Similarly, she explains, "Treatises on anatomy, physiology, and health, sustained by what is termed material law, are the promoters of sickness and disease. It should not be proverbial, that so long as you read medical works you will be sick."[66] Doctors' role in actually promoting illness became very important to the development of Christian Science because Christian Science healing claimed to provide health without emphasizing the weakness and fallibility of the body. By debunking the doctors, Eddy authorized herself as the knowledgeable professional and *Science and Health* as the source for information on how healing really works. Eddy posed a powerful challenge to established medical experts by centering her work in religion, which she claimed to be the source of all science and medicine and therefore more authoritative than the work of the physicians.

Eddy's assertions that medicine causes disease have a certain validity. In a very real sense, nineteenth-century medicine required disease in order to exist as a necessary practice. Thus, medicine relied on the sick body and may be said to have encouraged or promoted sick bodies through its naming and identification of illness. The sick body substantiated medicine's cultural authority, providing Scarry's "analogical verification." Medicine and Christian Science are contending forces in a particular crisis of substantiation, and the body of the sick woman is the ground on which this conflict is played out. Both sides take the sick body as proof of their own validity; however, Eddy's strategy has the effect of undermining her opponents. She grounds her argument not on the presence of the sick woman's body but on its absence. By eliminating the body, Eddy removes the basis by which professional medicine validated itself.

The main nineteenth-century physicians, known as "regular" physicians, operated on the basis of an allopathic theory of medicine, sometimes called heroic medicine. These physicians gave large or heroic doses of medicine; in addition, they made use of such invasive techniques as bleeding and purging sick patients. Because the field of medicine was only loosely based on any sort of scientific experimentation (the germ theory had not yet been formulated), regular physicians' work was often ineffectual or even damaging; for instance, Louisa May Alcott suffered mercury poisoning as the result of being administered the mercury-based emetic calomel during her service as a Civil War nurse.

Medical ineffectiveness was particularly dangerous to women. Theories of how women's bodies operated were by no means consistent, but most stressed an ideology of the body which supported the traditional true womanly view of women's behavior. As a recent historian explains, "Naturally enough, men hopeful of preserving existing social relationships, and in some cases threatened themselves both as individuals and as members of particular social groups, employed medical and biological arguments to rationalize traditional sex roles as rooted inevitably and irreversibly in the prescriptions of anatomy and physiology."[67] For instance, many in the field of regular medicine defined women's bodies as governed by the uterus. As one midcentury doctor put it, "Woman's reproductive organs are pre-eminent. They exercise a controlling influence upon her entire system, and entail upon her many painful and dangerous diseases. They are the source of her peculiarities, the centre of her sympathy, and the seat of her diseases. Everything that is peculiar to her, springs from her sexual organization." Another wrote, "The Uterus, it must be remembered, is the *controlling* organ in the female body, being the most excitable one of all, and so intimately connected, by the ramifications of its numerous nerves, with every other part."[68]

Women were seen by many regular physicians as bodies built around reproductive organs.

This definition of the woman as womb-centered supported women's supposed natural role as mothers and caretakers of the domestic space. It also allowed doctors to blame any illness on a dysfunction of the uterus and to ascribe the etiology to unwomanly behavior—or, in other words, any behavior that did not fit within the model of true womanhood. In the writings of many nineteenth-century physicians, uterine disease and "unwomanly" behavior are often interchangeable. William Goodell describes a patient whose moral decline was so significant that he refused to continue to see her. She and her husband practiced withdrawal as a form of birth control, which Goodell, in concert with other physicians at the time, found morally reprehensible. According to Goodell, this practice brought the woman to a continual state of arousal; Goodell explains, "In making a vaginal exam—to which she reluctantly submitted—I was struck with the excessive sensitiveness of her tissues, and with the uncontrollable excitement under which she labored—symptoms hitherto in my experience limited to unmarried women addicted to self-abuse." The uterine sensitivity Goodell notes is both a physical and moral disease, the two so interconnected in his assessment that he identifies this woman not as a sick patient needing treatment but as a potential prostitute.[69]

Women, according to physician Hugh Hodge, are especially susceptible to moral disease because of their naturally heightened sensitivity. He explains, "Women, compared to men, are impressible and sensitive. This is true of their organic, but especially of their animal life." He explains that women have "strong affections and passions" and that these passions, if not controlled, can cause physical damage to the brain: "Mental and moral affections excite the brain, and powerful passions, as anger, irritate this organ."[70] Thus, Hodge, like Goodell, does not differentiate between emotional, physical, and moral states of being; the three are intimately intertwined, at least where they concern women. According to many physicians, women's bodies are the site at which their moral destiny is worked out, and thus physicians' treatments often seem as much morally as physically driven. For example, in order to address uterine problems, regular physicians often used techniques which ranged from the gruesome to the horrifically painful—from the application of leeches to the cervix and vaginal wall to the cauterization of the uterus in an attempt to drive out infection. Ann Douglas Wood argues that regular physicians' "cures" were often veiled or subconscious punishments for women whose femininity had failed; she explains that this medical discourse "made a woman's womb very much a liability."[71]

Similarly, regular physicians' treatments often infantalized women and denied them any control over their bodies or their treatments. Mitchell explains in *Fat and Blood* (1878), his central text on women's health, that "the man who can insure belief in his opinions and obedience to his decrees secures very often most brilliant and sometimes easy success; and it is in such cases that women who are in all other ways capable doctors fail, because they do not obtain the needed control over those of their own sex." Similarly, Mitchell praises an ideal female patient (a fifty-two-year-old woman) who "obeyed, or tried to obey me, like a child."[72] Mitchell's medical theories required him to belittle his female patients and achieve mastery over them. Regular physicians were thus not only curative practitioners but were performing a role as social regulators, policing the boundaries of acceptable womanly behavior.[73]

Eddy's argument against the regular physicians in *Science and Health* begins with her assertion that the mind can affect the body, an argument the text supports with the testimony of several nineteenth-century physicians.[74] The text also presents Eddy's own testimony, explaining that she has "restored health in cases of both acute and chronic disease in their severest forms. Secretions have been changed, the structure has been renewed, shortened limbs have been elongated, ankylosed joints have been made supple, and carious bones have been restored to healthy condition."[75] By using medical terminology (ankylosed joints, carious bones) and writing in the passive voice, she maintains a detached manner aligned with the professional tone of nineteenth-century physicians and medical texts. By using their testimony and their forms, embedding their testimony strategically within her own, she authorizes herself on similar terms to nineteenth-century medicine and presents *Science and Health* as a kind of medical text.

Introducing herself as a medical colleague, Eddy explains that she has used traditional physicians' techniques and found them flawed: "Obedience to the so-called physical laws of health has not checked sickness. Diseases have multiplied, since man-made material theories took the place of spiritual truth."[76] She uses the very situation which drove many nineteenth-century sufferers to physicians—the perceived increase in illnesses—as evidence of regular medicine's failure. This failure opens the door, she argues, for Christian Science: "The author's medical researches and experiments had prepared her thought for the metaphysics of Christian Science. Every material dependence had failed her in her search for truth; and she can now understand why, and can see the means by which mortals are divinely driven to a spiritual source for health and happiness."[77]

While regular physicians belittled and objectified their patients, viewing them as children or reducing them to their sexual organs, Christian Science saw patients as spiritualized, Mind-centered beings, and gave them the authority to enact their own healing. Later editions of *Science and Health* contain a chapter called "Fruitage," which relates the testimony of patients whose health was restored through the principles of Christian Science. For instance, one patient, suffering from apparently incurable rheumatism, read *Science and Health* and explained, "I realized that the mental condition was what needed correcting, and that the Spirit of truth which inspired this book was my physician. My healing is complete, and my liberation in thought is manifest in a life of active usefulness rather than the bondage of helpless invalidism and suffering." Importantly, this patient, like many, noted, "I did not even have to apply to a practitioner."[78] Christian Science, as explained in *Science and Health*, gave this patient the agency for self-healing and "liberation." *Science and Health* repeatedly locates power in the Mind to overcome sickness. Eddy argues, "Sickness, sin, and death must at length quail before the divine rights of intelligence, and then the power of Mind over the entire functions and organs of the human system will be acknowledged."[79] The insubstantial body Eddy constructs is an empowered public force; her ideology brings the sick body together with the public female body to do battle with nineteenth-century medicine.

Science and Health's emphasis on experiment and patient testimony as evidence is effective, because this was a crucial way that medicine defined its field and its improvements. As early as 1830, European and American medicine began emphasizing disinterested analysis and the scientific method as the foundations for medical science.[80] As celebrated nineteenth-century physician William Osler explained in a late-century essay on the progress of medicine, "The most distinguished feature of the scientific medicine of the century has been the phenomenal results which have followed *experimental investigations*. While this method of research is not new . . . it was not until well into the middle of the century that, by the growth of research labs, the method exercised a deep influence on progress."

Similarly, physician John Shaw Billings explained, "All told, the most important feature in the progress of medicine during the century has been the discovery of new methods of scientific investigation."[81] Eddy presents *Science and Health* as a new kind of medical textbook, based on the very "medical research and experiments" which validated the work of traditional physicians.[82]

It was Eddy's commitment to and immersion in the culture of spirituality that enabled her to depart from the ideology of allopathic medicine. The criticisms of the medical establishment Eddy marshaled in *Science and Health* were not without precedent or without company. Many alternative medicines arose in the nineteenth century to address perceived and actual shortfalls in regular medicine. Hydropathy, or the water cure, was a popular alternative medicine which removed ill people from their homes, took them to water cure establishments, and encouraged frequent bathing, regular consumption of water, and wrapping the diseased body part in cold, wet compresses. This medical approach was much gentler than that enacted in allopathic medicine and was popular with all classes of society. Well-known figures such as Catharine Beecher, Fanny Fern, and Henry Longfellow were proponents of hydropathy. Dietary reform was also popular in the mid-nineteenth century; the most prominent reform, undertaken by Louisa May Alcott's family, was Grahamism, which promoted eating vegetables, whole grains, and cold water, stressing that consumption of meat inflamed the passions and the animal instincts.

Another popular reform, discussed in Mowatt's *Autobiography*, was mesmerism. Begun by Franz Anton Mesmer (1734–1815), mesmerism contended that all human bodies were affected by invisible magnetic fluid and that practitioners could heal the body by manipulating the fluid through magnets or by passing their hands over the afflicted body. As this form of medicine gained popularity in America, it began taking on characteristics of mind control; practitioners would place the patient in a trance-like state in which the body was more responsive to suggestion. Related to mesmerism was spiritualism, less an alternative medicine than a pseudo-science, which began in New York in 1848 "when two sisters, Margaret and Kate Fox, professed to have received intelligent communication, in the form of mysterious rappings, from the spirit of a murdered man."[83] Mesmerism and spiritualism were both quite popular, attracting such advocates as Margaret Fuller, Lydia Maria Child, Horace Greeley, and James Fenimore Cooper.

The major competitor for allopathic medicine, however, was homeopathic medicine. Samuel Hahnemann (1755–1843) founded this alternative medicine in Germany in the early nineteenth century, and its popularity quickly spread. While allopathic physicians recommended taking large doses of harsh drugs which were intended to counteract the patient's symptoms, homeopathic physicians recommended very small doses of drugs which produced in healthy people mild forms of the symptoms the patient was suffering. Homeopaths claimed that nature "often cures one disease by generating a milder one with similar symptoms," and this was the pattern they followed.[84] Because their doses were so low, homeopathic prescriptions did not produce many of the negative side effects of the heroic doses of drugs offered by allopaths, and homeopathy was thus quite popular.[85] All of these alternative medicines had substantial credibility in the nineteenth century, as regular medicine could not generally offer better results.

Gender, too, had become a crucial factor dividing the medical field in the nineteenth century. In addition to alternative medicines, the nineteenth century also saw the rise of a small but growing group of women physicians who stated in plain terms the errors of the male medical establishment, using these as justification for their own involvement in the field of medicine and as a reason to encourage other women to become doctors. One critic explains, "The women doctors who began to appear on the American scene in the 1850s saw women's diseases as a *result* of submission, and promoted independence from masculine domination, whether professional or sexual, as the cure for feminine ailments."[86] As the women physicians observed, many of their male counterparts kept their female patients deliberately uninformed and therefore reliant on the doctors themselves. When physician Harriot K. Hunt explained to her women patients what was wrong with them, male doctors would attempt to undercut the female physician's authority: "The slight and contempt with which some doctors spoke of us to their patients when they found them opening their eyes, deepened my conviction of their unfaithfulness."[87]

Hunt and many other women physicians seemed to have had a view of medicine which was more closely aligned with Christian Science than with the regular physicians. As Hunt explained, "The prevailing idea . . . is, that the *doctor* is to cure the disease. It is not so. The doctor and the patient *together*, are to cure or mitigate the disease. They must be coworkers." This kind of cooperative spirit between doctor and patient was clearly not operative in Mitchell's theory of medicine. Hunt also argued that "[h]oly unions within—reconciliations of jarring elements in the mind—have often broken up external maladies."[88] Woolson, too, asserted that "[t]his state of public opinion . . . is the chief cause of the ill-health so prevalent among us."[89] In recognition of the similarity of technique, Ann Douglas Wood refers to nineteenth-century doctor Elizabeth Blackwell as "an incipient Christian Scientist" because of Blackwell's emphasis on the patient's own role in healing.[90] By lessening the authority and power of the physician and increasing that of the patient—especially the female patient—and by focusing on mental or social causes of illnesses, women physicians as well as other female health reformers expressed their disagreement with a field in which women were denied power and were seen as controlled by their irrational and faulty bodies.[91]

Science and Health, however, repudiated the work even of reformist physicians, in this way differentiating its program from them. For instance, *Science and Health* compares alternative medicines to a kind of farcical religion by asking, "Is civilization only a higher form of idolatry, that man should bow down to a flesh-brush, to flannels, to baths, diets, exercise, and air?"[92] The text launches specific attacks against Grahamism, homeopathy, and other popular alternative medicines, indicting them for their continued reliance on the materiality of the body. Eddy was particularly critical of mesmerism or animal magnetism and spiritualism because these were the alternative medicines most often compared with Christian Science, and Eddy wanted to differentiate her program from theirs. She devotes two full chapters of *Science and Health* to what she calls the "unmasking" of these medicines, arguing of mesmerism in particular, "It is not a remedial agent, and . . . its effects upon those who practise it, and upon their subjects who do not resist it, lead to moral and to physical death."[93] While most of the nineteenth century's alternative medicines suggested a continuum between the material and spiritual worlds, positing that changes to the spiritual affect the physical, Christian Science went beyond the assertion of a continuum to the erasure of the material world. *Science and Health*'s most radical stance in relation to the medical world involves denying humans' corporeality. Eddy argues, "Man is not matter; he is not made up of brain, blood, bones, and other material elements. The Scriptures inform us that man is made in the image and likeness of God. Matter is not that likeness."[94]

Because the body is not real, medicine cannot be effective, and because of this belief, the text is able to treat nineteenth-century medicine lightly, dismissively. Eddy explains, "Physicians examine the pulse, tongue, lungs, to discover the condition of matter, when in fact all is Mind."[95] The physicians are mistaken; *Science and Health* provides the answer. Significantly, as *Science and Health* repudiates the body, it also presents explicitly detailed lists of bodily organs and illnesses, simultaneously bringing the material body into the text and negating its existence. This seeming contradiction is strategic, with the effect of bringing the reader's attention to her bodily ailments (or potential ailments) and then providing hope for relief through negation of the body itself. Eddy's strategy in this case is emblematic; this kind of technique, in which the text presents medical language and assumptions only to undercut them or turn them against themselves, is characteristic of the way *Science and Health* negotiates the varieties of competing discourses. Eddy's strategy here aligns with Mowatt's use of such double discourses as sensationalism and sentimentality. This polyvocality allows these women to challenge dominant models of womanhood and dominant discourses shaping women's bodies.

By destabilizing dominant discourses, Eddy's revision of the body effectively—although sometimes obliquely—challenges the notion that women are domestic beings at the mercy of more powerful cultural forces. For instance, she relates the following incident:

> A woman, whom I cured of consumption, always breathed with great difficulty when the wind was from the east. I sat silently by her side a few moments. Her breath came gently. The inspirations were deep and natural. I then requested her to look at the weather-vane. She looked and saw that it pointed due east. The wind had not changed, but her thought of it had and so her difficulty in breathing had gone. The wind had not produced the difficulty. My metaphysical treatment changed the action of her belief on the lungs, and she never suffered again from east winds, but was restored to health.[96]

This narrative is significant at several levels. The fact that Eddy's patient is a woman indicates Eddy's interest in redefining female corporeality. More importantly, this narrative demonstrates the many implications for Eddy and for other women of Eddy's denial of the body. In this incident, Eddy's insistence on the illusive nature of the body amplifies her own authority. The patient is introduced as "a woman, *whom I cured of consumption*": she is identified in terms of Eddy's curative abilities. Eddy is a powerful presence in the story; while the patient does nothing but breathe, Eddy cures, requests, and "change[s] the action of her belief on her lungs." The sick body of the woman, when subjected to Eddy's treatment and her textual retelling, makes Eddy into an active public presence. At the same time that this story emphasizes Eddy's agency, however, it also ascribes a certain degree of agency to the patient, whose own thoughts are ultimately responsible for the health of her lungs. The patient's body, too, becomes a public presence by its integration into *Science and Health*. In a sense, the dematerialized body of the patient becomes a text supportive of Christian Science, as well as a text supportive of a more fluid and broad-based social role for women.

Christian Science as a discourse emerged from the same kinds of dissatisfaction with the medical profession that inspired other medical reform movements. Although female physicians and alternative medical practitioners did not ally themselves with the policing role assumed by male regular physicians, their work affirmed the cultural belief in the sickness of the female body. According to *Science and Health*, the true religious approach to health relies on the insubstantiality of the body itself. The work of the health reformers, while in alignment with Christian Science beliefs on several levels, still were not as radical as the ideology put forth in *Science and Health* because reformist physicians maintained the belief in the physical body as a real thing. The denial of the body makes *Science and Health* one of the nineteenth century's most dramatic rewritings of these dominant discourses in relation to the female body. Because women were by far the majority of the participants in alternative medicines and in health reform, any discussion of medicine in the nineteenth century concerns women's worlds, but Eddy's book did more. By denying the body, Eddy could rewrite the woman herself.

SCIENCE

Science and Health engages not only medical discourses but also the discourses of science—from astronomy and physics to mathematics and biology—to counter the popular sentimental documents which valorize illness. By engaging the field of science, a male-dominated discourse, Eddy claims its authority for her assertions. She utilizes science to strengthen her text and give her assertions greater credibility within the public realm. Rather than crafting *Science and Health* as a sentimental or fictionalized document, genres implicated in the appropriately domestic realm of women, Eddy inserts it into particular male public realms. These realms do not encompass or overwhelm the text, however; Eddy works both within and against scientific discourses to make her argument about the body, aligning herself with scientific advances but utilizing her religious viewpoint to revise the scientific objectification of the body.

Nineteenth-century science was, in itself, a popular field; scientific documents such as Darwin's *On the Origin of Species by Means of Natural Selection* (1859) were written not for the professional scientists alone but for the larger educated public. As one critic explains, "Scientific knowledge was not the preserve of a special class. Neither the lack of a formal education nor that of an early scientific training could prevent intelligent men and women . . . from contributing powerfully to its advancement."[97] Although the nineteenth century saw the growing specialization—and proliferation—of scientific fields and the consequent professionalization of science, for most of the nineteenth century, science was a public concern and a field which, according to one historian of science, relied heavily on public approval.[98]

The public nature of scientific discourse led to a greater communication between scientific writing and other kinds of writing than is common today. "As long as nineteenth-century scientists remained in a shared discourse and culture, they used similar means to sway their readers . . . struggled with like problems of literary expression and wrote with an imaginative sense of fact, an ability to create potential truth, long thought typical of men and women of letters."[99] An understanding of this connection between science and other types of writing makes Eddy's appropriation of scientific language less surprising. Her endeavor in this regard was eminently practical; by engaging in the world of scientific discourse that invited involvement from the educated public, *Science and Health* both validated Christian Science as a truly scientific undertaking and defined science as the domain—even the responsibility—of women. In addition, *Science and Health* appropriated science's cultural capital, which was growing in the last half of the century. As one historian explains, after the Civil War, "More and more the public became aware of science as something affecting both intellectual attitudes and practical living. Science and things scientific were acquiring a status that gradually permeated all levels of society."[100]

In *Science and Health*, Eddy authorizes her own assertions through scientific discourse repeatedly; for instance, she connects Christian

Science to an astronomical investigation, arguing, "Our theories make the same mistake regarding the Soul and body that Ptolemy made regarding the solar system. They insist that soul is in body and mind [*sic*] therefore tributary to matter. Astronomical science has destroyed the false theory as to the relations of the celestial bodies, and Christian Science will surely destroy the greater error as to our terrestrial bodies. The true idea and Principle of man will then appear."[101] In this quote, the text's references to the world of science are multilayered. The martial imagery which asserts that Christian Science will enact destruction on false ideas fell in line with nineteenth-century physicist T. C. Mendenhall's assertion that "for the most part during the century just ended the advance of science was more of less of the nature of a guerilla warfare against ignorance."[102] Similarly, *Science and Health* partook of the rampant and seemingly exaggerated pride characteristic of nineteenth-century science. The confidence apparent in the previous passage affiliated this text with statements like that made by nineteenth-century astronomer Sir Joseph Norman Lockyer, who explained, "the results already obtained in expanding and perfecting man's view of nature in all her beauty and immensity are second to none which have been garnered during the last hundred years."[103]

Thus, *Science and Health* invokes not just the language of science but also the attitude of science—its assurance as well as its argumentative strategies. A *scientized* more than *scientific* document, *Science and Health* is full of lists, logical argumentation, and Socratic questions. For instance, the text explains, "If both the major and minor propositions of a syllogism are correct, the conclusion, if properly drawn, cannot be false. So in Christian Science there are no discords nor contradictions, because its logic is as harmonious as the reasoning of an accurately stated syllogism or of a properly computed sum in arithmetic."[104] Eddy validates her text by arguing that the ideas put forth in *Science and Health* are as accurate as syllogisms or math problems. On occasion, the text is even willing to use material science against itself, as when Eddy asserts,

> Natural history presents vegetables and animals as preserving their original species,—like reproducing like. A mineral is not produced by a vegetable nor the man by the brute. In reproduction, the order of genus and species is preserved throughout the entire round of nature. This points to the spiritual truth and Science of being. Error relies upon a reversal of this order, asserts

that Spirit produces matter and matter produces all the ills of flesh, and therefore that good is the origin of evil. These suppositions contradict even the order of material so-called science.[105]

Eddy uses this scientized discourse to argue for a picture of the world in which scientific and religious truths are congruent. She explains, "God never ordained a material law to annul the spiritual law"; Christian Science is a philosophical approach that provides, more accurately than the discourses of material science, a coherent view of the world.[106] While *Science and Health* does not duplicate nineteenth-century scientific discourses, it employs a scientized discourse that serves to legitimate the text's claims.

Science and Health defines its philosophical system as scientifically true, able to be proven empirically through experiments and able to be taught to others. Eddy explains, "Mind's control over the universe, including man, is no longer an open question, but is demonstrable Science." She also explains that her theories "were submitted to the broadest practical test, and everywhere, when honestly applied under circumstances where demonstration was humanly possible, this Science showed that Truth had lost none of its divine and healing efficacy."[107] The demonstrable quality of Christian Science was crucial; as several nineteenth-century physicians explained above, experimentation and replication were key elements of nineteenth-century scientific thought. *Science and Health* asserts its statements using scientific language. In addition, Eddy presents her own testimony and the testimony of other practitioners and patients who were healed using Christian Science techniques. These kinds of testimonies were crucial evidence which allowed new medical and scientific approaches to gain credibility. The text thus presents its own demonstrations of its scientific value.

Although the natural sciences, chemistry, and astronomy were among Eddy's favorite subjects in her early schooling, she was not, of course, a scientist. Her scientized language, characterized by broad assertions and simple concepts, aligns itself with the popular science and pseudo-science familiar to Eddy and her contemporaries in nineteenth-century magazines and public lectures.[108] While this pseudo-scientific bent could be viewed as a detriment to *Science and Health*, it could also be viewed as a strategic play for attention and legitimation. *Science and Health*, like other nineteenth-century popular scientific documents, was attempting to appeal to the broadest possible audience.

Although Eddy admits that "Christian Science differs from material science," she makes this difference an asset, asserting that Christian Science is "based on Truth, the Principle of all science" while physical science is "a blind belief, a Samson shorn of his strength." In fact, science, according to the definition in *Science and Health*, becomes the proper arena of a religious text like *Science and Health*: "The term Science, properly understood, refers only to the laws of God and to His government of the universe, inclusive of man."[109] By adapting the language and the ideas of scientific writing to her book, Eddy attempted to authorize her work as factual, believable, literal truth, which did not require a leap of faith but which should be as clear to any educated nineteenth-century person as the laws of gravity. By aligning her work with such notable scientific icons as Galileo and Newton, rather than more current names such as Louis Agassiz or James Dana, Eddy indicated her desire to be identified with figures who radically changed human perception and the course of history. She attempted to appeal to the intellect and rationality rather than primarily to the emotions, as sentimental literature did.

She did not, however, entirely repudiate sentimentalism. Significantly, *Science and Health* employs some of the techniques of sentimental literature, as when it explains that physicians are counterproductive when they "declare that the body is diseased, and picture this disease to the mind, rolling it under the tongue as a sweet morsel and holding it before the thought of both physician and patient."[110] This emotional, highly sensory, and metaphoric language is simultaneously at work with the scientific discourses that exist alongside it in *Science and Health*. Eddy wants to reach her readers by any means necessary, and she employs the multiplicity of nineteenth-century discourses available to her. Moving from the sentimental to the scientific and back, Eddy refuses to align herself with either pole of what her writing proves to be an invalid dichotomy. While the scientific and medical writing of the nineteenth century—writings affiliated with men—might seem to be completely opposite to the sentimental and domestic writings affiliated with women, *Science and Health* undercuts these distinctions and the gendered politics that accompany them. Through a strategic polyvocality and marshalling of multiple cultural discourses, Eddy challenges the limitations imposed on women and uses her culture's discourses against each other.

Eddy's appropriation of the language and rhetorical methods of science ultimately served her construction of the immaterial body, her alliance with the authority and public credibility of male discourses, and her alignment of women with *mind*. By making *Science and Health* a scientized text, Eddy demonstrated her break from the sentimental documents which formulated a virtuous, emphatically domesticated invalid body. By maintaining the subject-position of a *woman*, however, and by maintaining a link with sentimental, sensory rhetoric, Eddy undercut science and medicine's objectification of the female subject and the female body. The spiritualized body and mindful identity Eddy proposed are thus positioned both within and against key discourses, in a site of productive tension. Unable to be encompassed or fully defined by any single discursive mode, this body existed in a complex public space, as a multivalent text.

Ultimately, Eddy's deployment of key nineteenth-century discourses constitutive of women's bodies to construct her version of female embodiment made a significant intervention in her culture. By combining fields such as sentimental literature, which were associated with women, and fields such as professionalized medicine and science, which were male-dominated, *Science and Health* dislodged the gendered implications of these discourses. At the same time, the use of these discourses validated *Science and Health* as a socially significant document. The spiritualized body which Eddy deployed brought women and men to a literal equality by eliminating many of the impediments and cultural contradictions associated with nineteenth-century women's bodies. By eliminating the "Goliath" of material substance, Eddy proposed a true alternative to the available models of female embodiment.

3 As Strong as Any Man
Sojourner Truth's Tall-Tale Embodiment

I want to say a few words about this matter. I am a woman's rights. I have as much muscle as any man, and can do as much work as any man. I have plowed and reaped and husked and chopped and mowed, and can any man do more than that? I have heard much about the sexes being equal; I can carry as much as any man, and can eat as much too, if I can get it. I am as strong as any man that is now.
—Sojourner Truth, speech at the Akron Woman Rights Convention, 1851

Sojourner Truth's most famous speech is alternately called "Ar'n't I a Woman?" and "Ain't I a Woman?" This best-known of all Truth's public utterances has been widely anthologized in the twentieth century; it is the production for which Truth is best known. The first lines of this speech, cited in the epigraph to this chapter, demonstrate Truth's insistence on engaging with women's rights at the most literal level, the level of the body. Truth configures herself as a powerfully physical form, capable of feats of strength equal to that of any man. If Truth's words are interpreted within that most familiar of nineteenth-century constructs of womanly existence, true womanhood, her speech seems shocking, ahead of its time—and, indeed, it was. But true womanhood is not the most productive context within which to understand Truth's Akron speech or her other public acts. In this speech and elsewhere in her speeches and the reports of her life written by others, Truth uses and revises the tall-tale form to construct her bodily identity. Truth's Akron speech and her entire publicly constructed embodiment gain a richer legibility if interpreted within the context of the tall-tale genre of the early and mid-nineteenth century. Read alongside this folk literature, they seem less an anomaly than a strategic use of available discourses, which makes Truth into a heroic figure.

Truth, like Mowatt, was a figure literally on stage, physically on display before audiences. Truth was a public speaker for most of her life, traveling around the country first as a preacher and later as a political speaker in favor of abolition and women's rights. Thus her public body was configured on stage, before mostly white audiences. As an illiterate woman, she had limited control over the written texts which were produced in response to her speeches, so her voice became an important extension of her body, allowing her body to speak itself onstage. Through her speech acts, Truth constructed a public body that was unlike her literal body but that became a substitute for it.

The spaces Truth and Mowatt occupied were emphatically public. In addition, they utilized public discourses like that of sensational fiction and the tall tale to shape their audiences' interpretations of their bodies. Their presence does a great deal to undermine the notion of nineteenth-century women as domesticated beings; Truth and Mowatt found their "sphere" not in the home but on the stage and at the podium. While Mowatt's writing acknowledged the rhetorical power of domesticity and sentimentality for shaping women's bodies, Truth avoided these discourses altogether in her speeches, aligning her body with the heroism and power manifested as well in the tall tale.

The most distinguishing feature of the tall-tale body is its excessiveness. The body in the tall tale is often unattractive, even grotesque, due to its excessive features, including height and strength; these features generally find their fullest enactment in the kinds of conflict which propel tall-tale plots. Tall-tale characters are profoundly carnal; listeners have little other access to the characters than their bodies and their physical actions. The well-known tall-tale character Davy Crockett has no inner life in the stories which concern him; listeners know nothing but his physical self. Due to its excessive, grotesque physicality, the tall-tale body is essentially the body of the freak with a different defining discourse attached. Freaks are not preexisting formations, but are rhetorically constructed. So, too, are tall-tale characters. The tall tale offers an alternative formulation for the unusual body than that of freakdom. Crockett, differently described, could be a freak: "The Bear-Eating Man," "Half-Alligator, Half-Man," or even "The Wild Man of the American West." Instead, Crockett is defined as a tall-tale character, and thus his bodily excesses and abnormalities—his improper speech, his hunting prowess, and his backwoods origins—become heroic rather than grotesque, or in some instances heroic *because* grotesque. Truth employs the same dynamic, utilizing the tall-tale discourse to define her body not as freakish but as heroic.

Truth, like Mowatt, existed on the borderline dividing sensational womanhood from freakishness. Her body was dramatically different from traditional models of feminine embodiment, and Truth and those who wrote about her capitalized on these differences, emphasizing Truth's size, her strength, and her oratorical power. These characteristics could easily have led Truth's listeners and readers to categorize her as a freak, which, as was discussed earlier, is a subject-position of limited empowerment. Rather than allow this to happen, Truth utilized a different model to categorize herself. In her speeches, she did not attempt to inscribe her life or body within sentimental models of womanhood; instead, she described herself as a tall-tale character, using the discourse of the tall tale to give a particular meaning to her physical differences so that her body was defined not as freakish but as heroic.[1] Unlike Eddy, Truth did claim and employ her body, capitalizing on its materiality and using it as analogical verification for her arguments about race and gender. By utilizing the tall-tale discourse, Truth avoided negative models of black female embodiment as well as oppressive discourses of white female embodiment while still defining for herself a highly corporeal and dramatically public life.

The available models of black female embodiment in the nineteenth century were problematic, to say the least. Black women were represented in much scientific literature as overly sexual and animalistic. Proslavery rhetoric characterized blacks as having bodies especially suited for oppressive labor. Indeed, Carla Peterson notes that "nineteenth-century black women were conceptualized by the dominant culture chiefly in bodily terms . . . the black woman's body was always envisioned as public and exposed."[2] Even abolitionist discourse frequently characterized black women in terms of their deviation from the true womanly ideal and emphasized their victimization and their suffering. Thus, Truth faced a host of troubling representations of African American female bodies as she began her career as a public speaker, and she had to navigate her way through these models as she attempted to represent her own bodily identity.

The most positive model available, the one which least threatened Truth's safety—what one critic calls "the already canonized figure of the suffering slave, particularly the sexually degraded slave woman" fashioned by abolitionist writers—still carried with it many problematic implications, not least of which was the way the discourses of sentiment and suffering shaped black women's stories.[3] This discourse did intrude on Truth's self-representation. Olive Gilbert, the white woman who transcribed Truth's *Narrative*, attempted to amplify Truth's suffering, portraying her as a victim, as when she laments, "Of course, it was not in [Truth's] power to make to herself a home, around whose sacred hearthstone she could collect her family. . . . No—all this was far beyond her power of means."[4] Gilbert compares Truth to a sentimental ideal. Were Truth's narrative a sentimental one, this vision that Gilbert describes as impossible for Truth to achieve would form the novel's blissful conclusion. The last image of the novel would be Truth, husband at her side, children at her feet, secure in a vision of domestic sanctity. Because Truth was a slave and then a single parent, this sentimental ideal is unavailable to her, so Gilbert portrays her as a victim, unable to achieve the pinnacle her society offers women.

Critics tend to replicate this approach, interpreting the work of women writers, especially African American women, in terms of victimization. The models critics use to contextualize the discourse of women writers often emphasize sentimental suffering. However, this type of approach is inadequate to represent Truth, who deliberately positioned herself outside the discourses typically associated with nineteenth-century women, identifying herself with other discourses. Truth does not seem to see herself as a victim at all. Although she has certainly suffered, she does not emphasize her lack of power, her oppression by a system that will not allow her to hover around her own "sacred hearthstone."[5] Instead, she emphasizes her strength and her ability to get what she wants. Truth is neither fully victim nor fully agent; the question for her, as for the other women studied here, is how does she manifest acts of agency within an oppressive cultural context? What do her acts of agency look like? For Truth, the sentimentalized model of the suffering slave woman was rarely efficacious for her representation of herself; instead, she adopts a dramatically different model of embodiment than that provided by true womanhood or the sentimental. Truth presents herself as a tall-tale hero. The discourse of the tall tale allowed Truth to capitalize on the ways in which she deviated from the norms of true womanhood and sentimentalism while still making her an appealing figure to a white, middle-class audience.

By examining Truth's constructed embodiment in light of the tall-tale elements evident there, critics can more fully realize Truth's antisentimental configurations of her body and her life. This discourse allowed her to address, in Hazel Carby's terms, "the depth of the polarity between ideologies of black and white womanhood."[6] Truth could articulate this particular polarity by aligning herself with the tall tale which valued the very qualities true womanhood forbade: power, outspokenness, strength, even violence and vulgarity.

However, it is important to note that this particular polarity does not define Truth entirely. It has become customary in scholarship to position black women's writing *against* the dominant white ideologies; indeed, Peterson notes that the white women who "wrote" Truth's story in the nineteenth-century propagated this particular polarity in the form of binary oppositions: nature versus culture figured as black versus white. That binaric paradigm is of limited value here.[7] While the tension critics note between the ideological standards for black and white women is certainly an important component of nineteenth-century black women's experience, Truth's relationship to white ideologies is not entirely confrontational. By positioning herself within the tall-tale genre, Truth was identifying herself with a genre that was primarily peopled by white characters and which was familiar to most nineteenth-century white and black Americans. Her use of the tall tale thus allowed her to confront certain ideologies while remaining a familiar and friendly figure to her audience, and this dual standpoint helped her to establish the authority necessary to allow her to enact her critique of American culture.

It is well to recall that Truth functioned as a public speaker. Her career as a preacher in the public sphere depended upon her acceptance by mixed race as well as white audiences. She legitimated herself not by appearing utterly other but by appearing as a familiar figure. Not surprisingly, the speech act itself invited readers to see Truth working not only in opposition to but also within white cultural standards. Truth was well aware of the dominant cultural standards of the time, and by figuring herself as a heroic figure, a figure emerging from a tall tale, she both made herself familiar to her white audience and capitalized on her differences from them. Rather than capitulating to white, middle-class discourses of womanhood and femininity, Truth defined herself by a different set of standards; she made herself into a heroic, adventurous, and even life-saving body, and from her position within this constructed identity Truth criticized other discourses which shaped women's lives. The tall-tale discourse gave Truth a vocabulary with which to configure her body as powerful and strong and it allowed her to formulate a public life which did not conform to traditional models for women. However useful the tall-tale genre was, though, Truth did not adopt it unreservedly. She made strategic revisions of this model which allowed her to use it not only to heroicize herself but more effectively to propound her message of women's rights.

Truth is the subject of a growing body of research. Recent studies —including Nell Irvin Painter's biography, *Sojourner Truth: A Life, A Symbol* (1996), Carla Peterson's *"Doers of the Word": African-American Women Speakers and Writers in the North (1830–1880)* (1995), and Jean Fagan Yellin's *Women and Sisters: The Antislavery Feminists in American Culture* (1989)—are taking important steps to situate Truth in her proper place in the canon.[8] The insights of Painter, Peterson, Yellin, and other scholars are invaluable, documenting the facts of Truth's life insofar as they can be known and analyzing Truth's self-representation. Following in the footsteps of literary practitioners such as Peterson, I have grounded this study in a literary approach to Truth's words and public presence, taking interest in the textual nuances that can be ignored by social historians at work to verify data. Drawing from new historicism, this study attempts to be especially alert to the multiplicity of discourses evident in texts like Truth's and present also in the larger culture. Literary critical analysis can usefully be brought to bear on Truth's work, for Truth's engagement with discourses that may be surprising to critics—discourses like that of the tall tale—emerge when her words are examined within their cultural context. Close textual and cultural readings are necessary to reveal the complexity of Truth's cultural productions—productions of individual verbal artifacts and of the dominant discourses themselves.

This reading is not about formalism, nor is it about identifying Truth's sources of inspiration, whether they be tall tales or African folktales or something else entirely. Further, I am not suggesting that the tall-tale genre will explain Truth. Instead, I am interested in exploring what a reading of Truth's speeches *through* the genre of the tall tale may reveal about her public self-construction—what resonances we may find, and what perhaps surprising cultural linkages. Peterson notes that, for African American women writers in the nineteenth century, the question of genre was "not so much a choice of literary convention as an epistemological issue: how to represent the relationship of the self to the self and the Other." The choice of genre thus became a political choice. Although Peterson argues that Truth became "irrecoverably Other" because her biography was written by white women, I suggest that the question of Truth's choice of genre leads us to the tall tale, a convention which

Truth used to leverage her "otherness" into effective self-expression —to claim full personhood.[9] The point is not simply that Truth utilized the tall tale and that this genre somehow explains her work; instead, this study argues that this cultural mechanism—the tall-tale genre—allowed her to negotiate many dangerous discourses. It was a functional tool for corporeal self-construction and allowed her not only to abandon the public/private debate but also to enact agency.

A brief synopsis of Truth's cultural presence in nineteenth-century America may help position her discourse within the larger culture. A slave from her birth in New York state in 1797 until her release in 1827, Truth spent more than forty years traveling around the United States speaking and selling her narrative and her *Book of Life*. She was a fairly familiar public speaker within abolitionist and religious circles in the mid- to late nineteenth century, so much so that her fame reached the White House. When she met President Lincoln, she told him that she had not heard of him before he ran for president. She reports, "He smilingly replied, 'I had heard of you many times before that.'"[10] Truth received a calling from God in 1843, at which time God told her to abandon her birth name, Isabella, and become Sojourner Truth. She then began actively participating in the growing Northern reform movements. In 1850, Olive Gilbert transcribed Truth's *Narrative*, which initiated Truth's life in print. In 1878, the narrative was reprinted along with Truth's *Book of Life*, a compilation of newspaper reports about her, letters written to and about her, and signatures she had received from famous Americans. Truth, however, was first and foremost a speaker, and her status as "one of the great orators of the nineteenth century" is being increasingly recognized.[11]

One of Truth's best known speeches, commonly called "Ar'n't I a Woman?," is a contested site, because competing versions of her speech, primarily the one printed in the *Anti-Slavery Bugle* and the one recorded by Frances Gage, offer significantly different representations of Truth, although both versions are transcriptions of the same speech. For instance, the *Anti-Slavery Bugle* represents Truth as ending her speech by saying, "But man is in a tight place, the poor slave is coming on him, woman is coming on him, and he is surely between a hawk and a buzzard." Gage, on the other hand, shows Truth beginning her speech with, "I tink dat, 'twixt de niggers of de South and de women at de Norf, all a-talking 'bout rights, de white men will be in a fix pretty soon." These textual differences involve not only dialect but positions on exactly what Truth said and in what order. In the *Bugle* speech, Truth offers a vivid image of the white man being threatened by birds of prey, in danger of being torn apart and devoured. This harsh image completes the speech, lingering in the listeners' minds. In Gage's version, however, the white man will only "be in a fix pretty soon"—a much less vivid image, certainly one more palatable to Gage's middle-class white audience. Because Gage's version *begins* with this imagery, however, some of the major issues of the speech are evident at once. In addition, the version transcribed by the *Anti-Slavery Bugle* focuses primarily on Truth's words, while Gage's version includes Gage's commentary on Truth's gestures and on the reaction of her audience and also exhibits the dialect tradition that had become well known by the twentieth century through the regionalist dialect industry.[12]

These differences, however, need not deter us from the study of Truth's self-identifying statements; rather, examining the interactions of these voices within the moment of this text's cultural production offers insights into the multiplicity of discourses in nineteenth-century culture. In addition, such study reveals the ways in which a black woman's words are used and transformed within this culture as well as the ways these words interact with the culture. The different version of this speech have been the subject of analysis by Truth scholars including Mabee, Peterson, and Painter.[13] The two versions of Truth's speech may seem contradictory; however, the goal of this study is not to emphasize their opposition, much less to choose a "winner's version"; nor does this study consider, as Peterson's does, the ways the race and gender of the transcriber affect the written document. Instead, this study examines the two texts in concert, assessing their differences as productive of Truth's changing cultural presence. We must take these two versions of Truth's rhetoric as "a method for analyzing the *process* by which history unfolds through the struggles *within* and *between* discourses" rather than trying to locate her "real" discourse.[14]

To proceed on this basis is to relinquish the quest for the Ur-text of the black woman's "authentic" voice, discovering what she actually said as opposed to what she is represented as saying and doing. Aside from the fact that many narratives, including Truth's, are literally written down by someone else, such narratives are shaped within a set of cultural models which may block or obscure these women's voices. A poststructuralist awareness of the discursive construction of matter and the matrices of power which produce discourses themselves leads us to see that there is no elusive and essential "real" voice outside the world of cultural constraints, just as the notion of a "real" body unmediated by culture is a fiction. Ultimately, we cannot know what these women "really" said; all we have are the extant texts themselves, and the formulation of the history of which they are a part. Painter observes that "no means of knowing the past is objective, and none is transparent. The layers of interpretation between us and Sojourner Truth are simply different from those that separate us from people who document their own lives and try to supply their own meaning."[15] Although we cannot know how much of Truth's narrative or how much of her Akron speech are her "actual" words, we do know that these words attributed to her are important cultural documents which she played a critical role in crafting. The issue, therefore, is not what Truth "really" said or thought but what these words, which we assume to be an approximation of hers, say and do in negotiating the culture in which they are embedded, including entering the cultural discussion and becoming a part of public discourse. I do not by any means want to suggest that Truth's "authentic utterance" may not be of utmost importance for some critical projects. This project, however, examines two important documents that represent Truth and considers the cultural work these documents do.

Truth made her most famous speech at the 1851 Woman Rights Convention in Akron, Ohio. Shortly after the convention, several periodicals reported her speech. The *Anti-Slavery Bugle* printed the fullest transcription of the speech on June 21, 1851. Before this speech was reprinted in the Schomburg Library's 1991 edition of Truth's narrative, it was only available in the original *Anti-Slavery Bugle*. The full text from the *Anti-Slavery Bugle* follows:

> One of the most unique and interesting speeches of the Convention was made by Sojourner Truth, an emancipated slave. It is impossible to transfer it to paper, or convey any adequate idea of the effect it produced upon the audience. Those only can appreciate it who saw her powerful form, her whole-souled, earnest gestures, and listened to her strong and truthful tones. She came forward to the platform and addressing the President said with great simplicity:
>
> "May I say a few words?" Receiving an affirmative answer, she proceeded; "I want to say a few words about this matter. I am a woman's rights. I have as much muscle as any man, and can do as much work as any man. I have plowed and reaped and husked and

chopped and mowed, and can any man do more than that? I have heard much about the sexes being equal; I can carry as much as any man, and can eat as much too, if I can get it. I am as strong as any man that is now. As for intellect, all I can say is, if woman have a pint and man a quart—why can't she have her little pint full? You need not be afraid to give us our rights for fear we will take too much,—for we can't take more than our pint'll hold. The poor men seem to be all in confusion, and don't know what to do. Why children, if you have woman's rights give it to her and you will feel better. You will have your own rights, and they won't be so much trouble. I can't read, but I can hear. I have heard the bible and have learned that Eve caused man to sin. Well if woman upset the world, do give her a chance to set it right side up again. The Lady has spoken about Jesus, how he never spurned woman from him, and she was right. When Lazarus died, Mary and Martha came to him with faith and love and besought him to raise their brother. And Jesus wept—and Lazarus came forth. And how came Jesus into the world? Through God who created him and woman who bore him. Man, where is your part? But the women are coming up, blessed be God, and a few of the men are coming with them. But man is in a tight place, the poor slave is on him, woman is coming on him, and he is surely between a hawk and a buzzard."[16]

Anyone familiar with the popularized Truth will notice that this version is very different from the "Ar'n't I a Woman?" speech as it has made its way onto twentieth-century posters and into books. The *Bugle* version, in fact, appears nowhere in Truth's narrative or her *Book of Life*; the version that appears there is the "Ar'n't I a Woman?" version, which was recorded by Frances Gage. Gage presided over the Woman Rights Convention and therefore stands in a position of some authority in terms of Truth's words. Until this decade, most critics have assumed that she would surely not only know what Truth said but want to represent Truth positively, since Truth was speaking in favor of women's rights, the purpose of the convention. However, Gage's version of Truth's speech was not printed until 1863—twelve years after the convention itself—and it is significantly different than the version printed, as one critic notes, "less than thirty days after she delivered it."[17]

The textual issues surrounding these two versions of Truth's speech are complex.[18] Although Gage seems to have distorted Truth's words to fit the current stereotypes of black dialect,[19] Gage's is the well-known version of the speech, a version that many of Truth's nineteenth-century admirers would have read; it is through Gage, in fact, that the speech received the name by which it is still known.[20] Because of her distortion of Truth's language and the stereotypical images of black womanhood her speech employs, Gage's version of the speech is problematic, and I find the less well-known *Bugle* speech preferable, if a choice need be made. Even as Gage transformed Truth's voice, however, she brought that voice into circulation.[21] Gage offers physical description of Truth's vocal tone and physical gestures and thus deploys Truth's dramatic physical presence and her ideas; as Painter points out, twentieth-century "Americans of goodwill deeply need the colossal Sojourner Truth" deployed in Gage's version.[22] Thus, this discussion will have recourse to both versions of the speech. Rather than acting in opposition, the two versions work together to show the way one woman entered the nineteenth-century public consciousness and identified herself and her body with the tall tale in order to define herself as heroic and powerful rather than as either sentimental or freakish.

TRUTH AND THE TALL-TALE TRADITION

Truth's Akron speech shows Truth as an orator engaging with many different nineteenth-century discourses; critics such as Painter, Fitch, and Mandziuk have discussed Truth's negotiations of such discourses as religion and racial categorization in her speeches, and critics such as Franny Nudelman and Hazel Carby have discussed African American women's negotiations of the sentimental and true womanhood, discussions that have important bearings on Truth's work. The tall tale is a particularly vivid discourse which Truth utilizes to represent herself in her Akron speech, one which has not been noted by critics.[23] In the Akron speech, as well as in other speeches and in her narrative, Truth presents an image of herself as a tall-tale character: a heroic figure, physically strong, confronting seemingly insurmountable obstacles. She transforms her bodily distinctions from the white, middle-class ideal into tall-tale excesses, which thus confer on her a power that would be impossible were she to be defined in other terms.

Tall tales flourished in nineteenth-century American folklore. Tall humor emerged as a distinctly American form around the time of the Revolution and thrived during the nineteenth century. Although not a form of folk literature indigenous to America, tall humor and the tall tale became identified with America during the nineteenth century. As one critic asserts, "Americans adopted tall talk as a national idiom and the tall tale as a national form of humorous storytelling."[24] The exaggeration and boasting characteristic of tall humor were particularly suited to expressing the incongruity between America's expectations for itself and the realities of life in the new country.[25] Certainly noting this incongruity was one of Truth's major goals in her speeches, and this is a goal that fits well with the techniques of tall tales and tall talk. Although tall humor is often particularly identified with America's Southwest and with the western frontier, this genre was popular everywhere in America in the nineteenth century and would have been familiar to Truth and her audiences.

The tall tale is a particularly oral form, which made it an accessible and welcoming form for illiterate people like Truth. Carleton Mabee posits that Truth deployed her orality as a significant component of her public self-construction: "In a sense she molded her public image around her illiteracy, using it to dramatize herself and shape her life, turning her illiteracy from a handicap into a significant element of her charm."[26] Although the idea of illiteracy as "charm" is debatable, Mabee offers the valid suggestion that this aspect of Truth's public embodiment may have been a conscious cultural negotiation. Truth's orality could become a benefit within the world of the tall tale, which valorized acts of speaking and which circulated primarily through the spoken word.

In addition to its dissemination through oral channels, tall humor was also communicated through many newspapers, magazines, and comic almanacs; these printed forms enabled the tales to travel the country quickly, and they also provide a record of the kinds of stories which were being told and the ubiquity of this kind of humor. Walter Blair says of comic almanacs, a particularly friendly site for tall tales, "These illustrated pamphlets—the calendars, weather forecasts, feature sections, and comic books, so to speak, of that day—had huge readerships: few homes were without one."[27] Most nineteenth-century tall tales feature white men boasting about their feats of hunting, fishing, or brute strength; the protagonists may brag about prowess in such areas as holding their breath or eating an enormous amount of food. Some tall tales do not feature a human protagonist at all, involving livestock, wildlife, or the land itself, although the tale's teller is always implicitly a hero because of his ability to construct the tall tale. Dorson defines the tall-tale protagonist as "the eccentric frontiersman glorified, a braggart and a brawler, picaresque, earth-tainted, whimsically grotesque, not quite superman or hero or god in the accepted sense, but a comic embodiment of all three."[28]

Tall-tale bodies are the only access listeners have to the characters themselves; tall-tale characters are pure embodiment, with no inner life at all. They are the bodies of the frontier, confronting natural forces and negotiating often chaotic landscapes. They are thus figures in direct opposition to the goals and ideals of the developing nineteenth-century middle-class culture. Their physical brutality and the comedic tone of their tales make tall-tale characters a dramatic inversion of the ideals of sentimental womanhood. These rewritings of dominant cultural ideologies made the tall tale a potential site of authority; as Carroll Smith-Rosenberg notes, "Power emanated from the violation of categories and the fusion with chaos," evident in tall tales.[29] By aligning herself with the discourse of the tall tale, a speaker like Truth could access this power to enact a critique of particular cultural standards.

The protagonists or heroes of tall tales came in many forms, from the purely fictional like Paul Bunyan to those figures whose exploits might be fictional but whose existence as real people is verifiable.[30] Perhaps the epitome of the folk hero and the tall-tale protagonist who was both a real person and an exaggerated fictionalized character is David Crockett. Crockett was, of course, a real person who served in the military under Andrew Jackson in 1813 and 1814, and who was a representative to the United States Congress from 1827 until 1831 and again from 1833 until 1835. He later died at the Alamo in 1836. While his real-life exploits are somewhat notable, they do not compare to the legend that grew up around him both during his life and after his death.

Several important factors contributed to Crockett's fame: first, in 1831 James Kirke Paulding's very popular play *The Lion of the West* began production, featuring a backwoods hero named Colonel Nimrod Wildfire who was a fictionalized and heroicized version of Crockett. Second, between 1833 and 1836 two biographies and one autobiography of Crockett appeared, all supporting Crockett's campaign for Congress; these books document the facts of Crockett's life while also adding a great deal of tall embellishment. Third, and most important, in 1835 publishers began producing *Davy Crockett's Almanacks*, comic magazines which represented Crockett as a tall-tale hero. As Crockett critic Michael A. Lofaro notes, "There is no question that most scholars correctly view the comic Crockett almanacs of 1835 to 1856 as the single most influential genre in the creation and propagation of Davy's legendary life."[31] Crockett was thus a real person who fictionalized his own life through speeches and writings and allowed or inspired others to do the same. His legend was created both by his own speeches and personal presence in Congress and on the campaign trail, and by the narratives—both spoken and written—that emerged around him. In these ways, Crockett is an analogous figure to Sojourner Truth.

Truth's use of tall tales in constructing her public body is made clearer through comparison to the Crockett legend, which provides useful similarities to Truth's constructed corporeality. Crockett's legend was constructed around issues central to the tall tale in general: conflict and comedy, both of which played out and through the protagonist's excessive body. These are elements which Truth utilized in her public presentation of her body. The formation of Crockett's legend was happening at the time that Truth was beginning and solidifying her public speaking career, from the 1830s through the 1850s. While I do not draw a direct causal relationship—I am not suggesting, for instance, that Truth based her public embodiment on the Davy Crockett stories—I do think Truth was participating in or inserting herself into the same public discourse that characterized Crockett's legend.[32] As Mabee explains, "Truth often seemed willing to let friendly myths develop around her, myths that might make her a more fascinating advocate of the causes she supported." Painter, too, emphasizes Truth's role in developing her image, explaining that she "created and marketed the persona of a charismatic woman who had been a slave, and it is precisely through her marketing of herself or, as she put it, her selling the shadow to support her substance, that her name is known today."[33] By using and revising the tall-tale formula for constructing her own embodiment, Truth made use of a preexisting cultural site which validated the very physical differences that could otherwise have hindered her communication of her message.

Excessive Bodies

One of the cultural differences that could have hindered Truth's message was white observers' perception of her body: Peterson notes that many white authors reported Truth manifesting "an unruliness and excess of body and speech."[34] While this excessive and unruly body could be used to silence or negate Truth's message, within the discourse of the tall tale the unconventional, excessive body was normative. Truth begins the *Bugle* version of her speech by saying, "I am a woman's rights." This powerful statement, not only of personal identity, but of alliance with a struggle for justice, shows Truth not only striving for women's rights, but presenting herself as its incarnation. This is the sort of exaggerated, dramatic speech characteristic of tall tales; Truth's proclamation that she is "a woman's rights" is analogous to Crockett's claims to be "half-horse, half-alligator and a bit of snapping turtle."[35] She then proceeds to describe herself in terms sharply different from those espoused by the rhetoric of true womanhood and the sentimental. A true woman is delicate, unable to do physical labor, and governs the domestic realm. Truth defines herself in this part of her speech according to her labor, asserting that she can do all the physical acts a man can do, stressing, "I am as strong as any man that is now." Rather than skirting the issue of sexual equality, one which raises questions even today, she meets it head-on and brings it to the literal level, the level of the body, saying, "I have heard much about the sexes being equal; I can carry as much as any man, and can eat as much, too, if I can get it." In Gage's version of the speech her claims become more brutally physical as she claims she "can bear de lash as well" as any man, boasting her body's ability to withstand abuse.

This kind of bravado would be familiar to Truth's audience from the tall-tale genre of vernacular humor; bravado is one of the means by which the excessive body is defined. Characters like Davy Crockett assert their identities by boasting of their abilities; for instance, in the first Crockett comic almanac, Crockett is reported as saying he "can run faster,—jump higher,—squat lower,—dive deeper,—stay under longer,—and come out drier, than any man in the whole country."[36] Similarly, in an 1836 almanac Crockett faces an opponent with the following claim: "Says I, stranger! I'm the boy that can double up a dozen of you. I'm a whole team just from the roaring river.—I've rode through a crab apple orchard on a streak of lightning. I've squatted lower than a toad; and jumped higher than a maple tree; I'm all brimstone but my head, and that's aquafortis."[37] An important part of the tall-tale character's identity is his ability to intimidate his opponents through a show of confidence and braggadocio known as the "frontier boast." While the claims are generally so extreme as to be impossible and therefore humorous, within the world of the tale they are considered literally true, and outside the world of the tale they establish the speaker as a clever opponent.

By defining herself in terms which would have been so unwomanly as to be almost laughable in the mid-century—claiming to "have as much muscle as any man" and to be able to "carry as much as any man, and . . . eat as much too"—Truth utilizes tall-tale bravado in both versions of her speech and aligns herself with tall-tale characters. She defines her body according to the familiar tall-tale configuration of excessive strength. At the same time, Truth supersedes the tall-tale genre, because while her boasts may seem absurd to her audience, they have a grounding in literal truth. During her time as a slave, Truth was required to do physical labor that the average middle-class white woman would have found impossible. Although at the time of her Akron speech, Truth was probably no longer physically able to do this kind of labor, her assertions are more than empty or humorous boasts. The purpose of tall-tale exaggeration, or tall talk, is to show the distance between the real and the ideal worlds. Truth's "exaggeration" is true, so she herself presents a real body which contradicts the ideal and shows this ideal—true womanhood—to be lacking.

In addition to her claims to physical strength, Truth's boast that she "can eat as much as any man" identifies her with the discourse of the tall tale. Eating is a very important activity within tall tales; the tall-tale body is excessive in its ability to eat both grotesque kinds of food and massive quantities. Crockett, for instance, regularly describes a diet composed of bear's meat, eagle's eggnog, and rattlesnakes. The amount of food a character eats is also a means of emphasizing physical strength; Crockett describes a midday snack as "a sandwich, which was composed of half a bear's ham, two spare ribs, a loaf of bread, and a quart of whiskey."[38] Truth makes only one reference to food in her Akron speech, but this brief reference to her ability to eat would instantly have suggested the discourse of the tall tale to her listeners and would have further identified her body with excessive tall-tale bodies. At a time when middle-class table manners were being proclaimed in such documents as Catharine Beecher's *A Treatise on Domestic Economy* (1842) and in women's magazines like *Godey's Lady's Book*, Truth was participating in a discourse which flouted etiquette and validated eating as a show of carnal strength.

Rather than conforming to sentimental standards for women's embodiment, Truth defines herself within a genre that values physical excess and power. Gage's version makes this redefining of the female body particularly clear, for in this version Truth says, "'Look at me. Look at my arm,' and she bared her right arm to the shoulder, showing its tremendous muscular power." In this version, Truth actually displays her body, manifesting her physical strength. Because Gage's version of the speech is a document meant to be read, her description of Truth's "tremendous muscular power" has an even more emphatic effect, allowing her readers to imagine Truth as an almost superhuman body.

By showing her audience her muscular arm, Truth aligns herself with the bodily skill and power of Crockett and other tall-tale protagonists. In addition, as several critics have noted, she is taking the image of the slave woman on the auction block, whose body is displayed for purchase, and appropriating it for her own uses. She exposes her arm, not to demonstrate her value in the slave market but to illustrate her power and to define her body in terms different than those that might be applied to her. The force represented in her arm is not evidence of her ability to do physical labor for someone else but is, like Crockett and other tall-tale characters' bodies, evidence of her heroic status.

Without proper contextualization, Truth's claims to physical strength could be read as a reification of Truth's subaltern status as an African American woman whose bodily value was often based on her ability to work. As Carby explains, "Strength and ability to bear fatigue, argued to be so distasteful a presence in a white woman, were positive features to be emphasized in the promotion and selling of a black female field hand at slave auction."[39] Indeed, one of Truth's masters had bragged about Truth's strength, telling a friend, "'*that* wench' (pointing to Isabel [Truth]) 'is better to me than a *man*—for she will do a good family's washing in the night, and be ready in the morning to go into the field, where she will do as much at raking and binding as my best hands'"[40] His claim clearly demonstrates the dual role black women had to fulfill, that of male physical strength (working in the fields) and feminine domesticity (doing the laundry) and the value of their labor and strength within the context of both masculine and feminine arenas of work. However, rather than contradict her master's claim by emphasizing the ways in which she might fit within traditional models of womanhood, Truth embraces his characterization of her strength. Importantly, she appropriates this strength for her own purposes, to define herself as a hero and undercut the sexual stereotypes governing black and white women's lives.

By identifying herself with the strength of the tall-tale body, arguing, "I have as much muscle as any man, and can do as much work as any man," Truth undercuts dominant nineteenth-century assumptions about women's embodiment. Her self-definition in terms of strength and labor implies a new visioning of women's roles. Rather than simply reacting against the nineteenth-century agenda for women, Truth suggests an agenda of her own, one which presents women as a legitimate presence in the world of economic production. Her insistence that she has "plowed and planted and gathered into barns, and no man could head me" and that she "could work as much and eat as much as a man" positions her explicitly as a laborer. She explains that she herself can be responsible for the whole process of growing food, from the initial plowing and planting to the final harvesting and storing, presenting herself not as a worker on an assembly line but as an autonomous producer. Truth's speech works in direct contradiction to the ideals of true womanhood, not only through the actions she describes but through her repeated comparison of her body to the body of a man. Her forceful opposition of feminine ideals demystifies the ideals, showing that they are not natural attributes of women because she, as a woman, is not bound by them. She deploys a new ideal of womanhood by explicitly comparing her body to a male body, emphasizing that she has *the same* strength and ability as "any man" but that she is still a woman. She decommissions the male/female binary by challenging its discursive construction.

Just as Truth's rhetorically constructed physical strength aligns her with the tall tale, so, too, do other physical characteristics, including her height and her age. Gage and other commentators on Truth note that she was a very tall women. Gage describes her height in terms that make her an almost otherworldly figure, explaining that she "stood nearly six feet high, head erect, and eye piercing the upper air, like one in a dream"; she is not simply tall, but her height lifts her to "the upper air," placing her literally and figuratively above the audience to which she speaks. In "The Libyan Sibyl," Stowe explains, "Her tall form, as she rose up before me, is still vivid to my mind," suggesting that Truth's height is a particularly impressive feature of her physicality.[41] Her height helps to define her as physically intimidating, especially in Gage's version of Truth's Akron speech, which shows Truth slowly rising from a crouching position to her full size before the audience.

Height is an important physical feature within the discourse of the tall tale. This is an often-noted characteristic of male characters; the Crockett almanacs describe one of Crockett's foes as "so tall he could not tell when his feet were cold." However, this characteristic

Many visual images of black women's bodies in popular culture document the cultural expectation that they be as physically strong as black men. "Hoeing Rice" and "Planting Rice" offer an exoticized, anthropological view of black women laboring in the fields alongside black men. This was not the only way in which black women could enter the visual culture of the nineteenth century, however; "Noon at the Primary School" shows black children, male and female, engaging in appropriate, normalized physical play, and the bicycle image shows women embodying both physical activity and appropriate middle-class status.

"Hoeing Rice," Harper's New Monthly Magazine, *1878*

"Ploughing Rice," Harper's New Monthly Magazine, *1878*

"Noon at the Primary School," Harper's Weekly, *1866*

Group around a bicycle, ca. 1910
(Courtesy the Clarence Cameron White Photograph Collection, Schomburg Center for Research in Black Culture)

also appears in descriptions of women in many of these tales. For instance, as one almanac describes Lotty Ritchers, "She stood six foot in her shoes; but as she hadn't 'em on very often, she war not quite so high." Similarly, one story has Crockett describing his daughters and explaining with pride that "the oldest one growed so etarnally tall that her head had got nearly out o'sight."[42] Gage's description of Truth standing "nearly six feet high, head erect, and eye piercing the upper air" demonstrates significant similarities to the descriptions of height in the tall tales. While Truth was literally a taller-than-average woman, in reports about her, her height is described not as a simple, literal fact of her physicality but as a heroic feature that contributes to her almost mythical physical presence.

Truth's age, too, took on heroic significance in descriptions of her in the years after the Akron speech, with audiences reporting her to be over 100 years old or reporting her to be nearly 100 and still looking young. Indeed, the 1878 edition of Truth's narrative includes a preface by Frances Titus in which she reports, "Her health is good; her eyesight, for many years defective, has returned. Her gray locks are being succeeded by a luxuriant growth of black hair, without the use of any other renovator than that which kind Nature furnishes. She hopes that natural teeth will supersede the necessity of using false ones."[43] This image of Truth as forever young, her body regenerating itself in its old age, makes her a figure whose physical power is outside the realm of mortality and fits her, again, within the rubric of the tall tale. The Crockett almanacs have Crockett describing his grandmother as "an all-standin tough gal, in her 120th year"; she kills an attacking Indian with the force and volume of her "damned stubborn cough."[44] The combination of excessive age and persisting physical power would certainly have been familiar to the readers of tall tales, and would be a defining characteristic of a tall-tale hero. As Fitch and Mandziuk note, this was an aspect of her constructed physicality that Truth definitely supported, referring to her old age in lectures throughout the 1860s and 1870s. By seeming ageless, even immortal, Truth suggested that she was an almost superhuman figure.

Truth's literal body was probably five feet eleven, dark black, and somewhat muscular, although her right hand had been injured while she was a slave and so she was somewhat debilitated. Her public body, however, was formidable—extremely powerful, able to channel electricity, stun a crowd into silence, and soothe savage men. Truth presented her audience with an interpretive script, and this script was profoundly influential; through her self-presentation and representation as a tall-tale protagonist, Truth helped her audience and those who reported about her to see her not as a tired, injured older woman but as an Amazon who did not grow old and who "has a magnetic power over an audience perfectly astounding."[45] By aligning her body with the discourse of tall tales, Truth shaped not only her own words but the descriptions others gave of her.

The Body in Conflict

Tall-tale characters like Crockett are defined in terms of opposition or conflict. Tall tales are constructed around a moment of crisis in which the tall-tale protagonist must demonstrate prowess. Without conflict, the protagonist has no opportunity to identify himself or herself as a hero. Virtually every story in the Crockett almanacs shows a moment of conflict, either a fight between two characters, a character attacking or being attacked by a wild creature or natural force, or a confrontation taking place verbally.

Truth's Akron speech conforms to these criteria; like Crockett and other tall-tale heroes, Truth represents herself as a heroic figure facing opposition. Her Akron speech is a text explicitly framed in terms of contention, literal and figurative. Gage's report of the Woman Rights Convention describes men confronting the white female speakers and Truth countering the men. Gage explains, "Methodist, Baptist, Episcopal, Presbyterian, and Universalist ministers came in to hear and discuss the resolutions brought forth. One claimed superior rights and privileges for man because of superior intellect; another because of the manhood of Christ. . . . Another gave us a theological view of the awful sin of our first mother." The *Bugle* report describes no such confrontation at the convention, and Mabee has noted that none of the other published reports of the convention at that time noted any disturbance of any kind.[46] However, even if she was not speaking against actual men who were challenging her, it is significant that Gage represents Truth as a heroic figure who will flourish in the face of opposition, even opposition from white men, a group much more culturally powerful than Truth herself. This representation invests Truth with the cultural capital of the hero.

In addition, even if no actual men confronted the women at the convention, Truth's speech clearly shows that she was working against a rhetoric of woman's submissive place and circumscribed abilities, a rhetoric which would have been familiar to all the women at the convention; Truth was contesting this rhetoric even if she was not contesting actual men. While Truth's speech does gain some dramatic effect when positioned against these religious men's arguments, the possibility that no ministers challenged the conventioneers does not detract from Truth's intelligent and hard-hitting rebuttal. Truth is positioned as a figure who resists the ideologies of true womanhood in the same way that tall-tale protagonists challenge natural forces, threatening animals, or political competitors, and win.

In Gage's version of the speech, the conflict becomes the occasion for Truth's tall-tale body to emerge in its full power. Gage describes Truth's physical actions, as she "pointed her significant finger and sent a keen glance at the minister who had made the argument"; these bodily gestures show Truth responding directly to a confrontation, her body taking on a new set of meanings through the confrontation so that her finger becomes "significant" and her glance "keen." Later in the speech, when Truth asks the crowd about the origins of Christ, Gage explains, "she stood there with outstretched arms and eyes of fire." The conflict becomes Truth's motivation to become a huge, iconic figure whose "eyes of fire" suggest a power the reader can only imagine.

Not only Truth's speeches themselves, but the variety of abolitionist writings which feature her, position her as a character motivated by conflict, a mysterious person who sees trouble and rises just in time to end it. Her *Book of Life* contains numerous anecdotes from abolitionists explaining incidents in which Truth had saved a meeting or rebuked a proslavery speaker more effectively than any other abolitionist speaker could have. For instance, a writer to the *Bugle* describes a meeting in which a speaker denigrates blacks. The writer explains, "When he was about closing his inflammatory speech, Sojourner quietly drew near to the platform and whispered in the ear of the advocate of her people, 'Do n't dirty *your* hands wid dat critter; let *me* 'tend to him!' The speaker knew it was safe to trust her." It seems to be common knowledge in this anecdote that Truth is the most effective person to refute anti-abolitionist arguments; it is as though when Truth enters the anecdote, everyone knows that she will resolve the situation entirely. Truth then proceeds to compare addressing the speaker's arguments with "de scullionist and de dirtiest" work she has ever had to do, delighting the audience and humiliating the speaker.[47] This anecdote, which Truth approved to be included in her *Book of Life*, portrays Truth heroically; when a conflict arises, Truth emerges to solve the problem.

REVISIONS OF THE TALL TALE

Truth did not identify herself fully with the tall-tale genre; she manipulated the genre to meet her own specific needs as a public figure. Her rhetorical framing of her body, while aligned with tall tales in many significant ways, also strategically deviated from this model. Tall-tale characters are carnal, and their bodies are grotesque. While this carnality has potential benefits, allowing unusual bodies to be defined as heroic rather than freakish, the pure carnality of the tales does not accord with Truth's larger goals. She is not positioning herself as a tall-tale character merely for the sake of entertainment but to make a sustained argument about the rights of women and African Americans. She thus did not define herself as a frontier grotesque nor as a sexualized, carnal being but as a moral exemplar. This revision was aided by her use of religious or moral authorization within her tall-tale self-construction and her use of the conventions of elocution and oratory in combination with the tall-tale techniques.

Truth had to address several problematic elements of tall-tale discourse in her self-construction. One was the fact that tall tales were often racist texts, depicting acts of violence which glorified the white protagonist at the expense of racially identified others, including African Americans and Native Americans. This is a side of Crockett in particular that many scholars have been reluctant to acknowledge; Crockett almanacs abound with tales which range from mildly to viciously racist, particularly in the almanacs produced after 1843. For instance, Crockett claims he can "swallow a nigger whole without choking if you butter his head and pin his ears back."[48] Also, stories like "A Scentoriferous Fight with a Nigger" (which Dorson, in his reprinting, changes to "A Black Affair") are full of racist slurs. While these racist elements of the tall tales may not be familiar today, they were a common feature in the tall tales of the nineteenth century. Truth and her audience would certainly have been aware of this element of tall-tale humor.[49] This, then, is a way in which Truth is rewriting the discourse of the tall tale even as she uses this discourse: by defining herself as a tall-tale character and using the tall tale to communicate her message of equality, Truth asserts herself as a hero on par with such white characters as Crockett. She thus revises the tall-tale model which presents black characters as repulsive opponents and presents herself as the protagonist of her tales.

Gender configurations within tall tales are less blatantly offensive than the configurations of racial difference. Representations of women within tall tales are complex, and Truth works both within and against these representations when defining herself as a tall-tale protagonist. While the tall tale was a genre dominated by white men, female characters occasionally appeared in these narratives, particularly in the Crockett almanacs, and these female characters were in many ways similar to the men. According to Michael A. Lofaro, the only critic to analyze the female characters in Crockett's almanacs at length, fifty-eight almanac tales feature women in significant roles.[50] These women include figures already introduced in this chapter, including Crockett's daughter, grandmother, Lotty Ritchers, and Nance Bowers, along with characters like Sal Fink and Judy Coon. These women show themselves to be almost as physically powerful as their male counterparts; Judy Coon, for instance, stomped to death a "nest of young wild-cats," while Sal Fink burned alive a tribe of Indians who tried to capture her.[51] Women in tall tales are not limited to the Crockett almanacs; New England folklore also featured a few women tall-tale heroes like "Stout" Jeffrey Hazard's sister, "who used to take a full cider barrel by the chines and lifting it aloft drink at the bung," and Christian McNiel, who physically defeated a man who came to fight her husband.[52]

Perhaps the most famous female tall-tale character, the woman who appears most often in the Crockett almanacs, is Crockett's wife, Sally Ann Thunder Ann Whirlwind Crockett. She appears in eight tales, often providing crucial assistance to her husband, as when she helps Crockett to kill a bear.[53] She also kills a bear herself in one tale, and she and her daughter together kill a thirty-seven-foot alligator. In addition, she takes on a large family of eagles in order to get eggs to make eagle eggnog; according to Crockett, who narrates this tale, "The gal went into 'em bite, smite an' claw, an' made the feathers fly like a snow storm or a geese picken."[54] She is a tough, strong woman, like her compatriot women in the tales; however, Lofaro notes that she is never allowed to upstage her husband.[55] She and the other women in the tall tales are generally accorded secondary status.

This, then, is a key problem in the representation of women in tall tales. These women, whose excessive strength makes them noteworthy, are never accorded the heroic status that accrues to the male protagonists of the tales. In fact, they are often represented as characters even more emphatically carnal than their male counterparts. The unbridled physicality of tall-tale women is particularly evident in the woodcut pictures which accompanied many of the stories in the Crockett almanacs. Virtually all the characters represented in woodcuts are portrayed fairly harshly, with unappealing, sharp features and elements like wrinkles and blemishes emphasized; however, these woodcut images deal particularly harshly with female characters, as is evidenced by the different ways in which one female tall-tale figure, Crockett's wife Sally Ann Crockett, is represented in these pictures. In an 1837 woodcut, for instance, when she is assisting Crockett in killing a bear, she appears very stern and ugly; her face is distorted, mouth hanging open, and her body appears stocky and muscular. In the picture accompanying the eagle eggnog story in 1854, however, Sally Ann appears exaggeratedly feminine; the curves of her breasts are visible through her bodice, and she has long, flowing hair and a fairly nondescript face. One of her legs emerges from the folds of her skirt, and huge eagles reach their beaks toward her calves and thighs. This picture presents a sexualized Sally Ann very different from the grotesque, asexual image in earlier woodcuts. These visual differences point to the two ways in which tall-tale women could be objectified: they could either be made into asexual "shemales," as Lofaro calls them, or into objects of sexual desire.

These female characters demonstrate the benefits and dangers of the tall-tale discourse. On one hand, they represent powerful, independent female bodies. On the other hand, they are less heroic than their male counterparts; their representations verge on the freakish. As Carroll Smith-Rosenberg suggests, "The wild women of the West systematically violated the system of rigid proprieties which the Cult of True Womanhood imposed upon bourgeois women. . . . The women were ugly, boisterous, and autonomous."[56] Their autonomy and their ugliness are intertwined, making these characters problematic female models. While all tall-tale characters offer potential comedy, the women in tall tales often seem purely comic, as though they are the objects of ridicule without any counterpoint of admiration. They point to the reasons that Truth both utilized and revised the tall-tale genre in her own self-construction.

Probably the single most important element of Truth's revision of the tall-tale body is her use of her own voice. Although the female characters in the Crockett almanacs and other female tall-tale protagonists may provide same-gender models for Truth's tall-tale em-

The two contrasting images of Davy Crockett's wife, Sally Ann Thunder Ann Whirlwind Crockett, demonstrate different types of objectification of women in tall-tale imagery. Truth avoided such objectification by crafting her own image and acting as the teller of her own tales.

"A Desperate Contest with a Great Black Bear," Davy Crockett's Almanack, *1837*

"Perilous Situation of Mrs. Crockett," Davy Crockett Comic Almanac, *1854 (From the collections of the St. Louis Mercantile Library at the University of Missouri-St. Louis)*

These female tall-tale bodies were comical, excessive, and grotesque, but they were also powerful. They do not represent real bodies of athletic women but instead demonstrate one nineteenth-century cultural model that simultaneously ridiculed and validated women's bodily empowerment through strength and physical competence.

"A Tongariferous Fight with an Alligator," Davy Crockett's Almanack, *1837*

"Judy Finx Whipping a Catamount," The Crockett Almanac, *1839*

bodiment, they are problematic models, not only because of their carnality but because they are objects of the tales but not the tellers. As Lofaro makes clear, "The major male protagonists of the almanacs almost always tell their stories in the first person and, in so doing, build a closer bond between the reader and themselves as well as heightening the tale in the reader's mind. None of the She-males ever tells her own story; these superwomen of the frontier are always described."[57] This detail is significant. The women who are the objects of tales become laughable; the reader or audience can listen in amazement, interpreting the women's differences from the true womanhood standard as grotesque or horrific, while the tales' tellers are accorded authority and respect. The women in these tales are "as strong as any man"; the implicit comparison is to men like Crockett, and that comparison makes them freakish. Like Sally Ann, they may become sexualized or inappropriately asexual.

Truth, on the other hand, is defining herself. In true tall-tale style, she makes her opponents out to be the fools while she herself is heroic. The *telling* of one's own story is an important aspect of the construction of a persona; by having a voice, a character becomes more than an objectified body: he or she becomes a subject, able to shape the story and the audience's interpretation. This is what makes Truth's presentation of herself in the tall-tale model challenging; her speeches are in the first person, so she tells her own story and plays a large role in crafting her corporeality. Even the stories written about her by others show her speaking; like Crockett, she is represented as a subject rather than an object of her tales.

Truth as Tall-Tale Teller

Both in her role as a public lecturer and preacher, and in her dictation of her narrative, Truth was a woman speaking aloud, a role fraught with tension. Addressing groups of people was a fairly transgressive activity for a nineteenth-century woman to undertake, particularly an African American woman. Truth was able to authorize herself as a public speaker by framing herself simultaneously within the tall-tale discourse and the discourse of elocution, thus revising the tall-tale discourse. Her construction of her body contributed to her success as a public speaker; by offering her speeches as a highly physical, embodied act, she presented herself as a heroic body with a powerful, effective voice. At the same time, she utilized the moral intent associated with nineteenth-century elocution and oratory to mediate her emphasis on her heroic body.

The tall tale often functioned as an effective oratorical technique by binding the teller and his (or her) audience. The tall tale was first and foremost a verbal form; its translation into writing was a secondary process that, according to many critics, complicates much of the tale's cultural significance.[58] Not only was the tall tale itself a spoken form, but speaking was important to tall-tale heroes; the frontier boast is, of course, a feat of speaking represented within the tales, and in the case of Crockett, speaking was often one of the qualities he boasted about. The ability to speak effectively, convincingly, and even as a way of battle, appears in many tall tales as a characteristic of the hero. An early Crockett almanac features one of Crockett's speeches before Congress, in which he offers his famous boast that he can "run faster, dive deeper, stay longer under, and come out drier" than anyone else. However, even before he makes this boast, Crockett claims, "I can outspeak any man on this floor, and give him two hours start."[59] Clearly the act of public speaking is an important qualification within the world of the tall tale.

Public speaking was important not only within tall tales but within mainstream American culture. Oratory and its concomitant art, elocution, were extremely valued areas of study in nineteenth-century America. Frederick Douglass's powerful abolitionist speeches in the 1840s are a familiar example of the important role oratory played in American policy and social decision-making. Many books on grammar and on the use of the voice and the posturing of the body were available, including such titles as John Walker's *Elements of Elocution* (published in the United States in 1810), Noah Webster's *An American Selection of Lessons in Reading and Speaking: Calculated to Improve the Minds and Refine the Taste of Youth* (which went through at least fifteen editions between 1787 and 1800), and Caleb Bingham's *Columbian Orator* (1797), immortalized by Douglass. Samuel Kirkham informs the readers of his *Essay on Elocution* (1833) that his book of grammar went through fifty editions in six years.[60] The ability to use rhetoric and oratorical skills defined the well-educated person in the nineteenth century, and these skills were marketed as abilities practical for everyone.[61]

The intensity of the culture's interest in this field of study is revealed by the extremely detailed, technical analyses of voice, posture, and gesture in these popular books of elocution which were marketed not to the college student or professor but to the grade school pupil and to the average middle-class white male citizen. For instance, Kirkham's book, intended for grade school children, contains chapters called "Pronunciation of AND," "Errors in Modulation," and "Emphasis of Radical and Vanishing Stress." Other books spend a great deal of space analyzing the actual organs that make speech possible. All these elements together form a picture of a culture in which the way one spoke determined, in great part, the way he or she was received by others and, therefore, a culture in which elocutionary mistakes were to be studied and avoided.

While Truth had no rhetorical or oratorical training, she would certainly have been familiar with the common oratorical styles of her day and with the importance of oratory in general simply because of its cultural pervasiveness. Not only were public speeches and sermons very common, but oratory texts emphasized conversation as one of the best places to learn oratory, which shaped the way nineteenth-century Americans understood the act of speech, public and private, extending into the act of expression in general, whether in spoken or written form.[62] Truth would have been familiar with common oratorical styles and conventions through her attendance at political and religious meetings and revivals.

In addition to the more formal categories of oratory and elocution, Truth would have been familiar with vernacular speech, including such forms as tall talk; these forms, which emphasized orality rather than written texts, would have been particularly important to Truth since she was illiterate. Her illiteracy may, in fact, have facilitated her complex usage of both oratorical and tall-tale strategies. Recent biographers of Truth point to the value of Truth's illiteracy, arguing, "It is misguided to see Truth's orality as a pathology, a condition of negation. . . . She used her speaking voice as the unalienated inheritor of a great oral tradition."[63] Indeed, the oral traditions Truth utilized were not only American; many critics have noted the extent to which she remained wedded to African oral culture.[64] Truth utilized and balanced oral traditions and the middle-class model of oratory in her public speaking role and thus presented a complex embodied presence to her listeners.

The objectives of oratory in nineteenth-century America were moral and political. The nineteenth-century orator had "a central cultural role: to articulate a public moral consensus and bring it to bear on particular issues through forms of discourse—spoken or written."[65] More specifically, this moral consensus was identified with democracy: "Nineteenth-century rhetoricians equated the moral obligations of the rhetorician with the preservation of democratic culture."[66] In other words, the speaking person had a responsibility to uphold certain American moral ideals, ideals consistent with democratic culture. Oratory was never simply entertainment; the person who spoke had to speak for American culture and had to propound democratic values. Although this oratorical model was clearly aimed at white males, the goals of the nineteenth-century orator were goals that speakers like Truth fulfilled perfectly. In fact, Truth, a black woman who would be expected to have been silenced in nineteenth-century America, used the underlying rhetoric of American rhetoric itself to validate her act of speaking. She used her culture's own values to authorize herself as a public speaker, an orator.

She combined this oratorical patriotism and morality with the entertainment value of the tall tale. Tall-tale tellers entertained, and their tales also elevated speakers themselves. By combining both of these models, oratory and the tall-tale vernacular, Truth was able to construct a position of authority for herself as a speaker, validate her speaking within a model of democratic values, and configure her own body as simultaneously heroic and morally righteous.

This complex and effective configuration is all the more remarkable because of women's exclusion from public speaking in nineteenth-century American culture. Forbidden to address "promiscuous audiences," women who hoped to maintain respectability could speak only to other women in the public forum. Early women speakers, including Frances Wright and Maria Stewart, were controversial, drawing much public critique. The Grimké sisters were lecturing to female groups as early as 1838 but were harshly criticized when they did so to mixed groups.[67] In order to maintain their true womanly status, lecturers like Catharine Beecher, Emma Willard, Dorothea Dix, and Harriet Beecher Stowe all had men deliver their public addresses for them. In 1852, Horace Mann voiced the concerns of the American public when he said, "When a woman . . . appears on the forum and makes speeches she unsexes herself."[68]

Truth combated this notion of the unwomanliness of public speaking by constructing her own vision of the female body. She delivered her speeches in such a way that her body and her oratory were often inextricably linked in the minds of her audiences, and this linking is translated into the written documents about her. For instance, Olive Gilbert argues, "The impressions made by Isabella on her auditors, when moved by lofty or deep feeling, can never be transmitted to paper . . . till by some Daguerrian art, we are enabled to transfer the look, the gesture, the tones of voice, in connection with the quaint, yet fit expressions used, and the spirit-stirring animation that, at such a time, pervades all she says."[69] According to Gilbert, a more advanced technique must be found to convey Truth's impact as a public speaker; the written word is inadequate to the task, as are the common daguerreotype techniques which fail to capture "the gesture, the tones of voice . . . and the spirit-stirring animation" that are central to Truth's effectiveness as a speaker. Truth's body is a crucial element of her oratorical skill. Her visibility in a public forum is a necessary component of her cultural work.

The *Bugle* version of Truth's Akron speech begins with a similar disclaimer: "It is impossible to transfer [the speech] to paper, or to convey any adequate idea of the effect it produced upon the audience. Those only can appreciate it who saw her powerful form, her whole-souled, earnest gestures, and listened to her strong and truthful tones." Again, this writer insists that it is necessary for one to see and hear Truth presenting her words in order fully to understand her speeches. Her body is as important a component of her oratory as the words she speaks. This kind of disclaimer is common in descriptions of Truth; as Fitch and Mandziuk explain, "Those who tried to capture in words the effect she had on an audience frequently reverted to describing her physical form as well as her oratorical features, finding that one could not be explained adequately without the other."[70] Truth was not a disembodied orator; her physicality was a core constituent of her oratory, and she used this physicality to assert her bodily integrity in the face of the argument that women who spoke in public unsexed themselves. Peterson refers to this phenomenon as Truth's "bodied voice" and links it to her African origins.[71] Where unsexing suggests a dismemberment or loss, Truth puts herself forth as a *whole* body.[72]

While her body and voice were inextricably linked, Truth's voice itself commanded much attention from her listeners. Truth's voice is frequently described in transcriptions of her public speaking. The voice was an important aspect of an orator's performance, and Truth's voice apparently conveyed an authority and strength not often associated with women at this time. One newspaper quoted in Truth's *Book of Life* explained, "Her voice is strong, has no touch of shrillness, and she walked about as hale and hearty as a person of half her years." Another newspaper reported, "Her deep, powerful voice has the same effect as formerly in moving an audience."[73] Gage describes her voice as "like rolling thunder."[74] Her voice served to heighten her bodily presentation as a heroic, powerful figure. Her illiteracy comes into play here as well; because she spoke rather than wrote, her voice and her body were her texts, playing as large a role in her acts of communication as did her actual words.

The almost superhuman power attributed to Truth's voice—a voice "like rolling thunder"—serves further to establish the congruity between her voice and her body. This congruity works to Truth's advantage: Truth and those who write about her define her body and voice as powerful entities *made* for public speaking. When her body and voice threaten to be separated, Truth joins them forcibly; this is the case in one of the most famous stories emerging from her *Book of Life*. William Hayward describes this occurrence which took place in Indiana in 1858. Truth was speaking to a group of men who "demanded that Sojourner submit her breast to the inspection of some of the ladies present" because the group suspected her of being a man. When she demanded to know why they thought this, they responded, "'Your voice is not the voice of a woman, it is the voice of a man, and we believe you are a man.'"[75] This assertion presents two layers of meaning: in one sense, the speakers are commenting on Truth's literal voice, which was deep, strong, and authoritative; this is not the voice they expected to hear from a woman. In another sense, Truth's oratorical presence, her figurative voice, was powerful, public, and competent, and therefore the audience could not believe that she was a woman. The story continues that Truth reprimanded the group and proudly showed the congregation her breasts. Truth links her physical body and her voice, visually displaying her body when an audience does not recognize the congruity between her body and her voice. She demands this congruity and thus, as is often the case in her narratives, decommissions the male/female dichotomy by challenging its "naturalness."

Another story, second only to the Akron speech in its effective construction of Truth's tall-tale body and its demonstration of her revisions of the genre, is related in the *Narrative*, as transcribed by Olive Gilbert. Truth is a speaker at a religious camp meeting. The meeting is disrupted by "a party of wild young men" who insult the attendants and threaten to set the tents on fire; according to the *Narrative*, the whole meeting was paralyzed. Unlike a tall tale, this story relates Truth's fear: she says to herself, "I am the only colored person here, and on me, probably, their wicked mischief will fall first, and perhaps fatally." She quickly changes her mind, however, swayed by her belief in God and her own righteousness. It is, in fact, this righteousness that transforms her into an excessive tall-tale body; she explains, "I felt as if I had *three hearts*! and that they were so large, my body could hardly hold them!"[76] She becomes a tall-tale figure of compassion and Christian courage, characterized by the strength of her hearts rather than by her arms or height.

Her excessive tall-tale body then becomes vocal. When she goes before the disruptive crowd, her heroism emerges through her voice. This story emphasizes the importance of Truth's speaking ability as dramatically as any other story about her. To attract the crowd's attention, she sings to them, and Gilbert explains, "All who have ever heard her sing this hymn will probably remember it as long as they remember her. The hymn, the tune, the style, are too closely associated with to be easily separated from herself, and when sung in one of her most animated moods, in the open air, with the utmost strength of her most powerful voice, must have been truly thrilling."[77] Gilbert invokes the inseparability of Truth's body from her oral presentations and explicitly configures Truth's voice as heroic, manifesting strength and power.

The power of Truth's voice becomes even more explicit as the story progresses. She preaches to the crowd, and her singing and speaking have an effect on the "wild young men" that no amount of pleading, threatening, or exhorting by the white authorities of the camp meeting had accomplished: "Her speech had operated on the roused passions of the mob like oil on agitated waters; they were, as a whole, entirely subdued, and only clamored when she ceased to speak or sing." Her voice becomes an almost supernatural element, calming the men who are represented as little better than savage beasts. While she is speaking, she has them under her control. At the end of the evening, she tells the men that she will sing one more song to them if they will agree to leave afterward; when the crowd agrees to this proposal, Truth's voice again takes on heroic dimensions: "'AMEN! it is SEALED,' repeated Sojourner, in the deepest and most solemn tones of her powerful and sonorous voice. Its effect ran through the multitude, like an electric shock; and the most of them considered themselves bound by their promise, as they might have failed to do under less imposing circumstances."[78] Here Truth's voice becomes like the force of electricity, able to move through a crowd and affect each person individually. As an electric shock, Truth's voice has the power to ratify promises and disperse a dangerous mob. This story provides a particularly effective encapsulation of Truth's use of and revision of the tall tale in her construction of her body; in this story, she is a physically and vocally excessive body, but her excesses originate in her moral righteousness. Rather than being a purely carnal body, Truth is empowered by her religious beliefs; her heroism is mediated by her inner life, as represented by her three hearts.

Even as Truth's public physical presence was shaped to fit the tall-tale model, her moral purpose remained central. As Harriet Beecher Stowe reports in her article "The Libyan Sibyl," Truth asked God for her name to signify her purpose in life; she explains, "'And the Lord gave me Sojourner, because I was to travel up an' down the land, showin' the people their sins, an' bein' a sign unto them. Afterward I told the Lord I wanted another name, 'cause everybody else had two names; and the Lord gave me Truth, because I was to declare the truth to the people." Traveling, showing people their sins, being a sign, and declaring the truth were, thus, deemed by God to be Truth's roles in life. This is the role of the nineteenth-century orator, and Truth shows herself to be authorized by God to assume this role. She is the moral voice for her culture, for "the people," black and white.[79]

Truth is both the moral exemplar and the tall-tale hero. Truth's Akron speech combines humor and common-sense logical statements characteristic of tall tales with hard-hitting criticism of the country and the ideals shaping women's treatment and behavior. Her speech as it was recorded by the *Bugle* and by Gage is a masterpiece of oratory according to nineteenth-century standards (which to some extent explains its presence in twentieth-century popular culture): it is clever, rapidly paced, biting, and it responds intelligently and perceptively to the challenges the culture posed to women. She announces to the country's men, "Why children, if you have woman's rights give it to her and you will feel better. You will have your own rights, and they won't be so much trouble." This quote displays Truth's combination of humor and a manipulation of logic on a literal level, which was characteristic of many of her speeches. It is also a masterful use and revision of the tall tale.

As she is represented in her narrative and her *Book of Life*, she was a quick, witty woman, always able to think on her feet and knock down racist and sexist arguments with aphoristic statements. This is characteristic of the tall tale. In addition, Truth was a hard-hitting moral speaker, and nestled within her humor was a core of moral rectitude. Truth was very conscious of her role as an orator and of the moral responsibilities this role entailed. Although she utilized the humor and exaggeration characteristic of tall tales, her speeches were never pure entertainment in the way many of the stories in the Crockett almanacs were; instead, she was using her oratorical ability to change society, to force the United States to recognize its own democratic ideals.

Truth represented herself not in literal but in heroic terms. In this way she prevented herself from becoming a freakish figure, which was a possible outcome for unusual and visible nineteenth-century women's bodies. Rather than becoming identified, through her public presentations, with the tradition of Barnumesque performers like Joice Heth, Krao, or Julia Pastrana, Truth configured her body in terms of heroism, power, and moral fortitude. She used this discourse to dismantle many of the binary oppositions that would otherwise have blocked or disfigured her public self-representation. It is worth emphasizing that one of Truth's most obvious revisions of the tall tale was that the incidents she reported and the characteristics she attributed to herself, particularly in her Akron speech, had a foundation in literal truth. While she rhetorically constructed these incidents and characteristics within the discursive model of the tall tale, the incidents themselves were not intended to be tall-tale fictions. Like Mowatt, Truth was presenting an autobiographical text; and while autobiography is always fictionalized, readers must acknowledge the intended truth-value of these documents. Truth was manipulating available discourses not to elevate herself but to amplify her message of equality and Christian goodness. As a tall-tale figure, she was able to command a wider audience, assume authority as a speaker, and configure a public bodily presence which was far more powerful than her literal body.

The Supreme Right of American Citizenship

Ida B. Wells, the Lynch Narrative, and the Production of the American Body

4

The women of the race have not escaped the fury of the mob. In Jackson, Tennessee, in the summer of 1886, a white woman died of poisoning. Her black cook was suspected, and as a box of rat poison was found in her room, she was hurried away to jail. When the mob had worked itself to the lynching pitch, she was dragged out of jail, every stitch of clothing torn from her body, and she was hung in the public courthouse square in sight of everybody. Jackson is one of the oldest towns in the State, and the State Supreme Court holds its sittings there; but no one was arrested for the deed—not even a protest was uttered.

—Ida B. Wells, *The Reason Why the Colored American Is Not in the World's Columbian Exposition*, 1893

In this passage, journalist Ida B. Wells (1862–1931) relates the story—one of many in her articles and pamphlets—of a black female lynch victim. This woman is emphatically embodied by her nudity and her public display, and just as she is stripped of her clothes, she is also stripped of all agency: nameless, voiceless, identified only in terms of her relationship to her white employer, and acted on by a white lynch mob. Indeed, her body becomes a specular object, hung naked "in sight of everybody." Wells reveals this specular othering as a means of identity consolidation for white Americans.[1] By noting that the lynching takes place in a civic site, a location of civic formation, Wells suggests that this black woman's lynching functions to mark the boundaries of—and thereby create—a white community and white citizenry. Sojourner Truth narrated a black female embodiment characterized by power, vocality, and subjectivity, and upon first reading, Wells's text may seem to do the exact opposite, describing this "black cook" not as a self-possessed public actor but as a victim of the white public world. Wells does not reinforce cultural beliefs in black female victimization, however; on the contrary, Wells publicizes the brutalized black woman's body as a means of critiquing the American narrative which excludes black women from full personhood. Wells deploys the black female body in order to interrogate American notions of citizenship and identity, ultimately arguing for a new vision of black female embodied citizenship which she herself models. Like Truth, Wells deconstructs dominant narratives of black womanhood by proposing an alternative, a fully embodied black female citizen.

Wells's work had particular relevance in the late nineteenth century. Tensions over race and sex and their incorporation into the concept of American citizenship manifested themselves in this time period through lynchings. The torture and murder of thousands of blacks and the mutilation of their bodies as a public spectacle for enthusiastic white audiences are evidence of strains in the culture so serious and so threatening to dominant ideologies that in the minds of many prominent whites they necessitated—or at least justified—a public rhetoric and performance of ritual murder. Wells recognized lynching as a phenomenon that was actively defining the American body in the post-Reconstruction years. Rather than accepting the dominant explanation for lynchings, which asserted that black male rape of white women was a Southern epidemic which could be quelled only by violent community response, Wells identified the lynch narrative as a functional public text.[2] Through her publicly distributed pamphlets and newspaper articles, she argued that lynchings and, more importantly for this study, the rhetoric surrounding lynchings functioned to set a boundary for American citizenship at the black body, a boundary that excluded black women and men and used their bodies as a way of defining the absence of—and therefore the borders of—Americanness. Wells recognized that the familiar and often-repeated rhetoric surrounding lynching was a nationalizing narrative, a narrative constitutive of American personhood, and she intervened in this narrative in order to question its inevitability and evacuate its meaning.

Wells was the single most important writer about the widespread lynching of blacks from the late nineteenth century through the early twentieth, one of America's most horrific spectacles of violence. Up to 10,000 blacks were murdered by lynch mobs between 1870 and 1910, with the numbers peaking in the 1890s; what this meant was that, "on the average, a black man, woman, or child was murdered nearly once a week, every week, between 1882 and 1930."[3] The vast majority of those lynched were black men. According to historian Herbert Shapiro, "The phenomenon of lynching exhibited American society in its most ferocious and inhuman manifestation."[4]

Lynching was both a spectacle, enacted in cities and towns throughout the South, and a public narrative, described and explained in newspapers, political speeches, and sermons; and it was intensely embodied in both formats. The most obvious body involved was that of the black male—identified in the narrative as a rapist, bestial and savage—who was tortured, dismembered, and burned, and fragments of whose body were kept as mementoes by the white onlookers. The other conspicuous bodies were those of the white male perpetrators which the narrative identified as chivalric heroes, demonstrating "the strength of manly self-control," and the white female "rape victims," identified as passive, virtuous, and terrified.[5] The body left out of this scenario was that of the black woman, whom current critics have noted was both a "significant absence" and "*symbolically* present," but not a central figure.[6]

Wells is widely recognized as a crusader against the lynchings of the late 1800s; she began her career as a journalist in 1887 and began writing articles about lynchings shortly thereafter. After she was forced to leave Memphis because of a controversial antilynching editorial she had written, she consolidated her early newspaper articles about lynching into her first pamphlet, *Southern Horrors* (1892). While she continued as a journalist, she also wrote *The Reason Why the Colored American Is Not in the World's Columbian Exposition* (1893) and *A Red Record* (1895); each of her pamphlets combines statistics, her own essays, and excerpts from white press reports of lynchings. Her study of lynching through her articles, speeches, and pamphlets, is credited with revealing that "lynching was not simply a spontaneous punishment for crimes but an act of terror perpetrated against a race of people in order to maintain power and control"; most current critics of the post-Reconstruction South now agree with Wells's assessment that lynchings were "an excuse to get rid of Negroes who were acquiring wealth and property and thus keep the race terrorized and 'keep the nigger down.'"[7] Wells is a fairly well-known figure: she is generally represented in historical studies of black women writers of the nineteenth century and appears, as well, in texts which consider the post-Reconstruction period.[8] Any study of lynching must mention her writing,[9] and her texts—particularly *Southern Horrors* and *A Red Record*—are currently in print and widely available;[10] however, only in recent years has she begun to be considered as a historical figure in her own right.

Most scholarly studies still consider her as a kind of fringe character, providing local color but secondary to the "major" black figures of the late century, including Frederick Douglass, Booker T. Washington, and W. E. B. Du Bois.[11] She is considered secondary, as well, to the "major" women figures of the late century, including Susan B. Anthony and Elizabeth Cady Stanton, and to studies of nineteenth-century citizenship, even women's citizenship.

Historians, who might be expected to note the important interventions Wells made into the rhetoric of citizenship, often miss this aspect of her work because citizenship itself is not traditionally considered an embodied site; thus, many historians have overlooked Wells's intervention into the corporeal work of citizenship. What it meant to be an American citizen was highly contestable and unstable in the last years of the nineteenth century. Citizenship was a conflicted and embodied construct. At one level it was a legally defined construct, and legal definitions were ambiguous and controversial as they moved to exclude and maintain the exclusion of black men and all women. On another level it was an amorphous social organizational principle, which shaped the bodies and consciousness of those in the United States. Wells critiques the way the discourse of citizenship is deployed to idealize certain bodies and exclude others. In particular, she notes that the silenced and elided black female body plays a crucial, if veiled, role in organizing meanings accruing to bodies and citizenship.

Recent scholars who have emphasized citizenship as a set of abstract rights and ideals have worked in an opposite direction from Wells. Indeed, many recent studies of citizenship in the late nineteenth century emphasize an idealized version of American civic life and equality which bears no resemblance to the world in which Wells lived and worked. These critics and historians often validate the lip service Wells's white contemporaries gave to notions of equality and view the institutionalized enactment of exclusionary policies at all levels of American society as anomalous.[12] This study will attempt to correct some of these elisions by foregrounding Wells, considering her engagement not only with the issue of lynching but with the larger national discourse of citizenship, a concern which places her on par with such canonical figures as Douglass and Du Bois. This study will also bring the techniques of literary study to bear on Wells's writing, attending to textual nuances that broader historical studies may elide. Wells's work rewards this approach because her interventions into larger cultural discourses are narrative interventions, some of which are quite subtle. As Priscilla Wald notes in her study of narratives of nation, rhetorical and textual details such as odd phrasings or slips of grammar can "mark the pressure of untold stories"; thus, attention to formal elements of writing may yield insight into an author's confrontation of broader cultural logics. This approach is particularly beneficial for Wells because she herself exploited the textual slippages in the discursive construction of embodied citizenship.[13]

A number of recent studies of the post-Reconstruction South and the phenomenon of lynching do consider the profound inequalities of this time period and thus provide a context for this study. For instance, many current critics who analyze these areas are interested in how black and white *manhood* were constructed in this highly contested period.[14] Others explore how this time period brought into focus tensions surrounding white women's relationship to citizenship.[15] This study builds upon the insights of scholars exploring the intersection of race and gender, particularly as these discourses converge to shape American citizenship at the site of the body.[16] This is the very issue at the heart of much of Wells's writing, and it forms the focus of this study. In her most important texts, *Southern Horrors* (1892) and *A Red Record* (1895), Wells unpacks the raced and gendered bodies which undergird lynching; this strategy not only attempts to alter the country's understanding of lynching—an aspect of her work which critics have recognized—but also creates a representational vacuum in order to allow citizenship to become affiliated with a different set of bodies—black female bodies. Wells herself does not fully articulate the new vision of citizenship that her writing enables, but she puts into public circulation an image of fully civilized, empowered black female embodiment that resonates with and takes form in connection with her own publicly enactive body.[17]

Wells herself was in a position to recognize the tensions surrounding citizenship in the post-Reconstruction nation. Born to slaves in Mississippi, Wells, at the age of sixteen, fought to keep her siblings from being sent to live with different members of the community when her parents died in a yellow fever epidemic. To keep the family intact, she herself became head of the household, not taking on a maternal role but instead becoming the family wage-earner and establishing a personal precedent for leadership. She had taken courses at Shaw University, and after teaching school for several years, Wells entered the field of journalism, writing her first article under the pseudonym Iola. She quickly demonstrated her skill in this profession as well as her willingness to tackle controversial topics if she felt injustice was involved. As she wrote in her autobiography about one of her first controversial articles criticizing the Memphis school board, "I thought it was right to strike a blow against a glaring evil and I did not regret it."[18] Her journalism was quite influential in Memphis until she was banished by a white mob in 1892, at which point the black-owned *New York Age* hired her and she became a national—and international—author and speaker against lynching. Wells did not marry until 1895 and continued to write and speak against lynching and in promotion of racial justice even after she had children. In many ways, she is the quintessential example of the woman in public whose life is not legible within the traditional spheres model.

As the study of Sojourner Truth revealed, current critics as well as critics in the nineteenth century have been inclined to represent nineteenth-century black female embodiment exclusively in terms of victimization; indeed, as this study has previously noted, many critics interpret embodiment itself as victimizing, positing *lack* of corporeality as a strength, a position of agency. Wells, like Truth, demonstrates that this rubric is inadequate. Wells cannot be understood simply as a victim of her culture's mandates. While she certainly faced limitations due to cultural constraints, constraints which had particular sway over those whose bodies were both black and female, she defined her own existence not by limitation but by strategic manipulation of national narratives. Wells demanded a public platform. Working as a writer and as a public speaker, she rejected stereotypical representations of African American women and rejected, as well, the racial uplift models of womanhood promoted by many of her contemporaries. Even as she publicized the victimization of black women at the hands of rapists and lynch mobs, she utilized her analysis of the lynch narrative to create a public space for herself and to rewrite the black female body as empowered and civilized.

Just as Sojourner Truth made use of rhetorical strategies to shape public perception of her body, Wells's work makes clear the connection between rhetoric and the material body, revealing the powerful material consequences of particular rhetorical configurations of black bodies. Although narrative and rhetoric might seem to be poor weapons in a public battle in which thousands of blacks were killed, Wells engaged in this confrontation precisely at the level of narrative because the narrative justified and thus undergirded the material reality of lynching; if the narrative were deconstructed, a major support for the acts of lynching would be gone.[19] The lynch narrative articulates a set of interlocking corporeal configurations, an elaborate structure that is carefully calibrated and balanced: the coherence and credibility of the narrative is key to its efficacy and social functioning as a mechanism constructive of particular bodies, and it only maintains this coherence and credibility through the silencing of black women's stories and the discursive obscuring of their bodies. In addition, as Wells recognized and revealed, lynching involved not only the physical subjugation of thousands of black people but the mental subjugation, through fear, of all African Americans. Lynching worked powerfully at the level of public discourse to teach, as Wells put it, "the lesson of subordination" and to consolidate white supremacy and patriarchy nationally and internationally, creating a national myth that excluded black bodies.[20]

Wells was strategic in her writings, reprinting many white press reports of lynchings in her own pamphlets; one of her most effective methods for exposing the horrors of lynching was to allow the white press to indict itself.[21] She exploited the slippages and inconsistencies in white reporting and used "objective" white accounts against their authors in order to destabilize the three main characters in the lynch narrative, challenge the narrative's legitimacy, and create a kind of representational vacuum; by drawing attention to extant cultural instabilities surrounding citizenship and its definition, Wells re-envisioned the American national body.[22] This chapter will examine the discourse of citizenship in the late nineteenth century, considering how Wells intervened in and altered this discourse through her dismantling of the lynch narrative. It will highlight her strategies for undercutting the rhetorical and thus the political status of white and black women and men, and it will, finally, consider the new model of black female embodiment that Wells offered as a possible way to fill the vacuum of citizenship which she created.

LYNCHING AS A NATIONAL NARRATIVE

Wells attempted to change her society and to promote justice by intervening in the *discourse* of lynching. The dominant cultural discourse surrounding and justifying lynching, what I am calling the lynch narrative, was widely believed in the late nineteenth century because of its regular reiteration at all levels of society.[23] Not only whites but also blacks believed it; Wells herself explains, "Like many another person who had read of lynching in the South, I had accepted the idea meant to be conveyed—that although lynching was irregular and contrary to law and order, unreasoning anger over the terrible crime of rape led to the lynching."[24] She stopped believing this narrative when she had personal knowledge of a situation which led to a lynching: in 1892, three black Memphis businessmen were lynched for operating a grocery store which competed successfully with a white-owned business. The accusation of rape played no part in this lynching, which led Wells, who was a friend of one of the victims, to recognize that lynchings and the lynch narrative functioned to suppress black economic and political independence.

What Wells's analysis of lynching reveals is that the lynch narrative was one way in which the boundaries of citizenship were corporealized, defined, and policed. As current scholars such as Hazel Carby have noted, "Hegemony is never finally and utterly won but needs to be continually worked on and reconstructed, and sexual and racial ideologies are crucial mechanisms in the maintenance of power."[25] Wells's writing identifies the lynch narrative and its regular reiteration as part of the maintenance and functioning of a white supremacist hegemony. In particular, the lynch narrative was one way in which the dominant group identified and publicly announced which bodies were worthy of citizenship and which were not. By intervening in the lynch narrative and disrupting its reiteration and reception, Wells altered the meaning of the bodies in this narrative and the larger discourse of citizenship itself.

The post-Reconstruction period in which Wells was writing was a time in which notions of citizenship and Americanness were extraordinarily contested, played out—sometimes violently—in the court system, state and federal legislatures, and in community and interpersonal relationships or encounters. Although the term suggests a legally established and defined state of being, citizenship was and is, in fact, a troubled and contingent concept. Feminist historians have noted that "the status of citizen, which in stable times we tend to assume is permanent and fixed, [in unstable times becomes] contested, variable, fluid." Rather than being a historical constant, citizenship is "purposefully constructed, all the more reason that its meanings and the rewards and obligations it conveys may vary over time and among citizens." Historians note that "throughout the nineteenth century, lawyers, political writers, legislators, and women themselves struggled to establish the limits of citizenship and, by implication, personhood in the context of defining and redefining the American state," but this project became especially fraught in the post-Reconstruction period, when nation building was not simply a metaphor but a literal project.[26]

Nineteenth-century law grappled with the idea of citizenship and with the question of which bodies were allowed to be citizens. The purpose of citizenship law is to define and thus construct a polity; these laws bring together large aggregate groups of people under one unifying heading of "citizen" and simultaneously exclude groups from this designation. The practice of inclusion or exclusion in America has often been predicated on corporeal differences, namely the racial designation assigned to blacks and whites. Wells scholar Patricia Schechter notes that a key question for late-nineteenth-century law was, "Exactly what or who was a rights-bearing 'body' entitled to full citizenship and the authority to make claims on the state?"[27] Wells's parents were still slaves when the *Dred Scott* Supreme Court case of 1856 explicitly addressed the question of whether blacks were citizens, and the opinion of the court, written by Chief Justice Taney, explained, "We think that they are not, and that they are not included, and were not intended to be included, under the word 'citizens' in the Constitution, and can therefore claim none of the rights and privileges which that instrument provides for and secures to citizens of the United States."[28]

Although legal reforms introduced during Reconstruction, including the Fourteenth Amendment, moved to make black and white men legally equal, these changes were short-lived; indeed, social historian Martha Hodes and other scholars note that these legal reforms triggered more intense cultural differentiation of blackness and whiteness as whites strove to fortify the color line and consolidate white identity in order to protect white supremacy. By the time Wells began her career, post-Reconstruction reform efforts began revoking these many changes, shifting the country back to the ideal of exclusively white citizenship articulated in the *Dred Scott* case. Supreme Court cases from the *Slaughterhouse* cases and *Civil Rights* cases of the 1870s through the *Plessy v. Ferguson* case of the 1890s grappled with legal definitions of citizenship, ultimately fortifying white male citizenship while leaving blacks disenfranchised and legally disempowered.[29] The dominant legal attitude toward non-white citizenship was exclusionary; in fact, as the century progressed, and Wells grew into adulthood, laws moved to demarcate more and more overtly a legal boundary between full citizenship, exemplified in white male bodies, and secondary or partial citizenship, citizenship in name only—if that—for men of color and all women.[30]

The Supreme Court's decision in *Plessy v. Ferguson* did not create this dynamic but simply articulated an already manifest trend in American legal affairs.

Although the legal discourse of citizenship is significant for the way it elided black women entirely, negating their bodily existence while creating the conditions conducive to their abuse and exploitation at the hands of white men, even more important is the lived experience of citizenship and the larger symbolic relevance ideas of citizenship acquire in a given cultural moment. While Wells was critical of the laws and was the plaintiff in a racial discrimination court case early in her career, her intervention into the national narrative, rather than the legal construction, of citizenship provided her with the means to reclaim black female embodiment. As Wells recognized, citizenship is not based simply on laws; the larger cultural ideas about citizenship underlie and may in fact supersede the laws or create the climate in which certain laws come to seem necessary or inevitable, and it is at this level that Wells made her most significant contribution.

The lynch narrative is only fully legible when viewed in the context of the chaos surrounding the notion of citizenship in nineteenth-century America. Wells's work documents the fact that the murders of African Americans by lynch mobs was the material parallel to—or the material enactment of—the legal exclusion of African Americans from American citizenship. Citizenship clearly means more than legal status: citizenship is one way in which people in a country feel themselves fully part of their society and thus fully human. Citizenship creates solidarity, a sense of common identity and shared struggle. Nineteenth-century commentators on the idea of citizenship articulated this solidarity, voicing a necessary interconnectedness that defined belonging to America: "The good of every American is the good of all; the hurt of one is the loss or hurt of the whole people." This feeling of interdependence is the function of citizenship laws; these laws "literally constitute—they create with legal words—a collective civic identity. They proclaim the existence of a political 'people' and designate who those persons are as people, in ways that often become integral to individuals' senses of personal identity as well."[31]

This affective and corporeal sense of belonging to, of being part of, a larger whole creates the nation, and the feeling is created not simply by laws but also by narratives, persuasive stories alternately called "civic myths," "national fantasy," and "official stories" by current historians and cultural critics.[32] These stories, propagated widely until they are familiar to most people in the country, provide coherence in a diverse population by, for instance, constructing national origins, common enemies, and heroes. American myths like John Smith and Pocahontas, or George Washington and the cherry tree, are often deliberately constructed and circulated as a means of articulating and formulating national unity and thereby the nation itself. Literary and historical scholar Priscilla Wald explains, "Official stories constitute Americans. . . . They determine the status of an individual in the community. Neither static nor monolithic, they change in response to competing narratives of the nation that must be engaged, absorbed, and retold: the fashioning and endless refashioning of 'a people.' "[33] These narratives describe and define citizenship. Although critics have not yet explicitly identified it as such, the lynch narrative was a nationalizing story. Wells recognized the function of the lynch narrative, its power to construct a polity, and her writing not only reveals and undercuts this official story but crafts a competing "narrative of the nation."

The nationalizing narratives which create citizenship also shape the bodily identity of the narrative's participants; citizenship is thus not simply an idea but also a force formative of particular corporeal configurations. As current body critics have noted, rhetoric shapes lived bodily experiences. National discourses, in particular, often function as *nationalizing* discourses, constructing the bodies of those who live in or identify with a particular country. Wells was particularly interested in how these discourses functioned to shape black women's bodies. Throughout her writing, Wells insisted on foregrounding the black female body, emphasizing the reality of black women's experiences of racist and sexist violence as an unrecognized element of the national phenomenon of lynching; publicizing black women's corporeal experiences was a means of undercutting dominant cultural narratives and exposing the machinations of the lynch narrative. The description of the lynching of the black cook excerpted in the epigraph to this chapter speaks to two of Wells's main goals: her dismantling of the lynch narrative and her critique of citizenship, both of which she attains through insisting on the material, corporeal existence of the black woman. The black cook whose story Wells relates is emphatically embodied, and her embodiment combines violence and sexuality; her public presence conflates the criminal, the erotic, and the Other. These characteristics are evidence of what Elizabeth Grosz calls "modes of corporeal inscription," the specific ways bodies—in this case black female bodies—are marked and shaped by the national narratives of a cultural and historical moment. Grosz notes the ways in which all bodies are marked by their culture and history, explaining, "There is nothing natural or ahistorical about these modes of corporeal inscription. Through them, bodies are made amenable to the prevailing exigencies of power. They make the flesh into a particular type of body—pagan, primitive, medieval, capitalist, Italian, American, Australian."[34] Citizenship discourses are means by which "bodies are made amendable to the prevailing exigencies of power," and various retellings of lynch stories create American bodies. This story, however, and others involving the victimization of black women both expose these corporeal inscriptions and challenge them.

This woman's public murder calls to mind Mowatt's description of the flaming ballet girl, whose onstage mutilation was similarly a punishment and a scene of erotic violation. The lynched woman serves a different function in Wells's text, however, than the ballet girl does in Mowatt's: while Mowatt differentiates herself from and simultaneously borrows from the erotic power of the ballet girl, Wells presents the lynched woman as an indictment of the national narrative of citizenship. Wells mutes the erotic and sensational power of the lynched cook and instead capitalizes on how this body undercuts the "official story" of lynching. The woman's naked, murdered body gives the lie to the lynch narrative, which identified black rape of white women as the cause of lynching. This woman was not accused of rape or any sexual crime but was herself a victim, her naked body calling to mind the rapes of black women which were, as Wells often notes, common and ignored. Her story, in fact, has broad relevance, as her experience of sexualized violence and victimization are indicative of dominant cultural dynamics surrounding and shaping black women's embodiment in the late nineteenth century. Significantly, the lynch narrative not only does not tell her story but in fact erases her experience altogether, because the narrative is unable to stand if her story is known. Even as the cultural *process* of lynching operated to kill this woman and thereby threaten the community of blacks and maintain the boundaries of citizenship, the *narrative* of lynching subsumes her story and not only invalidates her experience but makes it seem a logical impossibility because the narrative is based on the black male rape of white women. By telling her story, Wells undermines the lynch narrative and its rewriting of history.

Moreover, Wells presents the lynched woman's story as a challenge to the national fantasy of citizenship. In her description of the lynching, Wells invokes and indicts the justice system. She notes that the woman was hung in the public courthouse square. Furthermore, the city in which the lynching took place, Jackson, Tennessee, was the seat of the Tennessee Supreme Court. By calling attention to these public sites symbolic of justice, Wells reveals the emptiness of American ideals and reveals that the foundational connective tissue of the nation, the concept of citizenship, was corrupt to such an extent that particular bodies had to be destroyed to maintain the fiction of national unity. By publicizing these putatively erased bodies, Wells confronts the national narrative. Wald notes that "national narratives of identity seek to harness the anxiety surrounding questions of personhood, but what they leave out resurfaces when the experiences of individuals conspicuously fail to conform to the definition of personhood offered in the narrative"; the body of Wells's writing is an attempt to refute the lynch narrative by publicizing "untold stories" and thereby allowing them to resurface.[35] Her writing reveals that white male supremacy, the denigration of the black male, and the domestic idealization of the white woman were all predicated on the erasure of the black female body from the national narrative.

Twentieth-century historians often portray citizenship as a disembodied construct, consisting of abstract ideals, rights, and responsibilities which are not explicitly affiliated with the bodies of actual citizens or the material reality of the nation itself; however, in nineteenth-century writing, the nation is often figured as a body into which individual citizens' bodies become literally incorporated.[36] Turn-of-the-century statesman Elihu Root explained in a speech on citizenship that civic virtue comes from all men "regarding their nation as a great organic whole," and an 1892 high school textbook called *The American Citizen* argued, "It does not work to treat men as machines or rivals; but as the famous Roman emperor said, 'We are made for cooperation, like feet, like hands, like eyelids.'"[37] However, citizenship discourses do not simply incorporate bodies; they may also violently expel certain bodies, and the process of incorporation or expulsion is mutually formative. Wells's work identifies actual lynchings and the widespread lynch narrative as "modes of corporeal inscription" which produce particular kinds of bodies: not only the black bodies which were politically and economically as well as physically subordinate, reviled, and abjected, but also the bodies of those who marshal this dominant rhetoric, white women and men.[38] She reveals these dynamics most clearly through her discussions of black female bodies.

A number of current critics have noted that nineteenth-century hegemonic discourse created particular corporeal configurations relevant to citizenship.[39] Wells's writings reveal that this nationalizing discourse emerged with particular force in the lynch narrative. She exposes the mechanisms by which white men come to stand for the nation while black men and women come to be "anticitizens," challenging the white male body's representative status through her work with lynch narratives.[40] Wells's work links the acts of lynching and the narrative surrounding lynchings to a larger, veiled national project constituting citizenship. Her work reveals lynchings not only as an act enforcing the economic disempowerment of blacks but also as a public spectacle that consolidates and creates white civilization. By fragmenting, degrading, and destroying the black lynched body, white men's own bodily integrity—and, further, their bodily congruence with the American nation—was performed and fortified. In other words, because black men and all women were identified with the body, white men came to seem noncorporeal and therefore wholly rational, and their claim to American citizenship was unquestionable, untainted by ulterior motives or base personal objectives tied to individual embodied identity. Wells demonstrates that lynchings were a performance of white male citizenship; these acts and the rhetoric that accompanied them in effect *created* white male citizenship and created the white male body as the unquestioned carrier of civilization, the representative American body. She challenges this construction of citizenship most powerfully through her descriptions of black women's experiences.

The rhetoric and practice of lynchings were emphatically public. At the same time that lynchings made use of public means of communication and public locations, however, they also tacitly worked to remove from the public realm such key national issues as the nature of citizenship and the uses of public space. As critics such as Gunning and Duggan have argued, the lynch narrative was a means by which a public debate surrounding race and sex became transformed into or subsumed within "private" discourses of morality, the "natural" characteristics and differences implicit in white and black bodies, and the vulnerability of domestic locations.[41] The public staging of lynchings thus foreclosed public debate of the issues underlying and fueling the lynchings. This interpretation of lynching as an intervention into the spheres debate is compelling because of its sensitivity to the ways the public and private may be deployed and manipulated as sites that organize meanings; it recognizes the dynamic nature of the spheres discourse and its political inflections. Wells's work intervened in the lynch narrative publicly, forcing the implicit categories to become explicit and thus disallowing the tacit foreclosure of the public debate over citizenship and national bodies.

Wells's writings achieve greatest legibility and reveal most fully their cultural force and significance when they are contextualized in terms of late nineteenth-century discourses of citizenship. The lynch narrative was one key element constitutive of American citizenship, and dismantling the lynch narrative enabled Wells to reconceptualize citizenship and the American body, a move which had profound implications for black womanhood. Wells's writings simultaneously respond to citizenship discourses and *produce* them; her writing is not simply reactionary but is also generative, altering and reconstructing the until-then implicit corporeal image of the American citizen. Like Mowatt, Eddy, and Truth, Wells operated within the confines of her cultural moment but also helped to transform that cultural moment, using her public presence to mobilize the cultural discourses and artifacts that surrounded her in order to create a space for change. While Mowatt utilized sensational rhetoric to formulate a public body, Eddy used a congeries of medical and scientific discourses, and Truth manipulated the language and images of the tall tale, Wells intervened in the public and legal discourse of citizenship in order to question the accepted models of embodiment and to propose a new envisioning of the black female body in particular.

Both Mowatt and Wells enlisted sensational discourses in their self-fashioning and their configuration of their own bodies, but they treated sensational tropes differently—and carefully. As was discussed in the chapter on Mowatt, sensational discourses were both powerful and dangerous. Mowatt insulated herself from the dangers of these tropes by emphasizing her respectable status as a middle-class white woman; she engaged with the concept of the sentimental and thus benefited from the culture's unspoken notions of white female citizenship. Wells, on the other hand, protected herself from the dangers of sensationalism by turning the sensational, even melodramatic, rhetoric surrounding lynchings against the whites who mobilized these discourses. In so doing, Wells did not accede to implicit notions of citizenship but argued for a more complete citizenship for blacks and women. Rather than try to engage with the sentimental ideal of embodiment—a model many of Wells's contemporaries attempted to utilize—Wells posited a revisioning of citizenship in general.

Wells's resistant depictions of the figures in the lynch narrative—white men, white women, and black men—and her discussion of the figure excluded from this narrative—black women—are the predominant means by which she intervenes in the national/nationalizing discourse of citizenship. Berlant explains that an effective nationalizing narrative or civic myth "sutures the body and subjectivity to the public sphere of discourse, time, and space that constitutes the 'objective' official political reality of the nation."[42] The lynch narrative attempts to operate in this way, demarcating the bodies which fit with the official master narrative of the nation, but Wells disrupts this process and this performance of embodied American citizenship by refiguring the bodies involved. The white male is no longer civilized as in the official national rhetoric but savage and bestial; the white woman, too, is removed from a pedestal and revealed to be ruled by passions. Black men become objects of sympathy, which means that their bodies' meanings are changed substantially from the hegemonic discourse, but they still do not stand as unmarked, representative bodies. Black women, excluded from the narrative, assume a place as victims along with their male counterparts, but Wells also suggests a powerful refiguring of black female corporeality, one that posits black women as capable of national leadership.

DISMANTLING THE LYNCH NARRATIVE

In order to rewrite the discourse of citizenship and configure the black female body as culturally central, Wells had to decommission the lynch narrative. Wells was a keen cultural critic who revealed and exploited cleavages or fissures within the discourse of lynching as a means of dismantling the narrative. By targeting awkward moments within the lynch narrative, moments Wald suggests "mark the pressure of untold stories," Wells is able to unearth and publicize these untold stories.[43] In publicizing black women's victimization at the hands of lynch mobs, Wells gives voice to one particularly important untold story; however, her project involves more than this significant recovery work. Revealing this untold story destabilizes the lynch narrative itself, and by undercutting each figure's cultural script, Wells creates a representational vacuum that becomes a space for her own construction of a new black female embodiment.

Early in her career, Wells had a professional experience which revealed the lynch narrative's power to shape black women's public lives and embodiment. In 1892, Wells wrote a significant antilynching editorial for the *Memphis Free Speech and Headlight*, a black paper of which she was part owner. Although she had written against lynching before, in this editorial she began her major assault against the narrative underpinnings of lynching, challenging one major element justifying lynchings—the ideology of absolutely pure Southern womanhood—by stating, "Nobody in this section of the country believes the old threadbare lie that Negro men rape white women. If Southern white men are not careful, they will over-reach themselves and public sentiment will have a reaction; a conclusion will then be reached which will be very damaging to the moral reputation of their women."[44] As was characteristic of Wells's writing, her tone was unapologetic and straightforward, offering no concessions to dominant ideologies of womanhood or of the appropriate behavior of blacks. Her editorial was not conciliatory but challenging, presenting her not as a supplicant but as an opponent who called Southern white men on their "old threadbare lie" and dared them to defend their ideology.

The white-owned Memphis *Evening Scimitar* responded immediately and harshly, misidentifying Wells as male and incorporating "her" into a lynch narrative. They printed an article in which they proposed lynching the author of the offending editorial; the *Scimitar* article called on the black community to expel the antilynching author who wrote such "calumnies" and threatened that if the black community did not respond, the white community would take possession of the "wretch," "brand him in the forehead with a hot iron and perform upon him a surgical operation with a pair of tailor's shears."[45] A mob ultimately did destroy the *Free Speech* headquarters and warned Wells, who was out of state at the time, not to return to Memphis, but it is the rhetorical response that is most revealing. Two aspects of this response are particularly telling. First of all, this respectable white newspaper makes a very public demand for the lynching of a black newspaper editor. Although Wells has done nothing but write an editorial, the paper is able to make an apparently uncontroversial call for her murder, even making the somewhat joking reference to castration as "a surgical operation with a pair of tailor's shears," the sardonic tone of which implies that the author(s) were confident in receiving full approbation from the paper's white readers. This aspect of the *Scimitar* article speaks to the broad-based popular approval for lynchings as well as to the public nature of the act of lynching itself—an act that would take place not in secret but "at the intersection of Main and Madison Streets"—and the rhetoric surrounding lynching.[46] Lynching was not a shameful act that should be hidden or concealed; rather, it was an act of public policing, of boundary fortification, and of citizenship formation. Lynching consolidated and protected the white community; because Wells challenged white womanhood—a challenge which was figured as an "attack"[47] in the *Scimitar* piece—she had become a significant threat, and lynching was the response. Notably, her threat was not physical but symbolic; the borders of the white community and white self-definition, white citizenship, were at stake.

Second, it is significant—and impossible to ignore—that the body the white writers plan to lynch is male. Although the white papers remained overtly hostile to Wells after they discovered that she was female, still threatening to lynch her, their initial reading of her body identified her as male—not just rhetorically or incidentally male, using "he" to identify her, but materially, physically male, alluding to the presence of and public removal of male genitals. The narrative surrounding lynching was so powerful that it imposed black manhood on Wells's print identity simply because she had posed a verbal threat to the ideology of pure white womanhood. Thus, Wells's black female body was erased—it was not even a possibility. Wells incorporated this quote into the text of her book *Southern Horrors* without commentary, allowing the irony of the text to speak for itself. Even as Wells entered and began to reshape the public discourse of lynching, the possibility of her public identity as a black woman was being foreclosed; there was no space in the official public narrative of lynchings—and, by extension, in the nation-building which these narratives invoked—for a black female body.[48] By placing this quoted passage from the *Scimitar* within her own text, Wells invokes the silenced and invisible black female presence. She uses this reclaimed black female body to denaturalize the *Scimitar*'s rhetoric, silently revealing the absurdity of the article's smug threat; clearly the "surgical operation" cannot be performed on her because she does not have male genitalia. In disarming the article in this way, she draws attention to the constructed and inaccurate nature of the larger lynch narrative in which the article is grounded, thus challenging its legitimacy, and implicitly calls into question the erasure of black womanhood from this narrative and from public discourse. This quote shows how—by elision and by particular textual configurations—certain bodies are excluded from citizenship and portrayed as antithetical to the community, which is figured corporeally as white and male.

Wells worked to counter black women's erasure from the lynch narrative by recovering and publicizing the stories of black women who were victims of lynch mobs. While her contemporaries and recent critics have rightly noted Wells's memorializing of male lynching victims,[49] little attention has been given to Wells's public memorializing of female victims.[50] In each of her books Wells reported on the lynching of black women, from young girls to pregnant women to elderly grandmothers. By bringing the bodies of black women into the foreground in her writings, Wells did more than simply publicize a profoundly marginalized group and reveal their suffering at the hands of a violent white majority; she enacted this publicizing as a means of rewriting American citizenship and the American national body, presenting a new embodied citizenship that was inclusive of and represented by the black female body.

Significantly, she did not revictimize black women through voyeuristic recountings of their lynchings. Rather than using the graphic detail that characterizes her reports on black male victims, with women victims Wells emphasized their humanity, often strategically using the language of true womanhood and sentimental literature to structure her descriptions. For instance, she ends *Southern Horrors* with the story of "poor little thirteen year old Mildred Brown," who was lynched on suspicion of poisoning a white infant. The rhetoric of sympathy and sentiment she employs—"poor little" Mildred Brown—runs directly counter to the rhetoric of the white press which casts black men as "a race of cut-throats, robbers and lustful wild beasts" and ignores black women altogether.[51] Her focus is not on offering up the graphic details of Mildred Brown and other women's victimization but on emphasizing their status as sentimental female figures on par with white women. While the female lynch victims literally experience the same fate as the male lynch victims—death at the hands of the white mob—she does not "offer up for public display the details of black female victims' bodily suffering"; instead, she emphasizes their true womanly suffering.[52] She maintains this emphasis in her descriptions of widows of male lynch victims, using sentimental rhetoric: "His wife holds Thomas Moss, Jr., in her arms, upon whose unconscious baby face the tears fall thick and fast when she is thinking of the sad fate of the father he will never see, and of the two helpless children who cling to her for support she cannot give."[53] In this passage, Wells does articulate the black female's bodily suffering, but this suffering—the body's permeability and vulnerability to the outside world—is manifested through tears rather than blood, unlike her descriptions of black male victims.

Wells deploys this somewhat sentimental black female body as well in some of her public presentations. Tears were occasionally part of Wells's lectures; indeed, in her autobiography, Wells reports crying during an early public lecture and describes the experience as one of losing control of her body: "A feeling of loneliness and homesickness for the days and friends that were gone came over me and I felt the tears coming"; and she explains that, afterward, "I was mortified that I had not been able to prevent such an exhibition of weakness. It came on me unawares."[54] Similarly, during her first trip to England she learned of a woman being brutally lynched, and she explained in a column in the *Chicago Inter-Ocean,* "And I sat there as if turned to stone, with the tears rolling down my cheeks at this new evidence of outrage upon my people, and apathy of the American white people."[55] Both these scenes show marked similarities to some of Mowatt's descriptions of the difficulties and debilitations of public presentations; both women even use the metaphor of feeling their bodies turned to stone, a metaphor that suggests the removal of the woman's agency over her body.

Wells mediates the sensational with the sentimental in ways similar to Mowatt's careful use of these discourses to describe her own embodiment. Even as Wells characterizes her experience of tears in terms of lack of agency—the tears "[coming] on me unawares"—her tears ultimately demonstrate her own strategic manipulations of black female public embodiment. She admits that the audience for her first speech found the tears very moving and effective, and although Wells disparages these bodily emotions as "stage business," Schechter notes that Wells often engaged in "talking through tears" in her public speaking as "a public demonstration of feminine bona fides."[56] While she often tried to present herself publicly as an objective and dispassionate observer, Wells knew the potential *power* of tears to communicate to her audiences and readers.[57] Not only did the tears help to characterize her as an appropriately feminine woman, but they also conveyed the bodily impact of the horrors Wells discussed.

By humanizing and feminizing Mrs. Thomas Moss, Mildred Brown, and other female victims, as well as herself as public figure, Wells asserts their reality and their identity as women, fighting the erasure of black womanhood; seen as merely *black*, she argues, many victims are not acknowledged as *women*. She writes of lynching victim Emma Fair, "One of the prisoners charged was a woman, and if the Nineteenth Century has shown any advancement upon any lines of human action, it is pre-eminently shown in its reverence, respect and protection of its womanhood. But the people of Alabama failed to have any regard for womanhood whatsoever."[58] She thus uses women's stories to challenge the dominant culture's ignorance and rejection of black womanhood; the "people of Alabama" belie their claim to civilized humanity by their treatment of women like Fair, and Wells's declamation of this treatment both makes black womanhood a public presence and invokes black female humanity.

In addition to calling public attention to the black women victimized by lynch mobs, Wells also explicitly decries white men's rape of black women. As critics like Bettina Aptheker and Sandra Gunning have observed, the white rape of black women is the unspoken national parallel to lynchings. As Aptheker noted as early as 1982, "When I let go of the conventional use of the categories 'lynching' and 'rape,' for example, it seemed to me that the antilynching crusade of Black women was also a movement—a Black women's movement—against rape. It was forged with the materials, resources, consciousness, and forms of argument and support that Black women had available to them at the turn of the century." Gunning, too, links the acts of lynching and rape in the lives of black women, arguing that "in white supremacist thinking black women are invisible and their experience of lynching and rape completely denied."[59] Black women's elision from the lynch narrative meant that their experiences were invisible and the effects of lynching and rape on them were erased. Their bodies' erasure ensured the perpetuation of the dominant national understanding of white male bodies.

Throughout her writings Wells addresses this elision by documenting the white double standard which makes the threat of black rape of white women a national emergency and the actual rape of black women unremarkable. Very early in *A Red Record*, Wells addresses the common white prolynching argument that rape is such an intolerable abomination that it compels otherwise civilized white men to acts of violence. Taking a very detached and professional tone, Wells asserts of white men,

> To justify their own barbarism they assume a chivalry which they do not possess. True chivalry respects all womanhood, and no one who reads the record, as it is written in the faces of the million mulattoes in the South, will for a moment conceive that the southern white man had a very chivalrous regard for the honor due the women of his own race or respect for the womanhood which circumstances placed in his power. . . . Virtue knows no color line, and the chivalry which depends upon complexion of skin and texture of hair can command no honest respect.[60]

Bodies here very literally become texts, texts which the informed and willing reader can interpret as documenting the morally corrupt nature of white male models of chivalry and civilization and documenting as well the bodily suffering of the black women victims. By identifying and corporealizing mulattoes as evidence of white men's rape of black women, Wells interprets light skin and hair as signs not simply of difference but of the emptiness of white narratives.[61] These bodies have been inscribed upon by acts of rape. She also reduces racial difference to such small matters—"complexion of skin and texture of hair"—as to be ridiculous. As with the other aspects of the lynch narrative, Wells's interpretations of these bodies enable her to undercut white ideologies of personhood and citizenship. This is also a means by which she foregrounds black female bodies, enlisting the materiality of black women's corporeality to provide substance to her arguments; black women's bodily experiences speak a different story of America than the dominant national narratives.

In both *Southern Horrors* and *A Red Record,* Wells gives voice to the different story by listing several pages of incidents of white men raping black women and girls and receiving no punishment. For example, she describes the community's response to a white man raping an eight-year-old black girl, Maggie Reese: "The outrage upon helpless childhood needed no avenging in this case; she was black." Similarly, she describes another rape as "a deed dastardly enough to arouse Southern blood, which gives its horror of rape as excuse for lawlessness, but she was a colored woman." She lists these events alongside descriptions of the community's immediate and violent response to any black man accused of raping a white woman, making the double standard explicitly visible for her readers. She discusses a case in which "the wives and daughters of . . . lynched men were horribly and brutally outraged by the murderers of their husbands and fathers," and another in which "a white man . . . inflicted such injuries upon another Afro-American child that she died. He was not punished." In another case she allows the white press to indict itself: "A leading journal in South Carolina openly said some months ago that 'it is not the same thing for a white man to assault a colored woman as for a colored man to assault a white woman, because the colored woman had no finer feelings nor virtue to be outraged!' Yet colored women have always had far more reason to complain of white men in this respect than ever white women have had of Negroes."[62] By placing this passage in her own text, a text which documents the offenses against black women and which, moreover, by its very existence, verifies the virtue and outrage of one black woman, Wells reveals the emptiness of this claim and the double standard it upholds. Wells's work discloses the fact that "lynching and rape formed a web of racist sexual politics designed to subjugate all African Americans."[63]

Documenting these rapes and unveiling the double standard also enables Wells to argue into visibility the interlocking and interdependent nature of dominant bodily configurations. White male virtue was a corporeal construction predicated on white female passivity and black male bestiality; similarly, the rhetoric of white female purity and black male savagery depended for their propagation on a particular configuration of the white male body as aligned with civilization. All of these bodily constructions, manifested in the lynch narrative, relied on the silencing of the black female experience and the erasure of the black female body. Revelations of black women's victimization, Wells knew, would be profoundly destabilizing to the whole narrative, potentially collapsing it like a house of cards. Thus by revealing black women's suffering, Wells made another significant intervention into the lynch narrative and the national narrative of which it was part. The black female body was simultaneously exploited and ignored; by asserting and documenting black female bodily existence, Wells undercut the lynch narrative and laid the groundwork for her new vision of embodied citizenship.

Wells's intervention into the lynch narrative did not only confront black women's depictions, it also addressed the narrative's representation of its three key figures: white women, white men, and black women. Each of her pamphlets identifies and exploits fissures and slippages in the official story of lynching, using these moments to allow the lynch narrative to undermine itself. One such fissure is the representation of white women in white press reports; this aspect of Wells's writing has received limited critical attention. Although the description of white womanhood is not a major emphasis for Wells, it was a significant aspect of her dismantling of the lynch narrative and her intervention into citizenship discourse. By examining representations of white women in white papers, Wells demonstrated that the lynch narrative was unstable, since the white papers themselves could not contain the stories they related within the lynch narrative, and this therefore destabilized the rhetorical status of the white woman.

In *Southern Horrors*, Wells quotes from white newspapers which document white women's consensual relationships with black men. In each case, the white texts register the inconsistency and instability of the discourse of proper white womanhood. For instance, Wells quotes a white paper: "If Lillie Bailey, a rather pretty white girl seventeen years of age . . . would be somewhat less reserved about her disgrace there would be some very nauseating details in the story of her life. She is the mother of a little coon. The truth might reveal fearful depravity or it might reveal the evidence of a rank outrage."[64] The newspaper seems to be unable to reconcile the contradictory categories Bailey occupies; she is both "a rather pretty white girl" and a person whose life story is "nauseating": she simultaneously occupies a traditional position of white womanly beauty and delicacy (the fact that she is "pretty" and may be the victim of "a rank outrage") and of inhumanity. The paper calls for Bailey to be "somewhat less reserved"; the word "reserved" suggests true womanly discretion—rather than "recalcitrant" or "uncooperative," Bailey is characterized in this way as a properly discreet, feminine woman. At the same time, by using the racist epithet "little coon," the white paper characterizes Bailey's child as monstrous and thus, by extension, the mother as monstrous, also. Bailey occupies a profoundly unstable position and thus reveals the rifts in the white narrative of white womanhood. The instability of their characterization emerges in contrasting bodily imagery—the monstrous woman versus the pretty white girl. The authors' inability to categorize Bailey safely within the category of victim of rape leads to tensions within the text; Bailey is both victimized white child and depraved whore.

Similarly, Wells notes the case of Mrs. J. S. Underwood, who was the white wife of a minister. After claiming she was raped by a black man, Underwood reports to her husband that the relationship was consensual, explaining, "He had a strange fascination for me. . . . I did not care after the first time. In fact I could not have resisted, and had no desire to resist."[65] When Underwood refers to her "strange fascination" and the fact that she did not want to stop the encounter from happening, her language evokes romance and passion rather than victimization at the hands of a rapist. Underwood's testimony suggests overpowering desire and lack of self control. She is the wife of a minister and thus in a position to embody the true womanly purity required for the white notion of civilization, but instead she is overcome by passion or lust. By positioning Underwood in this way, Wells allows her readers to identify the white woman as propelled by corporeal longings, longings which the dominant discourse connected to black women only. Perhaps more importantly, she documents the white press's inconsistency, a sign of its inability to maintain this fractured narrative.

Consensual sexual relations between black men and white women are a key site of this instability because the existence of these relationships undercuts the clear corporeal distinctions drawn between the races and the sexes. Wells explains, "The Southern white man says that it is impossible for a voluntary alliance to exist between a white woman and a colored man, and therefore, the fact of an alliance is a proof of force."[66] Publicizing these consensual relationships allowed Wells simultaneously to give the lie to three components of the lynch narrative: the cultural rhetoric pronouncing the inviolable purity of the white woman and her almost disembodied chastity, the lust-driven bestiality of the black men seen as rapist, and the consequent argument that because of these essential, corporeal differences, no white woman could ever willingly engage in sexual acts with a black man. In this rhetoric the black man and white woman are positioned as polar opposites, their literal corporeal differences magnified and distorted by popular discourse and made to stand for broad social and symbolic differences.[67]

Significantly, as Wells's writing reveals, this polar positioning effaces the black woman, who is deeply implicated in the rhetorical fashionings of black men and white women. Black women's bodies become the cultural repository of excessive sexuality, both the sexuality eschewed by the bodies of white women and that identified with the bodies of black men.[68] The spectacle of Sartje Bartmann from which Sojourner Truth had to differentiate her own public embodiment lingered to the end of the nineteenth century. Black women in the post-Reconstruction period were still—and perhaps even more emphatically—defined by excessive sexuality. One critic explains, "White women were characterized as pure, passionless, and de-sexed, while black women were the epitome of immorality, pathology, impurity, and sex itself. . . . Buttressed by the doctrine of the Cult of True Womanhood, this binary opposition seemed to lock black women forever outside the ideology of womanhood so celebrated in the Victorian era."[69] While Truth dealt with this binary by sidestepping it, identifying her body with a different model of corporeality—the tall tale—Wells addressed the binary and argued forcefully against it by identifying white women with sexuality, even excessive sexuality. In so doing, Wells destabilized the cultural narratives defining black and white womanhood. These consensual relations also undermined the picture of the black beast rapist, arguing that many of these women had *chosen* black partners, often then to abandon them when the relationship was suspected. Wells famously refers to this phenomenon when she laments "the poor blind Afro-American Sampsons who suffer themselves to be betrayed by white Delilahs," here exposing white women's manipulative, controlling use of their sexuality.[70]

In addition to indicting white women for their sexuality, Wells's writing also served a less accusatory purpose, that of showing the female body—black and white—as erotically legitimated. By acknowledging consensual interracial relationships, Wells gave sexual agency to black and white women and thus challenged the dominant culture's exaggeration or negation of female sexuality. As Duggan notes, "The suppressed agency of the white woman, her passivity and victimization, was refigured in Wells's version as the white woman's *choice* to engage in consensual sex with a black man."[71] While Wells used this notion of choice strategically, as a means of reforming public discourse surrounding black female corporeality, her writing nonetheless mobilized these ideas. In this way Wells's writing is linked to a cohort of late nineteenth-century and turn-of-the-century authors whose work attempted to normalize certain types of prohibited sex. Wells can certainly be read alongside Kate Chopin, whose miscegenation story "Desirée's Baby" and sexually-charged *The Awakening* offer new cultural visions of women's sexuality; so, too, Theodore Dreiser's *Sister Carrie*.[72] Indeed, Duggan positions the lynch narrative alongside an 1892 lesbian murder scandal as "parallel tales of sexual pathology"[73] that reveal relationships of power and the workings of the public sphere. The erotic, while not a main focus for Wells, does emerge in her construction of white and black female corporeality, and in this particular challenge to the dominant culture, Wells was not anomalous but on the forefront of social change surrounding sexuality that would emerge in the twentieth century.

Wells's refiguring of white and black female bodies functioned as part of her challenge to nineteenth-century citizenship. All women, white and black, were excluded from citizenship in the nineteenth century, with even white women classified as "members" but not citizens of the nation.[74] Although Wells did not lobby for women's suffrage, her emphatic reclaiming of black female bodies and her particular spin on white female embodied identity confirmed women as fully human. According to dominant discourses, the soft, delicate body of the white woman was not qualified for citizenship because of weakness and purity, and the coarse body of the black woman was doubly unqualified because of race and gender. Wells's writings destabilize both bodily configurations, allowing for the possibility of citizenship.

The notions of "savagery" and "bestiality" were key concepts used to organize bodies and delineate citizenship and the national body in the late nineteenth century. These notions were deployed by the lynch narrative and then redeployed by Wells. As we have seen, she challenged the savage/civilized dichotomy as it related to white and black women; this rewriting was perhaps more emphatic in her treatment of white and black men. Dominant discourses explicitly identified savagery with the black body, particularly the black male body, and aligned white masculinity with citizenship, and the lynch narrative was one of the public spaces where this model of black and white bodies played out, though not seamlessly. By intervening in representations of the white men who formed lynch mobs, Wells challenged dominant corporeal configurations. She reserved some of her harshest judgments for the lynch mobs and for the white men who comprised them and consistently rewrote the white male mob as the truly savage body in the lynching scenarios by allowing the white papers' descriptions of lynch mobs to document their cruelty. In this way she dislodged white male supremacy, showing white men to be uncivilized and thus incapable of national leadership. This strategy, documented by such critics as Sandra Gunning and Gail Bederman, is a means by which Wells undercut the "inevitability" of the white male national body.

In her numerous descriptions of lynchings, many taken directly from white news reports of the events, Wells repeatedly presents the white mob as savage, bestial, frightening, and beyond the pale of humanity. She refers to "the many inhuman and fiendish lynchings" and repeatedly calls the mobs "bloodthirsty," a term which assumes a literal cast in the context of the killings she documents. Wells is careful not to allow any reader to believe that the lynchings are perpetrated by a few anomalous and unrepresentative characters within the white community; instead, she often explains that lynchings are done "not by the lawless element upon which the deviltry of the South is usually saddled—but by the leading business men, in the leading business centre."[75] The press reports she reprints also emphasize the white lack of civilization; for instance, one report of a white mob killing an insane black man and his pregnant wife in Arkansas in 1892 notes, "The killing of a woman with the child at her breast and in her condition . . . was extremely brutal."[76] Wells thus provides a kind of textual background of white male cruelty and savagery, a background which suggests that savagery is the norm for white men; however, this background does not preclude certain horrific white male acts from emerging as a kind of relief portrait of white male brutality.

Wells's presentation of the lynching of Henry Smith in Paris, Texas, in 1893 presents a number of particularly vivid examples of the bestiality of white citizens and shows, as well, Wells's strategies for publicizing this bestiality. Wells introduces this case by asserting, "Never in the history of civilization has any Christian people stooped to such shocking brutality and indescribable barbarism as that which characterized the people of Paris, Texas, and adjacent communities." Her juxtaposition, even conflation, of the "civilization" of "Christian people" with "shocking brutality and indescribable barbarism" sets the profoundly ironic tone for this description. She will not allow a clear distinction between the lynchers and the black man they have identified as the object of their rage; in fact, she explains that the whites "proceeded to carry out their purpose with unspeakably greater ferocity than that which characterized the half crazy object of their revenge."[77] While the white male body culturally assumes a place of inherent leadership, Wells questions this designation, suggesting that there are no lines of separation between lynchers and lynched in terms of their humanity and civilization and arguing that the lynchers actually manifest "unspeakably greater ferocity." She then proceeds to quote at length from an account of the event which corroborates her assertion, offering sickening, graphic details about the lynching which attempt to celebrate the event but ultimately fail in this project.

Placed in the context of the image of white bestiality that Wells mobilizes, the white-authored texts she excerpts are unable to maintain a clear emphasis on the virtuous white citizen. Through these texts, Wells unveils the internal rifts in the lynch narrative for her readers. For instance, the white reporter on the Smith case whom Wells quotes at length asserts that "everything was done in a business-like manner" and yet describes the white community as being in "a wild frenzy of excitement" at the prospect of the lynching. Here and throughout the news report Wells reprints, the white press articulates contradiction, identifying the white lynchers as frenzied and eliding the supposedly clear difference between the white citizens and the abjected black body they lynch.[78] The distinction between the black "beast" and the white citizens becomes even slipperier as the reporter describes a carnivalesque scene in which Smith "was escorted through the city so that all might see the most inhuman monster known in current history."[79] This white-authored passage offers a moment of rich, almost certainly unintentional irony within Wells's text because, of course, the white mob which assembles to enact and celebrate the lynching of Smith is, itself, shown to be the "inhuman monster" in this text. Smith, in fact, becomes a kind of cipher in this report, mentioned only in passing. His symbolic significance as a black beast rapist is so codified that the reporter need not articulate or argue this point; instead, the main focus of the report is on the white mob itself and the horrific violence they enact, and Wells capitalizes on this slippage.[80]

The reporter offers graphic descriptions of Smith's torture and murder, and although he registers the sickening nature of the events he observed, saying, "Words to describe the awful torture inflicted upon Smith cannot be found" and "It was horrible," he gives a detailed description of each event and explains that "every groan from the fiend, every contortion of his body was cheered by the thickly packed crowd of 10,000 persons." The reader presumably begins to be sickened by the white reporter's descriptions of how the lynchers "thrust hot irons into [Smith's] quivering flesh" and the explanation that "after burning the feet and legs, the hot irons—plenty of fresh ones being at hand—were rolled up and down Smith's stomach, back, and arms. Then the eyes were burned out and irons were thrust down his throat."[81] Removed from its original context in a white newspaper, the report's graphic descriptions of violence become less predictable and more unfamiliar. Indeed, the reader may begin to empathize with the black victim, feeling twinges of his bodily suffering in his or her own body. Furthermore, because the description has been preceded by statistics which Wells lists to show the emptiness of the rape myth used to justify these acts, the reader has reason at the very least for skepticism about the lynch narrative. Wells thus leads the reader to uncertainty about the nature of the white mob.

Although the crowd of whites finds entertainment in viewing these acts of torture and violence—and there is some suggestion that the reporter does as well—the reader registers a discontinuity between the "horrible," "awful torture" and the crowd of cheering white citizens, a discontinuity that destabilizes the civilized, somewhat disembodied status of the white crowd. Thus, although the terms "fiend" and "inhuman monster" are used to identify Smith, the white mob itself comes to fit these descriptions, particularly because this report is situated within Wells's text. By taking control of white press reports and using them to eviscerate the image of white men, Wells undercut the easy connection of white men and citizenship. Wells here pulled the curtain away from the otherwise invisible reconstruction of white hegemonic ideologies, revealing the complex and only partially effective machinations that go into formulating the lynch narrative's valorization of white men and the disembodied white male citizen.

The lynch narrative heightened the cultural importance of white male valor and white female passive purity, especially in the South. White male and female bodies had to bear the weight of the white supremacist need to differentiate between blacks and whites. Because the legal reforms of Reconstruction had threatened too much similarity between the races, the post-Reconstruction project of legal and racial differentiation necessitated that white bodies manifest a purity and valor that could then be characterized as distinctly white virtues. Writing for the court in *Plessy v. Ferguson*, Justice Henry Billings Brown argued that the law cannot intervene in racial discrimination because "legislation is powerless to eradicate racial instincts, or to abolish distinctions based upon physical differences."[82] This statement articulated and fortified the widespread belief that blacks and whites were inherently different, differences that were figured as "physical differences" and "racial instincts" and were identified in the bodies of blacks and whites. *Plessy* represents the culmination of the *legal* process of stripping blacks of citizenship.[83] It is not, however, the apex of the *cultural* process; the cultural discourse of citizenship was much more pervasive, and therefore the means by which blacks were expelled from the national body were more visible, publicly enactive, and repetitive. Lynching represented the culmination of this cultural process; it was the material parallel to *Plessy*.

White purity and valor, then, were of great importance. As Sundquist notes, the maintenance of white Southern masculinity became a "national enterprise" in the late nineteenth century, as "civilization" was continually articulated as a characteristic embodied in white men. Indeed, Bederman explains, "By harnessing male supremacy to white supremacy and celebrating both as essential to human perfection, hegemonic versions of civilization maintained the power of Victorian gender ideologies by presenting male power as natural and inevitable."[84] White female purity also occupied a privileged space in dominant ideologies; the editorial that caused Wells to be banished from Memphis warned white men that "the moral reputation of their women" would be damaged by the revelation that many white women selected black male lovers.[85] White female purity stood, in many ways, for the validity of the dominant national narratives; Hodes notes that "white ideologies about the purity of white women" intensified after emancipation, and Dana Nelson explains that, in periods of nation-building and transition, "anxieties about impurities within the (male) civic body can be transferred to the sexuality of women."[86] Wells's revelation of the tenuous construction of white male and female embodiment, then, had profound implications.

While Wells's publicizing of white bestiality undercut the status of white men and women, she altered the lynch narrative's picture of black men by reframing them as victims, a move which enabled her to emphasize the inhumanity of the act of lynching, to counteract the apathy of the United States and other countries, and to refute the image of black men as vicious, villainous, and inhuman. Indeed, Wells's texts promoted sympathy for black men. However, her emphasis on black male victimization simultaneously undermined the ideology, propounded by a number of her black male contemporaries, that black men should be and were the leaders of the race. Wells's emphasis on black male victimization can be read as another way that she dislodged the main characters in the lynch narrative.

Wells's portrayal of black men as victims operates in her depiction of Henry Smith as well as her description of the lynching of Lee Walker in Memphis in 1892.[87] These two descriptions, the most graphic and extensive in her pamphlets, are damning to the white mob. Equally obvious, although often not recognized as a rhetorical strategy, is that, in both of these lynchings, Wells emphasizes the victimization and powerlessness of the black men. Although the white paper she quotes initially states that Walker "made a desperate resistance," within the same paragraph it undermines this agency, reporting that "his power to resist was gone."[88] He is shown being attacked, dragged bodily out of jail, and animated entirely at the whim of the white mob.

Indeed, the white press reports that Wells excerpts reduce Walker and Smith to nothing but bodies, pure physicality on display for the benefit of the white mob. By providing exhaustive details about the lynchings, these press reports give numerous examples of this reduction to the base corporeal. For instance, after Walker is dead, the report explains, "The body fell in a ghastly heap, and the crowd laughed at the sound and crowded around the prostrate body, a few kicking the inanimate carcass." The reporter seems to go to great lengths to emphasize the body's passivity, describing it as a "heap," "prostrate," and an "inanimate carcass." Further evidence of the reduction of a person to powerless flesh was the mob's propensity to divide up the body of the dead victim among themselves as souvenirs; the reporter on Walker's lynching notes, "The relic hunters remained until the ashes cooled to obtain such ghastly relics as the teeth, nails, and bits of charred skin of the immolated victim of his own lust. . . . The teeth were knocked out and the finger nails cut off as souvenirs."[89] Current critics of lynching and of Wells's work have examined this phenomenon from psychoanalytical and historical frameworks, with particular attention to the white mob's fascination with black male genitalia as evidence of homoerotic fascination with the abjected other.[90] More important for this study, however, is the fact that Wells does not shy from reproducing these images of black men's dehumanization in her texts. As I have noted, Wells documents but does not capitalize on black women's lack of agency; where black men are concerned, Wells provides more sensationalistic detail. By reprinting such graphic reports in the context of her own challenge to the lynch narrative, Wells does not entirely replicate the lynch narrative's process of dehumanization. She does, however, continue to circulate images of a black male lack of agency, and as she displays the lynch mob's brutality, she highlights the victimized black male body. This strategy allows her to rewrite another piece of the lynch narrative, portraying black men as victims rather than as beasts. By locating black men in the role of victim, Wells displaces black and white women from this role. White women, as we have seen, assume a more sinister agency; black women, conversely, come to embody the power, control, and moral righteousness of American citizens.

This refiguring of black male embodiment, along with her refusal to defer to black patriarchy as an appropriate response to the racism of the post-Reconstruction United States, may explain some of the antagonism Wells encountered from many contemporary black men who were public figures. Although she generally received support from Frederick Douglass,[91] many other black male leaders, including a number of newspaper editors, were critical of her work.[92] As one scholar explains, "Black proponents of uplift proposed accessing full citizenship by subscribing to dominant bourgeois class and gender codes," including patriarchal dominance of black women and black women's enactment of true womanhood.[93] This was a version of "racial uplift" to which Wells did not adhere; she did not assume a true womanly approach in her own activism, nor, as we shall see, did she concede to a vision of black male leadership of "the race." Thus, both the context and content of Wells's activism were threatening to many black male leaders, some of whom responded by belittling her with diminutive descriptions such as "a defenseless woman" or "solitary little woman," or by calling her reputation into question.[94] Her work was controversial even within the black community, but Wells had a larger vision of social transformation toward which she strove, although it often meant encountering hostility from black men.

There are ways in which Wells does mitigate the wholesale dehumanization of black men in the lynch narrative. For instance, she is careful in her discussion of the crimes of which black men were accused. She does not claim that all lynch victims are innocent of all criminality, but she cites precisely what the crimes are.[95] Wells's strategy in these instances is perhaps more effective than if she had denied all wrongdoing on the part of those lynched; because the black male body in the lynch narrative signifies monstrosity, bestiality, and unspeakable crimes, Wells's identification of actual acts—accosting two women on the road, consensual sex, and even the murder of a girl—offers a vision of black men as people, shifting their bodily representation somewhat. By offering her own detailed and objective assessment of the crimes, Wells humanizes the black men, demonstrates her own reliability as a narrator, and reveals how out of proportion the lynchings—and the lynch narrative—may be to the crimes themselves.

Furthermore, in her writings Wells does periodically identify black men not with victimization but with agency and even heroism.[96] For instance, her major pamphlets featured introductions by Frederick Douglass, who emphasized black manhood, arguing in one case, "We are men, and our aim is perfect manhood, to be men among men. Our situation demands faith in ourselves, faith in the power of truth, faith in the work and faith in the influence of manly character."[97] As I will discuss, however, Wells routinely used her assertions of black male heroism as a way of structuring her own arguments about black women. Bederman emphasizes the fact that Wells made many black men into emblems of manly virtue; in comparison to the white men in her text, the black men clearly appear more humane, sane, and sympathetic. The predominant image of the black man in her writing, however, is the victimized, dead body. By offering graphic details, Wells leaves the reader with the images of black men dissected into body parts, immolated, variously mutilated. *The Reason Why* and *A Red Record* even feature photographs and engravings of lynched bodies, generally reprints of souvenir postcards that were made to celebrate the event.[98] These images in particular feature smiling white faces around a destroyed black male body, and they linger in the reader's mind. These images—both rhetorical and visual—are horrifying, and this is, of course, the point: Wells wants to shock her readers into recognizing the inhumanity and injustice in the act of lynching. She is also attempting to dislodge the lynch narrative's image of the bestial black man by replacing that image with that of the victim. By propagating these images of black men, however, Wells also undercut black male leadership rhetoric and provided a key prerequisite for her reclaiming of black female embodiment.

RE-CREATING BLACK FEMALE EMBODIMENT

Wells used her writing systematically to dislodge the symbolic significance of each of the three key players in the lynch narrative: the white woman embodies not victimization but desire and sexual longing, the white man is no longer the defender of womanly purity but is a frightening savage, and the black man is not a beast but an oppressed victim. Wells's writing also reveals that black women are effaced in the lynch narrative, their experiences not publicized and their political status absorbed into the category "black" or "woman," each inadequate. By reclaiming and publicizing black women's experiences of lynching and of rape, experiences felt and conveyed corporeally, Wells calls into question the interarticulation of bodies and identities, which the lynch narrative perpetuated and reinforced.

In her attempt to manifest a black female national presence, Wells was not alone: black female domestic novelists were also involved in this reclamation of black womanhood. Recent critics Claudia Tate and Ann duCille have brought critical attention to the strategic manipulation of domestic discourses in black women's writing in the late nineteenth century; by declaring dominant gender roles as their own, black women authors such as Frances Harper, Emma Dunham Kelley, and Pauline Hopkins demanded the full humanity implicit in those roles. As many critics have noted, however, claiming the status of "true black woman" also meant claiming the patriarchal baggage that came along with this role, including male dominance in the family and female relegation to a secondary role, typically domestic.[99] These domestic novelists utilized and manipulated—but still subscribed to—the public and private spheres model of civilized behavior and community organization. According to this model, male leadership and citizenship was of primary importance. The domestic novelists also often relied on decorporealization as a strategy for inscribing black women within dominant discourses, muting the bodily specificities of their characters and even "normalizing" them by making them indistinguishable from characters in white-authored domestic and sentimental texts.

Wells's strategies did not align with those of most black women who worked for racial uplift, particularly domestic novelists. Even in her use of sentimental rhetoric, Wells kept the black female body visible. More important, the representational vacuum she created in the lynch narrative and the larger rhetoric of American citizenship provided her with a space to construct her own vision of embodied black female leadership. As Schechter notes, Wells "burst the gender roles held out to black women of her generation."[100] Rather than being wholly reactive, Wells manifested agency in her shaping of civic myths and national fantasies, moving beyond the simplistic dichotomies—dichotomies of male and female, agent and victim, as well as public and private. Critics have claimed that Wells "argued that African American women had to organize themselves politically to effect inclusion in the category of protected womanhood"; this is not entirely accurate.[101] Wells's writing does more than attempt to convince the larger culture to accept black women as needing as much protection as white women; she pushes beyond the binary, beyond the private and public spheres model, arguing into existence a black female embodiment which cannot invoke protection because there is no one there to protect her. The cultural landscape Wells maps out is populated by savages and victims; thus, black women themselves must embody their own courage and power, and in Wells's world they do so.

Although black women are subaltern bodies, vulnerable to official discourses of power and citizenship, Wells is able to utilize her own subaltern status as a critical entry into the larger discourse of national belonging, a vantage point from which she can disrupt and resist the dominant narratives of citizenship. Lauren Berlant's model of Diva Citizenship is one example of this resistance and disruption, and it is a useful means of understanding Wells's activism. Diva Citizenship is a model which does not subscribe to reductive binaries but instead brings into focus the fluid way power operates and can be shifted and mobilized simultaneously by dominant groups and those who are members of "politically distressed populations."[102] Berlant explains Diva Citizenship as "a dramatic coup" in which a nonprivileged woman "puts the dominant story into suspended animation; as though recording an estranged voice-over to a film we have all already seen, she renarrates the dominant history as one that the abjected people have once lived sotto voce, but no more; and she challenges her audience to identify with the enormity of the suffering she has narrated and the courage she has had to produce, calling on people to change the social and institutional practices of citizenship to which they currently consent."[103] Although Berlant does not include Wells in her consideration of Diva Citizenship, this is a model that Wells fits perfectly.[104] Wells's writing and her attempts to tell a different story of American nationhood fit Berlant's definition because they give voice to the abjected and subaltern African American women whose stories and bodies are continually overlooked or violated, and they reinvent American citizenship. Wells certainly narrates and publicizes the suffering of African Americans, but more than this, she also alters the playing field and encourages her readers to reimagine citizenship. Diva Citizenship is not a passive model; it does not describe an attempt to blend with current practices. Instead, it stages a coup, flashes up, challenges, and invokes change; thus, this model makes visible Wells's work to overthrow dominant narratives and construct a new way for African American women to be publicly embodied citizens. While the domestic novelists' model relies on the hegemonic narratives already in existence, Wells moves beyond that model; the concept of Diva Citizenship reframes and thereby brings into focus this aspect of Wells's cultural project.

Wells does not entirely reinvent citizenship; rather, she offers hints, suggestions, and glimpses of an alternative to the current models. Because she has emptied the dominant corporeal configurations of citizenship, she has created a space for new configurations, and her own body often steps into this space. One key moment of this new envisioning of black female embodied citizenship occurs in Wells's encounter with the Chesapeake and Ohio Railroad: in 1884, early in Wells's adult life, she attempted to make the court system work on her behalf, initiating legal proceedings against the Chesapeake and Ohio Railroad for discrimination when they excluded her from first class train accommodations because of her race. Wells was successful initially, but when the railroad appealed the case to the Tennessee Supreme Court, the Court ruled against Wells. This event is often represented in biographical sketches of Wells as a touchstone for her political activism, the moment at which she came to the realization that she could fight the institutionalized racism of the dominant culture.[105] More importantly for this study, this event also serves as an effective example of how Wells exploited cultural elisions and tensions in order to define black womanhood as fully embodied and powerful, though it has rarely been read in this way. At the time there were no segregated train cars, so blacks were expected to ride in the smoking car; Wells, however, was riding in the ladies' car. In her autobiography, Wells describes the event:

> When the train started and the conductor came along to collect tickets, he took my ticket, then handed it back to me and told me that he couldn't take my ticket there. . . . [H]e came back and told me I would have to go in the other car. I refused, saying that the forward car was a smoker, and as I was in the ladies' car I proposed to stay. He tried to drag me out of the seat, but the moment he caught hold of my arm I fastened my teeth in the back of his hand.
>
> I had braced my feet against the seat in front and was holding to the back, and as he had already been badly bitten he didn't try it again by himself.[106]

Wells was eventually dragged bodily from the car by the conductor and the baggage carrier, to the applause of the white passengers. This event, and Wells's description of it, suggests the complexity of black women's public embodiment in the late nineteenth century. The fact that this encounter took place on a train car makes the story particularly resonant with post-Reconstruction discourse. As Sundquist notes, "The train car was easily one of the most charged symbols of racial politics in American culture, a field of ritual drama." In fact, the train was a highly charged site for citizenship discourse in particular because it was the site for much legal conflict over the definition of full citizenship and the question of which bodies were qualified for citizenship.[107] This event in Wells's life thus carries the weight of both personal experience and symbolic significance. Wells demanded a seat in the ladies' car because she was a woman; in this way, she defined herself as legally and morally equivalent to the white women on the train car. She was excluded from this car because of her race; according to the conductor and the passengers, Wells's ethnic status as an African American superseded or encompassed her sexed status as a woman. Her womanhood was elided by the racist discourse of the time and her right to full personhood and belonging in a public space was disavowed.

Wells's response to this erasure of black womanhood was significant and characteristic of her antilynching activism and her writing and public speaking throughout her life. Rather than concede quietly, or attempt to maintain a decorum and demeanor appropriate to a true woman, Wells enacted the courage and challenge implicit in Diva Citizenship: she fought back. By biting the conductor and bracing herself in her seat so that it took two men to pull her from the train, Wells emphasized her own corporeality, her own bodily existence. This act was a refusal to be erased. She manifested her bodily integrity by engaging physically with the conductor. She draws attention to her body in her description of the event: "The moment he caught hold of my arm I fastened my teeth in the back of his hand." She mentions her arm and teeth in addition to the conductor's hand, in this way making them bodily equals. Her rhetoric is careful; the verb "fastened" suggests a deliberate, precise action, not a passionate lashing out; she is clearly avoiding discourses that would fall in line with the dominant discourse of blacks as bestial.[108] Her language also demonstrates control which can then be mapped onto her body: when describing the encounter, Wells employs an almost detached tone, seen in the passive voice of "he had already been badly bitten," which frames her as an omniscient, objective observer.

This particular event in Wells's life and her description of it offer a pattern for Wells's literary resuscitation of black female selfhood and corporeality. While biographers and critics of Wells have often emphasized the court cases that followed the event on the train as pivotal moments in Wells's professional life, I believe that the encounter on the train itself is a pivotal event, more so than the court cases which resulted. During this event, her construction of her own identity was emphatically corporeal; rather than obscuring or effacing her distinct material reality, Wells argued into public discourse and consciousness the black woman as a fully embodied national presence. Her approach to black women's embodiment was complex. As we have seen, she occasionally emphasized victimization—even in her own infrequent tears during public lectures—but she also promoted a vision of black female selfhood which was vocal and physically powerful; indeed, this periodically emerging black female subject was more civilized and more qualified for national leadership than the white male and female and black male models of selfhood mapped out in the cultural narrative of lynching. This envisioning of black womanhood resonates with Wells's own authorial presence, which is dramatically public—necessarily so, because the lynch narrative played out in public journalism, political speeches, and actual public spaces in towns and cities throughout the South. Wells uses her authority as a writer not only to dismantle the lynch narrative's key players but also to put into circulation the possibility of a different bodily configuration of black women. Her own bodily reality as a civilized, intelligent, self-controlled, and relentlessly righteous black woman was a continual subtext in her writings, and was foregrounded in her public lectures; she presented a complex corporeal identity, characterized not only by feminine tears and rational self-control but also by outrage at injustice. She was often described as "full of fire."[109] This complex embodiment, although not always explicitly articulated as such, made the case for black women as civilized people able to embody citizenship.

One significant means by which Wells asserted the civilized status of black women was by associating cultural leadership with black men, and then assuming this role, sometimes seemingly inadvertently, herself. Although it may seem ironic that Wells would promote, as part of her cultural project to create black female embodied citizenship, the racial leadership of men, a careful reading reveals that Wells assumes the leadership role herself. Her apparent claims for black male leadership of the race are evidence of discursive tension—Wald's "untold stories," textual sites which reveal hidden narratives of identity. Since there is no language for the kind of black female embodied citizenship, or Diva Citizenship, Wells is enacting, she reverts to the available language of patriarchal control and manipulates it to fit her needs. She may be forced to rely on old language, but she appropriates this rhetoric as a means to communicate her own agenda.

Repeatedly in *Southern Horrors* and *A Red Record* she calls for a powerful black manhood; like Frederick Douglass, she articulates a vision of black community that features a powerful patriarch. For instance, in *Southern Horrors* she inveighs against the South for its attempts to enact "the subjugation of the young manhood of the race. They have cheated him out of his ballot, deprived him of civil rights or redress therefore in the civil courts, robbed him of the fruits of his labor, and are still murdering, burning, and lynching him."[110] This passage describes a masculine leadership of the race, decrying the treatment of the "young manhood" and calling for masculine violence; most critics have taken this statement and others like it at face value, reading them as evidence that Wells's writing "bolsters black patriarchal authority under attack by white supremacists; thus black male agency becomes the solution to safeguard the black family and American civilization."[111]

This interpretation, however, only considers the literal level of Wells's assertions, missing the underlying significance of these apparent defenses of black patriarchy: most of Wells's statements in support of black manhood, including the excerpt cited above, demand to be read as describing Wells herself. She defends herself through physical aggression as she bites the conductor; she has been denied her civil rights and redress in the courts in her suit against the railroad; she has no access to the ballots; and she was robbed of the "fruits of her labor" when her newspaper headquarters and equipment were burned down by a lynch mob. Therefore, although her indignation is apparently voiced for black men as leaders of the race, she herself meets these criteria for leadership. Wells's own resistant readings of white newspaper reports throughout her pamphlets provide the model for a resistant reading of her calls for patriarchal leadership; her pamphlets reward this kind of reading.

In a very telling passage in *A Red Record*, Wells argues that the black community has reached a turning point: "If he did not, now, defend his name and manhood from this vile accusation, he would be unworthy even of the contempt of mankind. It is to this charge he now feels he must make answer."[112] Not only does she use the male pronoun, but she defines the problems facing the black community as threats specifically to the manhood of the race, threats to which the men of the race must respond. It is significant, therefore, that *she* is the one rising to the defense; *she* is answering her own call, embodying in her own public discourse the black manhood she calls for. Although she appeals for a kind of powerful black patriarchal leadership, ultimately she herself embodies the citizenship and full humanity of the black race. The leadership she invokes and manifests is corporeally powerful; by silently identifying herself with this model of leadership, she evacuates the public/private binary as well as the stereotypes of masculine and feminine behavior, not challenging them head-on but invalidating them through her resistant usage.

The same dynamic takes place in another passage from *A Red Record*: mimicking white newspapers' condemnation of black male "rapists" but calling attention to white attacks on black women, she asserts, "Humanity abhors the assailant of womanhood."[113] This statement works at multiple levels; on one level, she is simply reiterating a societal truism. She undercuts its standard meaning, however, by showing that white men are more likely than black men to be the "assailants of womanhood," and thus claims the mantle of humanity for blacks. Her statement operates at another level as well, because it is *she* who articulates this emotion and who indicts publicly the white "assailants"—*she* abhors the assailants; thus, although she is claiming the mantle of humanity for blacks broadly conceived, her writing and activism denote Wells herself as the deserving recipient of this label. The most powerful, articulate, civilized, and corporeally self-controlled figure in Wells's writing is Wells herself; thus, although there is not a popular rhetoric of black female leadership and embodied citizenship, she uses the language available to her to formulate this notion of the black woman as the nation's unofficial carrier of civilization.

While Wells's embodiment of cultural leadership was typically implicit and subtextual in her writing, on occasion it surfaced more explicitly, as in an 1894 editorial in the *Indianapolis Freeman* that documents a broader recognition of Wells's resistant role. The article notes that lynchings were continuing and that the black community could expect

> no assistance from churches, nor politicians except in the face of defeat or in the perfunctory statement of a newly elected president.

The hour had come, where was the man?

Unfortunately, the man was not forthcoming—Miss Wells was![114]

Although this article laments the lack of an appropriate black patriarchal presence to speak out against lynchings, it locates Wells in this position of cultural leadership and thus validates her revisioning of black womanhood. The adverb "unfortunately" registers the discursive tension surrounding black female assumption of a leadership role, but Wells's own demonstrated competence and authority create a space for this new black female body.

In the absence of an appropriate model of the black female body—publicly enactive, authoritative, civilized, and empowered—Wells did what the other authors considered here did as well: she made use of the cultural tools available to her to construct her own model of embodiment. As the Diva Citizenship model would suggest, Wells did not accede to current cultural configurations of blackness or of womanhood but instead used them resistantly, presenting herself as a figure representative of a new kind of citizenship, an embodied black female citizenship. Although late nineteenth-century culture circumscribed black female bodies in profound and crippling ways, Wells challenged these cultural proscriptions and distortions in order to create a space for her full corporeal engagement with American nationhood.

Wells challenged her culture's tacit understanding of black womanhood and its insidious deployment of the lynch narrative to protect white supremacy. By undercutting the lynch narrative's main characters, destabilizing the bodily configurations which accompanied them in the dominant cultural discourse, Wells offered a resistant reading of the nation's beliefs about citizenship in the late nineteenth century, a move which allowed her, at least rhetorically, to validate and protect the black female body. Her work did more than challenge the justifications for lynchings in the United States; it also confronted the civic myths—which she revealed to be corporeal myths—underlying the legal and social beliefs about the bodily identities of American citizens.

Ultimately, Wells demanded black citizenship as a marker of full black personhood. In an 1892 essay from the *AME Church Review*, Wells argues black citizenship into existence, here as elsewhere explicitly identifying this citizenship as masculine but implicitly offering validations that she herself meets: "The Afro-American, as a race, would not return to Africa if he could, and could not if he would. We would not be true to the race if we conceded for a moment that any other race, the Anglo-Saxon not excepted, had more right to claim this country as home than the Afro-American race. The blood he has shed for liberty's sake, the toil he has given for improvement's sake, and the sacrifices he has made for the cause of progress, give him the supreme right of American citizenship."[115] She identifies American citizenship as a "supreme right" of African Americans because of their bodily investment in America as a nation. Their citizenship is produced corporeally through bodily effort: blood, toil, and sacrifices. Blacks do not simply deserve citizenship; according to Wells, they *already embody* citizenship because of their material, corporeal contribution to American nationhood. The material reality of America—American soil, industry, infrastructure—has been shaped by the bodies of blacks, and thus the American body is the black body as much as it is the body of any other group. Wells argues that citizenship is experienced as a sense of bodily belonging to a place, the "right to claim this country as home." She rejects the notion of a "return" to Africa because the African American homeland is America. Indeed, she invokes a bodily equality between African Americans and whites, arguing that "the Anglo-Saxon" race is no more entitled to American citizenship than the African American.

In this passage Wells also engages with the lynch narrative, connecting lynching to the demand for African American citizenship through her reference to black "blood" and "sacrifices."[116] She suggests that, although lynching is a practice aimed at separating blacks from American citizenship, black suffering at the hands of whites is a justification for their belonging to the nation. Furthermore, as the body of her work documents, black women, herself included, are particular victims of violence at the hands of whites, and their blood, toil, and sacrifices make them deserving of citizenship. A closer reading connects these corporeal qualifications for American citizenship with Wells herself. Her life's work was dedicated to the "liberty . . . improvement . . . and progress" she invokes in this passage. Lynchings and the lynch narrative were white interventions into the formation of national fantasy, a means of expelling black bodies from the ideation of Americanness. Thus, what was at stake in Wells's writing was the body of the American citizen itself, a body which she claimed for blacks, for black women, and for herself, as a "supreme right."

5 We Have Hardly Had Time to Mend Our Pen

Sarah Hale, *Godey's Lady's Book*, and the Body as Print

At thy return my blushing was not small,
My rambling brat (in print) should mother call . . .
I washed thy face, but more defects I saw,
And rubbing off a spot still made a flaw.
I stretched thy joints to make thee even feet,
Yet still thou run'st more hobbling than is meet. . . .
—Anne Bradstreet, "The Author to Her Book," 1678

The body of
B. Franklin, Printer
Like the Cover of an Old Book
Its Contents torn Out
And Stript of its Lettering and Gilding
Lies Here, Food for Worms.
But the Work shall not be Lost;
For it will (as he Believ'd) Appear once More
In a New and More Elegant Edition
Revised and Corrected
By the Author.
—Benjamin Franklin, "Benjamin Franklin's Epitaph," 1728

We want short, racy, spirited essays; stories and sketches that embody pages of narrative and sentiment in a single paragraph.
—Sarah Hale, *Godey's Lady's Book*, 1839

The incarnation of the body in book form has a substantial history in American literature, beginning in the early days of the colonies with the writings of Anne Bradstreet, moving through Benjamin Franklin's familiar textualizing of his life, and appearing also in the work of Sarah Hale, a less recognized member of this tradition. Sarah Josepha Hale (1788–1879), editress (her preferred term) of the popular nineteenth-century magazine *Godey's Lady's Book* for forty years, was a woman thoroughly enmeshed in the print culture of the nineteenth century. As an editor, writer, and anthologist, Hale exerted a powerful influence on her culture through her manipulations of printed words, demanding texts for her magazine that presented a specific kind of corporeality—"racy, spirited." By calling for these texts to *embody* a certain narrative structure, Hale both asserted her authority as an editor and articulated an important aspect of nineteenth-century print culture: the world of print was an embodied space.

Hale's epigraph to this chapter indicates the interconnectedness of texts and bodies in *Godey's Lady's Book.* She requires "spirited" essays, essays as corporeal sites which contain an enlivening consciousness. Not only are texts themselves corporeal sites, which she explicitly configures as bodies, but manuscripts reveal traces of the labor that has gone into their construction and thus reveal the *authors'* bodies, as well. Her demand for a certain kind of essay implicitly indicts the authorial body responsible for producing this writing. By mentioning pages and paragraphs, the building blocks of an essay, Hale emphasizes the materiality of the text, which is made up, in her estimation, not of insubstantial ideas but of concrete grammatical, syntactical, and material structures. Each of these smaller structures is required to enact a certain embodiment, and this embodiment then extends to the larger text—the *Lady's Book* itself. Indeed, under Hale's control the magazine as a whole becomes a kind of body, a speaking body that "both writes and is written," and this print body is a representation of and a surrogate for Hale's own corporeality.[1] By utilizing *Godey's Lady's Book* as a substitute for her body, Hale capitalized on print culture as a site responsive to her acts of agency and self-construction and a site with the potential to decommission binaries such as the separate spheres; for instance, print afforded Hale the same kinds of bodily mobility that Mowatt experienced through travel.

Hale actually traveled very little. Born in New Hampshire, she moved only out of necessity—first to Boston where she edited the *Ladies' Magazine* for ten years, and then very reluctantly to Philadelphia after four years of editing *Godey's Lady's Book* from a distance. She is known for asserting, in her first article for *Godey's Lady's Book,* "We are always at home," and in fact, she was at home much of the time.[2] Early in her career as an editor, her magazine did not have an office, so she edited from her apartment. Later in her life, when her age prevented her from traveling, she conducted the business of the *Lady's Book* from her daughter's home in Philadelphia, using her grandson as a courier.[3] Indeed, she might seem to have been the least likely candidate for a traveling body; unlike Mowatt, whose stagecoach careened through icy ditches and who pulled wool socks over her shoes to tramp through the snow, Hale remained fairly stationary—even domestically located—throughout her life.

Hale's apparent rootedness, however, only applied to her physical body. Hale did not identify herself solely with her corporeal being; her life's energy was focused on the *Lady's Book*, and she utilized the magazine as a surrogate for her own body.[4] By doing so, she made herself a remarkable traveler. *Godey's Lady's Book*, with a circulation that exceeded any other magazine of the early and mid-nineteenth century, was sped to tens and even hundreds of thousands of homes across the country every month, packed into rail cars and canal barges. According to Louis Godey, "From Maine to the Rocky Mountains there is scarcely a hamlet, however inconsiderable, where it is not received and read; and, in larger towns and cities, it is universally distributed."[5] By identifying her own corporeality and professional life with the magazine, Hale gained a bodily mobility and expansiveness even Mowatt could not dream of. Mobility was, however, only one aspect of Hale's print embodiment. By identifying her corporeality with the *Lady's Book*, Hale benefited from the destabilizing of the binary of the public versus private spheres. Because of the transitional character of popular print media in the 1840s and 1850s, Hale was able to maintain allegiance to the rhetoric of the private sphere and construct a presence that, while emphatically public, was often read as domestic and submissive. The point is not that Hale was public instead of private; the point is that her engagement with the world of print culture allowed her to exceed the boundaries of that binary and call it into question.

Hale's identification of herself with *Godey's Lady's Book* provides an entry into a revisioning of nineteenth-century print culture and women's relation to the world of print. Many of the major studies of American print culture have examined men's contributions and work within this arena.[6] These studies, foundational to current considerations of American print, do not address women's place within print culture and women's use of print media, particularly in the nineteenth century; their insights need to be extended into gender-specific uses of print culture.

This omission is addressed somewhat by recent feminist criticism, which has often approached issues of print culture tangentially; those feminist critics who have analyzed women's role within

American print culture have posited text somewhat simplistically as a freeing site. For instance, according to Nina Baym, the world of print culture is "a sphere that enables women to imagine themselves out of their bodies." Similarly, Nicole Tonkovich asserts, "The gender, race, and authority of the originator of the discourse no longer were evident in the speaker's presence and embodied voice; thus women might construct a public voice in print even while remaining bodily in the 'private sphere.'"[7] These critics assert that the world of print could offer a woman writer a kind of protected space where her actual physicality was masked; her readers encountered her words and her constructed world rather than her physical body. The implication of these assertions is that the female body is somehow entrapping, and print allows women to escape from their embodiment; print, therefore, is liberating.

Hale's work provides an important corrective to those studies of print culture that exclude women; in addition, her negotiations with print and print technologies reveal the complex relationship between the female body and print which is obscured by critical assertions of the freeing nature of print. This chapter argues that, for Hale, print was not a space which liberated her from the imprisonment of her body; rather, her work reveals that print is a space which can create syncretic, multivalent embodiment. Indeed, the materiality of print media and its reliance on the marketplace and the machinations of labor and consumption provided Hale with tools for negotiating and shaping her own public corporeal presence. As theorists such as Susan Bordo suggest, limitations can be formative of embodiment; in Hale's case, she leveraged the tensions and conflicts in the print marketplace to create a powerful, mobile, and effectively active body.[8]

The positing of print as a bodily surrogate recurs in scholarship of American literature, although it is less familiar in studies centered on the nineteenth century.[9] The representation of bodily identity as a printed text—or of printed texts as having a bodily identity—emerges initially in early modern English literature. Although the usages of this trope are historically contingent, its reiteration in different historical periods suggests its larger importance as a means of accommodating print culture; the identification of body and text in nineteenth-century print culture may become more visible when this trope is traced from the early modern period. In the early years of print technology, texts were often compared to the body, and vice versa. Because print was a new phenomenon, the culture attempted to familiarize this new technology by aligning the apparatus of print with the human body. According to Leah Marcus, "In the early modern era, there was a tendency to assimilate the human organism to print technology: not only were some of the parts of the printing press named after parts of the human body, but people in early print culture often thought of themselves . . . as writing, or as half-human, half-book. The image of the beloved as a book to be perused is so common in early modern culture that we have perhaps failed to recognize its strangeness."[10] The identification of print with the human body appears in Shakespeare, for example, as when Hamlet refers to "the book and volume of my brain," and in numerous other early modern texts.

Readers of American literature have encountered this construct before, as well. The epigraphs to this chapter present familiar American literary configurations of text as body. In "The Author to Her Book" (1678), Bradstreet describes her written works as her children, each poem a "rambling brat (in print)." This conceit characterizes the printed words of her poems as a body. Her pun on the metric feet of her poems as literal feet with joints that can be stretched emphasizes the materiality of texts. While Bradstreet does not describe the poems as her body, she does introduce the conflation of body and print into American literature, and she makes this conflation specifically female: the poems are children that she has given birth to. As a mother, she feels particular responsibility for the upkeep of their bodies as they go into the world.

This idea does not disappear in Enlightenment writings. Franklin's "Epitaph" (1728), which he wrote as a young man and disseminated among his friends, envisions his body as the material makings of a book, its contents removed; resurrection is imagined as a new edition, with God as an invisible printer responsible for the work.[11] The body as text configuration appears again in a more extended form in Franklin's 1791 autobiography, in which he delineates his life as a printed text with its errata. Franklin's profession as a printer immerses him in the world of print culture; his extended metaphor of life as text establishes this trope as an appropriate one for the self-made American man who can write his own life and acknowledge—and thus potentially change—his errors.

Hale regularly refers to *Godey's Lady's Book* in corporeal terms, as when she demands stories that "embody" great amounts of information in a small space. This identification of body and text is central to the nineteenth-century understanding of texts, although it may be so familiar that it proves difficult to recognize. Marcus argues, "We have inherited a strong tendency in our culture to think of the printed book as somehow organic, a surrogate self of its author, whose spirit or intellect is embodied within it."[12] The idea of body as text or of text and printing apparatus as body is less common within critical commentary on nineteenth-century American literature, but it may have been a useful construct to those involved in nineteenth-century print culture. For instance, a minister giving a toast at a meeting of New York publishers in 1855 described the steam-powered printing press as "more like an intelligent being than a machine" and "the best hand they have in the shop."[13] This piece of printing equipment becomes analogous not just to a human worker but to a hand; this bodily categorization of laborers, when applied to a machine, demonstrates the constructed corporeality inherent in the world of work and the world of print. Hale, drawing, perhaps, from the earlier traditions or simply from the print culture of her time, links her body to her text. Appropriate models of womanhood offered little in the way of a self-made woman, so Hale—like Franklin—turned to the world of print to express her life's work and configure her body.

Hale constructs her identity within the pages of the *Lady's Book*, identifying her body not with the world of the sentimental heroine or with other available models of women's embodiment but with the materiality of the magazine itself. In *The Letters of the Republic*, Michael Warner argues that print culture is not a monolithic entity but a historically contingent space. An analysis of Hale's use of print reveals a particular enactment of that space. As the stage and the stagecoach provided Mowatt with sites to configure her body as sensational, the printed page of the *Lady's Book* was Hale's site to configure her body in terms of materiality, labor, and power. While Mowatt wrote about her traveling body and thus used the printed page to construct her public self, for Hale the printed page was representative of her public self, allowing her body to travel. The *Lady's Book* is a space in which she could create herself as a businesswoman and laborer without subjecting her physical body to the kinds of damage working women could suffer in the nineteenth century. The magazine was constituted not only of signed and unsigned stories, essays, and poems by Hale but also editorials and the marks of Hale's choices as an editor, such as the works she chose to publish and the order in which she published them; it was a space where Hale could work through what it meant to be a public body.

This space, however, is complicated, even contradictory, as is the embodiment Hale constructs here. Isabel Lehuu's analysis of the "exuberant print culture" of the antebellum decades emphasizes the world of the popular print media as transitional, carnivalesque, and rife with conflict. She notes that the print market was responsive to many voices and registered a "multiplicity of publics" as well as complicated social stratifications developing at the time.[14] The world of print, therefore, was not monolithic; neither was Hale's embodiment in this world. Hale's multivalent print body, then, can be seen as emblematic of the time. Like Mowatt and Eddy, Hale utilized different stylistic modalities in her writing, shifting from the sentimental to the scientific to the critical. Unlike the other women studied here, however, Hale split her voice even further. She often wrote herself into multiple-person conversations where every voice was her own. More than this, by identifying with the *Lady's Book*, Hale broadened her modes of embodiment and, thus, her influence and power. Just as *Godey's Lady's Book* itself was fragmented, composed of a congeries of genres, topics, and formats, so, too, was Hale's print corporeality. In fashioning this corporeality, Hale not only responded to cultural prescriptions for appropriate womanhood but also to the marketplace. Ultimately, what the carnivalesque site of print culture enabled was a bodily identity for Hale that is not legible within the traditional binaric categories of public versus private or agent versus victim. The "sphere" of the domestic world does not encapsulate Hale's business acumen, public authority, and realm of influence; nor does the notion of the marketplace as an exclusively public realm explain Hale's adherence to and promotion of many of the discourses surrounding appropriate femininity.

This complexity and tension is demonstrated in Hale's interactions with the magazine's fashion plates. Hale's *Ladies' Magazine*, which she edited from 1827 to 1836, did not have fashion plates for many years, but Hale was eventually forced to incorporate them into the magazine because of their tremendous popularity. They were always a feature of the *Lady's Book*. These images of middle-class, leisured women in the latest fashionable dresses and hats were not only engraved especially for the magazine, they were hand-colored with watercolor paints. Louis Godey frequently noted that he paid a staff of young women, first working from home and then later working in an office the magazine established for this purpose, to hand paint each and every fashion plate in each and every magazine. The plates were common in many magazines at the time, but the *Lady's Book*'s plates were particularly elaborate.

Hale was a moderate fashion reformer; she argued that women should wear clothes that were comfortable and healthy rather than fashionable. Not surprisingly, the *Lady's Book* documents a tension between Hale and the fashion plates, a tension between Hale's invisible, multivalent editorial body and the visible, voiceless women of the fashion plates which framed the magazine. These silent, decorative women stand in contrast to Hale, who was outspoken and deliberately not fashionable; yet these textual female bodies are in some ways analogous to Hale's own body. In their emphatic visibility, the female bodies featured in the fashion plates destabilize any simplistic public/private binary. Although, as Lehuu notes, the most familiar fashion plates reinforced true womanhood and domesticity through the content of the scenes depicted—frequently women convening in a parlor, their bodies rigid and contained within fashionable gowns—the magazine also often featured women in public situations, such as riding bicycles or swimming.[15] In these scenes, the women's bodies, while still rigid and mannequin-like in their display of fashionable clothing, suggest the possibility of assertive physicality and explicitly public positioning. In addition, all the fashion plates, regardless of content, made women's bodies publicly visible without the concomitant threat of transgressiveness or freakishness. In their simultaneous enactment of public embodiment and appropriate feminine domesticity, then, the fashion plates are analogous to Hale herself.

Furthermore, they were part of the magazine that Hale constructed, the magazine through which she enacted her own embodiment; although she did not approve of them, she acknowledged their profitability and allowed them a prominent place in the magazine. Hale's relationship with the fashion plates indicates the complexity of her embodiment in print culture: her textual embodiment was shaped by the tension between the magazine's material needs and Hale's own voice. To add to the complexity, both of those elements, as well as existing in tension, were interdependent: Hale's voice was one of the magazine's needs, and Hale required the material substance of the magazine to provide her a site for her voice. While readers often referred to the *Lady's Book* as "Mrs. Hale's Book," suggesting a strong connection between Hale and her textual production, this connection—and thus Hale's textual embodiment—was

These images document one of the tensions in Godey's Lady's Book *fashion plates and in the larger magazine itself: the women here are ostensibly engaged in athletic activities ranging from horseback or bicycle riding to swimming to gymnastics; however, each woman's body is ultimately a mannequin, emphasizing the fashionable clothing rather than the activity itself.*

Fashion plate, Godey's Lady's Book, *1890*

"Ladies' Bathing Dresses," Godey's Lady's Book, *1871*

"The Metropolitan Gymnastic Costume," Godey's Lady's Book, *1858*

less a simple identification than a continual negotiation between Hale, the specific demands of the magazine, and the larger demands of the nineteenth-century print marketplace.

During her lifetime, Hale was one of the single most influential individuals of the nineteenth century. As editor first of the *Ladies' Magazine* and then of *Godey's Lady's Book*, Hale wielded a powerful influence over American readers for fifty years.[16] However, after the early part of this century, her work was all but forgotten; a few scholars wrote biographies of her and noted her importance, but in general if her name appeared at all it was as a fringe figure to nineteenth-century literature and culture. When feminist criticism began unearthing significant women from nineteenth-century obscurity, Hale's name was among them, but she was typically noted as a somewhat negative figure, as a woman who prevented other women from succeeding and who played an active role in preventing women from achieving their rights. Only in the last decade has Hale become a topic of serious, sustained critical inquiry, and she is being reevaluated as an influential author and editor whose life and career may help to reveal the complex political and social forces at work in the nineteenth-century womanhood she helped to shape. Even now her editorial career has been neglected because of the difficulties attendant on a study of such a substantial body of work; however, her work as the editor of the *Lady's Book* calls attention to issues of women's professional status and employment at midcentury and to one woman's sustained investment in the world of magazine publishing and print.[17]

Criticism of Hale, particularly recent feminist criticism, has mapped out a contested terrain. Hale's work is often seen in absolute terms: as conservative and apolitical or as feminist and politically active.[18] Critics have tended to take the all-or-nothing approach Lora Romero warns against in *Home Fronts*. It is important to apply Romero's warning here: Hale is neither absolutely apolitical nor absolutely politically active, neither antifeminist nor feminist, neither radical nor conservative. Similarly, her life and work are not legible through the binaric lenses of the public and private spheres nor the notions of victimization or agency. As Romero asserts, power is multiple, not binary: "Resistance may not transcend power relations altogether, but that does not mean that it merely reproduces the same power relations or that all power relations must reproduce the status quo."[19] Hale's work over the forty-year period during which she edited the Lady's Book presents a far more complex political picture than one which is merely oppressive or liberatory, terms which have meaning only from our current political perspective. Critics often want to position Hale in relation to late twentieth-century feminism, but this anachronistic kind of approach can only reveal Hale as an imperfect version of ourselves. It is much more important to attempt to reconstruct the historical context which gave Hale meaning in her own time. This contextualization and attention to history will allow us to see more clearly the complexities of Hale's life and work. As one recent essay argues, "From a political point of view . . . Hale must be seen in a context more nuanced than feminist or antifeminist."[20] By examining Hale's use of the *Lady's Book* as a body surrogate, this chapter avoids the question of Hale's "feminism" altogether and, instead, interrogates Hale's interactions with her textual and material culture. The magazine acts as a complex locus of multiple demands and desires in tension; this tension is productive, creating a space for Hale's construction of her public embodiment. Her embodiment was multivalent, even fragmentary; but just as Hale the editor unified the many separate components of the Lady's Book into one coherent magazine, so, too, did she exert control over the congeries of bodily manifestations the magazine enabled, transforming many seemingly contradictory elements into her own corporeal identity.

PRINT, MATERIALITY, AND THE MARKET

Print culture could be an inviting world for nineteenth-century American women, offering them many opportunities to identify themselves with their reading. Middle-class women were reading in much greater numbers as the century progressed, and these readers often read voraciously and aligned themselves with the characters they read about. Reading could provide women not only entertainment, it could also help shape their goals and beliefs. One need look no further than Ellen Montgomery in *The Wide, Wide World* (1851) for evidence of the important role books could play in the lives of women readers. Ellen's Bible, a gift from her mother, is her most treasured possession, and she relies on it to help her become the Christian woman her mother and her other mentors want her to be. When she gives a Bible as a gift to a friend, she explains its importance: "If you would only read it,—it would make you so happy and good."[21] Books could help shape women readers better to meet their culture's expectations for them.

Reading could have other results, as well; according to one critic,

"Reading provided space—physical, temporal, and psychological—that permitted women to exempt themselves from traditional gender expectations."[22] Regardless of whether their reading fortified or undermined traditional gender roles, many middle-class American women valued reading highly and were enmeshed in print culture in the middle of the nineteenth century. Women's identities—including their bodily identities—were being formed in great part in the rapidly growing world of the printed word and the printed page.

Hale's own life was thoroughly enmeshed with the print culture of her time. Educated by her mother, Hale learned a love of reading as a child and reports that she was very attracted to books by Americans and books by women. She writes of the first novel she read, *The Mysteries of Udolpho* by Ann Radcliffe, "I had remarked that of all the books I saw, few were written by Americans, and none by women. Here was a work, the most fascinating I had ever read, always excepting 'The Pilgrim's Progress,' written by a woman! How happy it made me! The wish to promote the reputation of my own sex, and do something for my own country, were among the earliest mental emotions I can recollect."[23] She explicitly figures her early years of reading as an attempt to find her own identity represented in the books she read. She was looking for herself in print culture. The world of print was central to her marriage, as well; she and her husband read every night for two hours, and she exclaimed, "Two hours in the twenty-four: how I enjoyed those hours!"[24]

After her husband's death in 1825, Hale's attempts to support her family revolved around the written word. She worked briefly as a milliner, but this employment was quickly succeeded by her work as a writer. She wrote a volume of poetry, which was moderately successful, and had a number of poems published in various periodicals; she then wrote *Northwood* (1827), a novel popular enough to win her the attention of the Reverend John L. Blake, who had been planning to start a women's magazine. He decided that Hale would be an ideal editor, and she accepted his offer. She edited this magazine, the *Ladies' Magazine*, for ten years, until Louis Godey hired her to edit the *Lady's Book* in 1836. In addition to her editorial work, Hale also wrote stories, poems, and essays for the *Ladies Magazine* and then for the *Lady's Book*. She also anthologized essays from the *Lady's Book*, did exhaustive historical research to write the biographical sketches of the world's notable women in *Woman's Record*, and throughout her life wrote children's books. It is difficult to think of anyone in the nineteenth century more enmeshed in print culture than Hale.

As editor, poet, essayist, fiction writer, and anthologist, her world revolved around the printed word.

Print culture is thus a key site to examine in terms of women's embodiment in general and Hale's in particular. While current feminist critics posit print as a freeing site, a number of nineteenth-century authors describe print culture as oppressively embodied. Hale's work aligns with neither of these viewpoints; she articulates print as a space which is both public and private and thus demands a complex embodiment. For Hale, print is a site that neither allows unfettered agency nor fully denies that agency. By employing the *Lady's Book* as a substitute for her own materiality, Hale constructed a body which existed in a site of tension between cultural mandates, her own subjectivity, and the material demands of the print marketplace.

Nineteenth-century writers explain the kinds of bodily victimization writers, particularly women, could face in print culture. What threatened any perceived textual safety or camouflage for many women writers was the extent to which women writers were identified with their writings. Columnist Fanny Fern, a contemporary of Hale's, experienced this effect. In one of her newspaper columns, she parodies the readers who would attempt to determine her character and her physical make-up through her writing; speaking in the voice of an imaginary critic, Fern writes, "We have never seen Fanny Fern, nor do we desire to do so. We imagine her, from her writings, to be a muscular, black-browed, grenadier-looking female, who would be more at home in a boxing gallery than in a parlor,—a vociferous, demonstrative, strong-minded horror,—a woman only by virtue of her dress."[25] Fern continues to parody this point of view and the assumptions that underlie it, skewering those critics who denounced her writing as unwomanly because of its humor, sarcasm, and societal critique. What her parody makes clear, however, is that women writers' texts were often taken as a kind of representation of the woman herself; according to some critics, Fern's writings were unwomanly and thus her body was assumed to be "muscular, black-browed," and only identifiable as female by the dress she wore. Basically, while writing could offer safety, the safety was always contingent upon the public's acceptance of the written work. As Tonkovich argues, the mid-century was "an age in which a woman's literary production was scrutinized as if she and her text were one."[26]

In his story "Tartarus of Maids" (1855), Melville provides a terrifying literalization of this cultural directive. Melville's narrator describes "the pallid faces of all the pallid girls" at the factory he visits. Significantly, these women are laborers at a paper factory; they are victims of the booming print culture, producing the paper that makes magazines like the *Lady's Book*. Their bodies are so identified with the factory that they actually start to resemble the paper they produce; as the narrator explains, "slowly, mournfully, beseechingly, yet unresistingly, they gleamed along, their agony dimly outlined on the imperfect paper, like the print of the tormented face on the handkerchief of Saint Veronica."[27] Their bodies become incorporated into print culture not like Hale's—through manipulation of words and self-determining production—but like the shreds of cotton that constitute the paper itself. They are sucked into the paper; it bears the imprints of their bodily agony. Melville presents women in print culture as excessively victimized, to the point of losing their bodily integrity.

Both Fern and Melville assert the dangers to nineteenth-century women who are too fully identified with their texts. What Hale's work demonstrates is that this bodily identification with texts need not be perceived as oppression or victimization. Hale's corporeality was invested in the *Lady's Book*; she consciously and continuously identified herself with the magazine. Rather than becoming eviscerated and depersonalized like the laborers at the paper factory Melville describes, Hale utilized the materiality of the *Lady's Book* to substitute for her own. The magazine provided a site for her to conceptualize and construct her own laboring body; this body is not fully free from cultural demands; neither is it fully victimized. It exists in a syncretic space which demands a more complicated kind of embodiment. The magazine's materiality and Hale's labor were interdependent; her labor creates the magazine as a substantive text, and the text in turn provides a material surrogate for Hale's body. By articulating the material underpinnings and daily organizational issues involved in the production of the *Lady's Book*, Hale called her readers' attention to the corporeality of the magazine and thus described and defined the material foundations of her textual body.

Hale's identity permeated the *Lady's Book*; within the magazine, she had power and authority, she could range freely among the pages, and she herself decided what was appropriate material and what was not. Hale wrote an editorial column in each issue of the magazine as well as writing fiction and poetry. In addition, she wrote small snippets of material to fill in the ends of columns and articles; thus, her presence permeated the entire magazine even as her editorial choices determined the content and structure of the magazine. She herself wrote about such diverse and atypically feminine topics as the daily workings of an arsenal and chemical experiments, along with more traditional sentimental literature. She was the highest literary power in the magazine, determining which articles were printed and which were disposed of. Hale's presence unified the magazine's many diverse elements; her voice was the magazine's voice, and the magazine thus became a surrogate body, entering people's homes and speaking for/as Hale.

LABORING BODIES

While the whole magazine represented Hale, she spoke to her readers directly in the "Editors' Tables" that she wrote for each issue of the magazine; this was the space in the magazine that was explicitly hers to discuss whatever topics she chose. This was the space in which she most fully configured her editorial role and gave voice to her textual body that was the magazine. This voice was not distinct from her embodiment in the magazine but was a crucial part of that embodiment. The voice is a bodily attribute, emerging from the body, and thus Hale's voice within the *Lady's Book*, particularly in the "Editors' Tables," demands analysis as a component of and a shaping element of Hale's textual embodiment.[28] Significantly, this was the site where she could describe her own labor to produce the magazine.

Located in the back of the magazine, only a few pages from the back cover, the "Editors' Table" was easy to find; readers could flip to Hale's column quickly each issue. The typeface used for these columns was considerably smaller than that used elsewhere in the magazine, which allowed Hale to include more of her own writing and gave her columns a compact, serious appearance. Within these editorials, Hale was able to construct her own persona in whatever way she chose; she could write about any topic that appealed to her, from the changing of the seasons to the opening of new schools for women (a favorite topic) to a speech or sermon she had recently heard. They provided a kind of liminal space where other voices could enter the magazine through letters Hale printed or through excerpts from contributors whose pieces were not strong enough to be printed in full. She used this column as her podium, bitterly complaining about the word "female" being included in the name of Vassar College, and promoting the adoption of Thanksgiving as a national holiday—two campaigns launched from this column which were ultimately successful. She could also advertise events and endeavors that she felt were worthwhile, such as the Bunker Hill Monument Society Fair.

Most importantly to her self-representation as an editor, these columns were the site in the magazine where Hale addressed the business of running the magazine itself. Here Hale could have a meta-conversation with her readers about their act of reading and about the text which they held in their hands. These articles were a site where Hale could most explicitly construct her editorial self; they were the space in the magazine which was most fully her own, where she could define and amplify her voice and the magazine's material surrogacy for her body.

The magazine's materiality is constructed through the written pieces that constitute it. In many of Hale's columns, she discusses the contributions to the magazine and characterizes the manuscripts as physical. She explains comically, "The bad articles are usually at the bottom [of the manuscript box], some weighed down by their own specific gravity, (dullness is heavy as the nightmare,) and others laid aside because unreadable, being written, as we opine, in humble imitation of the Chinese characters."[29] In this humorous description of the kinds of difficulties facing an editor, Hale both describes the physicality of the papers themselves—not disembodied ideas but papers which rest in a box, which are covered with illegible handwriting, which can be picked up and laid aside—and invokes the physical dimensions of her own work; the reader is invited to imagine Hale squinting at a manuscript, attempting to make out the characters, and finally putting the page down in disgust.

The issue of the illegibility of manuscripts recurs regularly; in another "Editor's Table," Hale praises an author by name for her penmanship even though she has not read the author's work. She writes, "The appearance of the article is very neat and lady-like. The writer has spared no pain to render it readable. We commend the example to all who write for periodicals; many an article is rejected because it is so difficult to be deciphered."[30] In this instance, because Hale has not read the text in question, she seems to be valuing the material form of the manuscript over its content, reversing what many readers assume is the natural hierarchy for written texts. In another column, Hale laments submissions "written with blue ink on blue paper"[31] and suggests that she might try burning the manuscripts and judging their merit by the brightness of the flames. By invoking the physical reality of the papers, Hale suggests not only the physicality of the *Lady's Book* but also the embodied nature of the authors themselves, people not only with ideas but with handwriting, a detail which points to the physical work involved in the act of writing, especially in the nineteenth century, when pens had to be mended, and when a manuscript had to be carefully copied by hand to be sent to a magazine.

Hale also discusses the manuscripts from the point of view of their style and content, explaining her standards for judging the magazine's submissions. Virtually every "Editors' Table" features at least minor commentary on the works submitted in the "To Our Correspondents" section; here Hale responded to her contributors. She would explain whose contributions she had accepted and would list the names of pieces she rejected, without including the authors' names. She regularly wrote criticism of the pieces rejected, explaining the criteria she had used and offering her contributors advice for future work. This commentary, read over the months and years of the magazine, establishes Hale's rigorous standards for the writing she accepted into her magazine. By voicing these expectations in her column, Hale makes explicit the framework that underpins the work printed in the *Lady's Book*. By demanding nothing but the highest quality writing within the *Lady's Book*, Hale establishes the magazine—and by extension, herself—as having unimpeachable integrity. She also suggests the work required both of the authors and of the editor to maintain this integrity.

The *Lady's Book*'s standards made it a trailblazer among nineteenth-century periodicals. Hale established stringent editorial policies as editor of the *Ladies' Magazine*, and when this magazine merged with the *Lady's Book* in 1836, these policies moved with her to the new magazine. For instance, Hale valued American writing and printed as much original work as possible. In a time when no copyright laws existed and periodicals could—and usually did—reprint articles from European publications for free, Hale insisted on soliciting original written work. Under her command, the *Lady's Book* featured American authors and women authors, and they were paid well for their writing.[32] While this made the magazine more expensive to produce, it allowed the *Lady's Book* to feature—and even inaugurate the careers of—many of the nineteenth century's most prominent writers, including Edgar Allan Poe, Harriet Beecher Stowe, Oliver Wendell Holmes, Lydia Sigourney, and others. Continuing with this valuation of writers' work, in 1845 the *Lady's Book* was the first American periodical to copyright its contents, preventing other magazines, newspapers, and gift books from reprinting the texts for free. These policies made the *Lady's Book* a more prestigious and reputable publication, and Hale and Godey emphasized their editorial policies regularly, as when they subtitled stories with the caption, "Written for the Lady's Book."

Hale was a stringent critic of submissions to the *Lady's Book*. One of her key demands was that submissions strive for brevity. Hale believed that short texts were more difficult to write than longer pieces, and she reminded her contributors that their job was to condense action, characterization, and plot into as short a space as possible. When contributed texts did not meet these standards, she told the authors so—plainly and often even harshly—but without listing their names. For instance, she writes of a stack of anonymous writing sent to the magazine, "We are obliged to do—what we wish the authors had done—consign the whole pile to the flames." She writes of another month's collection of contributions, "We regret to say, there is not much improvement in the quality of these communications." In the voice of a schoolmaster Hale evaluates one contribution by saying, "It is a pity they have spoiled so much good paper."[33] Again emphasizing the corporeality of the magazine and of writings that enter her office, Hale defends the standards of the *Lady's Book* and asserts her editorial voice powerfully and unapologetically. Although she is often identified unilaterally with sentimental true womanhood, her voice here is not what we might expect of a submissive, domestic figure.

Hale, however, was also a supporter of writing. She gave constructive criticism to many of her rejected authors, as when she wrote, "We would say as a friend, to the authors of these rejected articles, that they have not done justice to their own talents. Marks of haste are too visible." She also often encouraged individual authors, as when she wrote of one submitted story, "It has considerable power, and the young and unpretending authoress should be encouraged to cultivate her talent." She acknowledges the difficulty of writing short, effective articles, explaining, "In the labors of human intellect, those which present the least bulk are sometimes the result of superior talent or severer application."[34] She thus praises her own magazine as she articulates and upholds its standards; she simultaneously defines the kind of authorial presence she expects for the magazine.

Hale identified writing as a profession with rigorous standards, requiring determined effort and time as well as talent, and in so doing, she grounded her surrogate corporeality not only in the materiality of the printed page but in the print marketplace and the professionalization of authorship.[35] As Okker explains, "In these editorials, Hale repeatedly rejected the idea that anyone could become an author. Like any other occupation that required training, talent, and hard work, authorship, according to Hale, deserved professional respect."[36] Hale's responses to authors further emphasized writing as work and acknowledged the person—the body—responsible for this labor. By emphasizing the professional respect due to authors and establishing the criteria by which the authors' quality could be determined, Hale made explicit her editorial demands and undergirded the magazine's standards.

While many of the other characteristics examined here have hinted at the work involved in producing the *Lady's Book*, Hale often addressed this work directly. She used her "Editors' Tables" to characterize the labor that was responsible for producing the magazine and to continue her project of situating the magazine within the world of material production. For instance, she describes her own work as an editor. In a column from January 1838, Hale dramatizes for her readers and contributors the process she undergoes to read and select manuscripts for the magazine. She characterizes the *Lady's Book* as a kind of industry, writing,

> Thanks to the wise liberality of the Publisher, we have a larger list of contributors. Political economists have long been urging the benefits of a division of labour. They are right. Nothing great in physical improvement can be accomplished without co-operation. And intellectual improvement and literary excellence can also be greatly accelerated by the same means.
>
> For ten long years have we sat here alone, and so busied with the thousand and one cares of our duty, that we have hardly had time to mend our pen.[37]

Hale aligns "literary excellence" with the world of political economy, suggesting that the magazine is a product akin to the iron or fabric that emerged from mills in the nineteenth century. Just as factories and mills require division of labor, so, too, does the Lady's Book. She brings her own body into this discussion, as well; she represents herself as a laboring body, alone in an office "for ten long years" and continually busy, attempting to do all the editing of the *Lady's Book* and the previous *Ladies' Magazine*.

This is an important moment of embodiment: Hale is characterizing herself as a working body, and by enacting her body textually in this column and representing her own relationship to her work as physical, which she will continue to do throughout this article, she is in effect creating her textual body and identifying that body with the work that produces—work that is represented in and fully entwined with—the *Lady's Book*. She moves from a theoretical concept of division of labor to a concrete, physical representation of a tired body. She also suggests the practical, physical nature of the work of both editing and writing by mentioning her pen; she does not allow her readers to detach themselves from the physical labor that goes into making a manuscript or a magazine; articles are not born but are constructed by people with ink, paper, and pens—pens that must be mended occasionally.

Elsewhere in her columns, Hale propounds a similar message, revealing the labor other than her own that goes into producing the magazine. In an 1842 column, Hale, through the voice of a fictional character, describes the many working bodies which create the magazine: "'I sometimes think,' said Mrs. Marvin, 'that our 'Lady's Book' owes much of its unparalleled success to the blessings which the poor of our sex, who are benefited by its publication, are constantly calling down upon it. Not to reckon the host of female writers, who are promptly paid, there are besides more than one hundred females, who depend for their daily bread on the money they receive for colouring the plates of fashion, stitching, doing up the work, and so on.'"[38] While this statement makes the sentimental point that the success of the magazine is due to its charity in employing poor women workers, veiling the magazine's financial attainments with emphasis on its moral intent, an underlying message emerges: the *Lady's Book* is a material entity which does not simply appear but is constructed by the hands and bodies of hundreds of women workers. As was mentioned earlier, this large staff was often a point of pride; Godey boasted about the women workers who colored the fashion plates because the quality of the plates contributed to the success of the magazine. More important to Hale's self-construction, however, is the fact that the magazine gains its materiality in part from the bodies of the working women who construct it. In a sense, then, to the extent that Hale builds her own bodily identity on and through the magazine, utilizing the magazine's materiality to substitute for her own bodily corporeality, her body is maintained by the bodies of the working women who give the magazine its materiality. The labor that constructs the magazine also constructs Hale's public embodiment. What we see here is an image of the editor as a kind of parasitic body, built from the labor of others, particularly women. The bodies of the laborers and the material construction of the magazine perform a kind of analogical verification on Hale herself, allowing her to verify and validate a particular corporeal reality. Hale absorbs and transforms the unseemly manual labor of watercolor painters, binders, and paper makers, and even the labor of transcribing articles by hand, into a restrained, controlled, and powerful bodily identity.

Hale's insistence on the physicality of the *Lady's Book* undergirds her construction of her textual body. The physicality of the magazine gives a corporeal shape to her work as editor. Her discussions of her work call attention to the magazine as a physical entity. As a recent work on the history of the book explains, "Too often scholars, particularly literary scholars, have tended to idealize books as 'mere' texts—disembodied mental constructs transcending materiality, culture, and history. While the notion of a disembodied text may be a useful critical fiction, it is nevertheless an inherently distorting one, for there is no such thing after all as a text unmediated by its materiality."[39] Hale will not allow her readers to forget the materiality of the *Lady's Book* because the magazine's materiality becomes her own material being. The magazine's corporeal life becomes her own. At a certain level it is clear how Hale and the *Lady's Book* are connected: Hale's goals are the *Lady's Book*'s goals; the *Lady's Book*'s success is Hale's success. Beyond this, though, the magazine's embodied identity gives Hale an expanded physicality. The *Lady's Book* has greater mobility and reach than Hale herself. It travels across the country on a monthly basis and enters the homes of hundreds of thousands of families. Hale's famous assertion in her first *Lady's Book* article, "We are always at home," takes on an unusual meaning when read in this context. The magazine is always at home—at the homes of its readers—and therefore Hale's voice is permeating households and families across the nation. While Hale's literal body remained true to the traditional precepts of womanhood, her textual body could circulate freely and carry her ideas to places her literal body could never go. This was the power she gained through her identification with the magazine.

THE PRINT MARKETPLACE

Further emphasizing the fact that the *Lady's Book* was a material text reliant not only upon disembodied ideas but upon people, paper, and money, Hale often addressed financial issues in her "Editors' Tables." A consistent problem for the *Lady's Book* and all other nineteenth-century periodicals was subscribers' failure to pay for their subscriptions. The magazine's main source of income came from subscribers, and judging from Hale's columns, there were many who regularly neglected to pay.[40] Typically she used the end of the year as an occasion to prod her readers, explaining that the magazine was balancing its accounts and required its payments. Occasionally these requests for payment occurred at other times of the year, as well, as in September 1838 when Hale wrote an entire "Editors' Table" entitled "An Appeal to the Heart and Conscience of the Delinquent Subscribers of the Lady's Book."

She begins the article by differentiating herself from Godey, whom she identifies as the source of the financial demands: "Our publisher has appealed to us to write a DUN! But DUN is not a pretty word. It raises unpleasant images, and is altogether unbefitting the character of the Lady's Book."[41] Her differentiation from Godey has the effect of identifying Hale with the *Lady's Book* itself; the magazine has a character that, like that of a respectable middle-class woman, should not be troubled by financial concerns. Hale, significantly, is the one to decide what is and is not appropriate for the character of the magazine. Although she refuses to "write a dun," by capitalizing the word "dun" and repeating it, Hale emphasizes the importance of this word. This is an example of Hale's strategic compliance with the demands of true womanhood; she simultaneously manifests appropriate middle-class feminine distaste for financial matters as well as a keen awareness of the market. She calls her readers' attention to the financial needs of the magazine and points out the readers' own financial culpability, explaining, "the amount due to [Godey] on account of the Lady's Book, is so large, that we do not like to name the sum lest it should be thought incredible."[42]

Her role as editor allows her to show herself to be fully conversant with the financial issues surrounding both the magazine and the country in general. She writes, "During the late 'pressure' in the money market, the difficulty of obtaining current bills, no doubt prevented many of our southern and western friends from remitting their subscriptions. But the cause of such delay is now happily removed."[43] Writing in a friendly, intimate tone, Hale discusses the importance of money to the running of the *Lady's Book*. Stressing the financial needs of the magazine emphasizes its materiality; each issue costs money to produce, and that money is coming from a person, Godey himself. Hale identifies her subscribers as responsible for the support of the magazine, addressing her readers and subscribers as "our friends" while still exhorting them "no longer to withhold the amount they owe."[44] Her emphasis on money, in this column and others, identifies the magazine as a business; while her readers may be "friends," they are also and simultaneously business associates. Their money is required to keep the magazine in production.

Conversely, she also emphasized the financial success of the magazine, configuring it as a thriving business and thus a healthy material body. The *Lady's Book* was well-positioned in terms of nineteenth-century print culture and was reliant for its success on material changes in American culture and technology. The magazine experienced increasing popularity during a time of transformation in the world of American print culture. In the early decades of the nineteenth century, printed material was becoming more widely available than it had been in the eighteenth century, and much of this material was aimed at entertainment rather than at religious education. Fiction began increasing in popularity.[45] The reasons for this change are many: a decrease in the price of paper, better transportation systems to circulate texts once they were printed, better marketing techniques, and increasing secularization of American culture and therefore of American reading. These changes also led to consolidation of printing and publishing operations.[46] In addition to the wider accessibility of printed texts, other technological changes made reading more common, including the availability of better domestic lighting and corrective eyeglasses.[47] Thus during the years of the *Lady's Book*'s growth, the technologies for both printing and reading were improving.

In the year that Hale became editor of the magazine, the country experienced the Panic of 1837, the greatest financial crisis in the nation's history. While the Panic was devastating to many sectors of American business, including banks and mercantile houses, it was actually beneficial to the *Lady's Book*. Because the Panic put many book printers and publishers out of business, it opened the market for less expensive reading material, a niche which the *Lady's Book* filled perfectly. The magazine also benefited from the improvements in transportation and communication that helped to tie the nation together; rather than appealing to a local or regional market, the *Lady's Book* presented itself as—and was—a national periodical. The magazine always had readers from across the country.[48]

Hale publicized this national audience, advertising the magazine's popularity by keeping her readers abreast of the numbers of subscribers to the magazine. Since these numbers were dramatically higher than those of any competitors through the 1830s and 1840s, they established the *Lady's Book* as the nation's most successful magazine. The *Lady's Book* was an extremely popular magazine, by far the most popular and successful in the country from the 1830s through the Civil War, and still one of the nation's most popular magazines in the decades after the Civil War. While most magazines at mid-century had an average of 7,000 subscribers, with many like the *Southern Literary Messenger* weighing in with far fewer, the *Lady's Book* announced its subscription list to be at 40,000 in July 1849.[49] The number of readers surely exceeded the number of subscribers since subscribers regularly wrote the magazine to complain about their copies being borrowed by friends; by 1869, Godey himself claimed that the magazine had 500,000 readers.[50] The *Lady's Book* probably reached its pinnacle of subscribers just before the Civil War, with 150,000. The number of subscribers held steady in the 100,000 range throughout the 1860s and 1870s. Only after the Civil War did any magazine begin to surpass the *Lady's Book*'s number of subscribers.[51]

Hale advertised this success. She wrote to her readers in 1839, "It is no spirit of boasting, but because we wish to record a fact so honourable to the liberality of the public, that we mention that our list now exceeds the combined number of any other three monthly publications, and if we can judge of the future by the past it will reach by next year, the astonishing number of 25,000."[52] Hale frames this publicity by claiming to be expressing her gratitude to the public, but the fact that she reveals potential subscription numbers and compares her magazine with her competitors, suggests that this statement is less an expression of gratitude than one of publicity and pride. The magazine's subscription list continued to grow; in 1850 Hale asserted, "The *Lady's Book* shall be made worthy of its one hundred thousand patrons. Need we say more?"[53] The *Lady's Book* profited from the changing publishing marketplace; Hale's discussion of the magazine's success serves, again, to emphasize the materiality of the magazine by articulating its reliance on its subscribers and their funds, its competition with other magazines in the market, and its imbrication within the world of print advertising and sales. Further, her emphasis on the magazine's many subscribers was a means by which she heightened the public element of her embodiment.

By speaking as a gracious and grateful hostess, pleased with a positive reception from her guests, Hale conjoined two seemingly disparate personas—true woman and businesswoman—in one body, the *Lady's Book*.

Hale's statements of ambition and pride for the *Lady's Book*'s success, particularly her discussion of high subscription numbers, were evidence of changes happening in the marketing of publishing in the nineteenth century. Women were increasingly able to navigate the business of publishing.[54] In addition, publishers were striving for mass markets and were increasingly utilizing sensational tactics to sell their publications.[55] Publishers began using the numbers of texts sold as an advertising gimmick; as larger editions of books were able to be printed, transported, and sold, the numbers themselves became a selling point.[56] A book's popularity began to be advertised in order to promote its popularity. Positioning Hale within this framework gives an important context for her statements and demonstrates even further how she was identifying herself with the print culture of her time more than with stereotypes of female embodiment. For instance, while it would have been inappropriate for Hale to valorize herself and her own success, by explaining the circulation figures of the *Lady's Book*, she was simply participating in a mid-century trend in the marketing of printed materials. The material existence of the *Lady's Book* depended on and was shaped by the larger publishing marketplace; this marketplace, then, was a significant component of Hale's own bodily configuration, and her discussion of the market realities in her columns allows her both to intervene in the marketplace and to shape her own construction by the market. In combining the market and the home in one body, Hale did more than utilize both "spheres": she destabilized the binary itself and capitalized on the consequent carnivalesque energies released.

Laboring bodies, paper, and money create the magazine as a material entity. The magazine's materiality underwrites Hale's embodiment. Thus the material construction of the *Lady's Book* is a significant factor in Hale's own public body. The magazine's format, design, and even paper selection spoke to the fact that it was a high-quality publication targeting the middle classes. The *Lady's Book* was comparable in size to the other magazines of the day. In the early decades of its publication, it was six inches by nine and one-half inches. In the 1850s, the size decreased slightly to five and one-half inches by nine inches. This size distinguished the *Lady's Book* and other magazines from the less respectable popular weekly papers called "mammoth" and "leviathan" because of their enormity—often two feet tall by three or four feet wide.[57] Although the *Lady's Book*'s size was standard for a genteel family publication, the *Lady's Book* distinguished itself in terms of its visual and tactile presence in a number of ways. Probably the most notable visual features of the magazine were its fashion plates, noted earlier as one of the magazine's most popular components.

In addition to the fashion plates, the *Lady's Book* featured a variety of other illustrations, including highly detailed engravings done especially for the magazine by leading engravers of the day.[58] These engravings, protected by rice paper within the magazine's pages, often accompanied stories and featured such images as mothers and children, views of homes, and landscapes. The magazine also featured a number of less detailed, smaller images in each issue. In 1849, for instance, a representative issue of the magazine contained one color fashion plate, two detailed engravings accompanying stories, six other full-page illustrations, and several smaller images. The numerous images, particularly the time-intensive colored fashion plates, were expensive; Hale noted in one of her editorial columns that "the engravings in this last volume alone would, were they separately purchased, cost more than the year's subscription."[59] The most expensive of the plates could cost one thousand dollars to produce.[60] This expense was a selling-point for the magazine, however; through the quantity and quality of its beautiful images, the *Lady's Book* distinguished itself from other magazines and newspapers and demonstrated its quality and appropriateness for America's middle classes.

The magazine also utilized a higher quality of paper than that used in newspapers, as a sign of its quality and difference from these cheap publications. The magazine utilized paper of differing qualities: in addition to the strip of rice paper protecting engravings, the magazine featured a card-stock cover and a binding much like today's magazines which distinguished it from newspapers. Its length was also a distinguishing feature; the magazine gradually increased in length over the years of its publication, growing from forty-eight-page issues in the 1830s and 1840s to one-hundred-page issues in the 1850s and 1860s. While the length distinguished the magazine from cheap newspapers, it also distinguished it from longer, more self-consciously intellectual magazines like the *Atlantic Monthly*. This magazine, subtitled "A Magazine of Literature, Art, and Politics," weighed in with a first issue in 1857 of one hundred thirty pages and no illustrations.[61]

The material construction of the *Lady's Book* thus established its identity as a high-quality family magazine that targeted not the intellectual elite or the masses but the middle classes and those who strove to appear middle class. The magazine's material construction marked the site of yet another tension within the magazine: while the publication's appearance was middle class, Hale often characterized the magazine as a factory or as the product emerging from a factory, emphasizing the laboring bodies responsible for the publication. Thus the form and content of the *Lady's Book* offered opposing visions of the magazine itself, existing in a continual tension. This tension is emblematic of Hale's continual negotiations between the work the magazine required of her and the power it offered her—characteristics not typically associated with middle-class womanhood—and her attempts to make the magazine a model of middle-class respectability. Lehuu suggests that the world of popular print media dislodged the binary of the public and private spheres and inserted, instead, the binary of the popular versus the legitimate press.[62] Indeed, the carnivalesque world of antebellum print culture was a perfect site for the decommissioning of reductive binaries. I contend that neither of these binaries allows for a full understanding of the *Lady's Book*, which straddled the public and the private as well as the popular and the legitimate.[63] The *Lady's Book*'s mastery of the world of mid-century print culture suggests that Hale was able to navigate these tensions between and among binaries and capitalize on them, creating not only a successful product but also her own successful—and marketable—corporeal identity.

MULTIVALENT PRINT BODIES

The printed page offered Hale the opportunity to manipulate certain constraints which obtained for middle-class nineteenth-century women. It was a space where she had at least limited agency to define her own body and her career in terms not typically applicable to women of her time. In a brief note in one of her essays about Hale, Nina Baym comments on Hale and Godey's work within the *Lady's Book*, figuring the magazine as a body: "From the vantage point of the reading I give here, the division of responsibilities would correspond with Hale's idea of sexual difference: she was the mind and spirit, Godey the physical implementer, of the journal."[64] While

Godey may have been the magazine's physical implementer, providing the magazine's financial backing and much of its marketing, to identify Hale as the "mind and spirit" of the magazine ignores the actual physical work she did for the magazine and reifies standard nineteenth-century sexual stereotypes that would have us believe that women achieve their work in the world through amorphous and nurturing "influence." While Hale herself upheld a sexual division of labor, she mobilized the idea of sexual difference strategically, emphasizing her mind and spirit in conjunction with a multivalent and present physical editorial identity. The fragmentation—and even, at times, ambiguity—of Hale's embodiment through the *Lady's Book* facilitated her broadening of the roles and power available to her as a woman. Although her readers clearly knew that she was female, her comments on herself in her editorial role do not offer the reader stereotypically female imagery or even wording.

Hale's physical body, as differentiated from her textual body, aided her self-identification with the magazine. Hale wore mourning for her husband throughout the forty years of her life after he died. Effacing her own physical body with black clothes—providing, through her clothing, a clear representation of herself as a grieving widow—and wearing her hair throughout her life in the kind of sidecurls which were popular in the 1820s allowed Hale to construct a physical body that was less constrained by the changing world of fashion. Hale chose a style of dress which was eminently respectable, beyond reproach: her literal body became another text, a text which signified respectable, grieving widowhood and a kind of old-fashioned sensibility. As Tonkovich asserts, "It was perhaps the ultimate demonstration of Hale's contention that if dress were to be equated with character, a wise woman would use her dress to exemplify the character she wished her public to attribute to her."[65] Hale's body became a kind of constant which both shaped her public persona and allowed her to focus her energy on her text—and her textual self. Indeed, by freezing her body in time, she essentially erased it. Her body became a cipher, legible symbolically with no reference to her bodily specifics required.

This absent or symbolic body has had a profound impact on her reception by scholars. Hale is an excellent example of a nineteenth-century woman who has been read as manifesting a straightforward sentimental true womanhood when, in fact, her public presence was much more complex. Many twentieth-century critics of her work seem to have been distracted from her agency and her emphatically public power by her physical image or her emphasis on women's spirituality; few have noted what a keen businesswoman she was. For instance, Bardes and Gossett call her a "discriminating promoter and patroness of members of her own sex and especially of the writers among them," emphasizing her literary interests but describing her as a kind of professional cheerleader or supporter of the arts, not as a professional woman. Other critics, like Ruth Finley and Caroline Bird, have characterized Hale as a businesswoman who marketed femininity; while these critics note Hale's business acumen, they portray this business skill as a kind of elevated flirting or nagging.[66] Okker is one of the first critics to frame Hale's work within the context of the professionalization of writing in the nineteenth century, calling Hale "a master writer responsible for instructing apprentices and maintaining professional standards."[67] The world of words allowed Hale to manipulate the kinds of negative bodily configurations working women could face. Hale conformed herself outwardly to the traditional standards of middle-class womanhood through the clothing she wore and her emphasis on the virtue inherent in womanhood, and then created for herself a textual life which was not subject to those constraints.

Hale's use of print culture to address the problematics of nineteenth-century business women's embodiment involved embedding a physical representation of herself within the magazine and using the magazine as a sign or representative of her physical self interacting with the larger world. As an editor she was not forced to conform to true womanly ways of speaking and behaving; her life in print was one of authority, force, power, and control. As we have seen, she constructed her editorial identity as financially savvy and critically demanding. More to the point, her *Lady's Book* columns describe and define not only her mental characteristics but also her textual body. It is perhaps significant that the title of Hale's columns was "Editors' Table" when it could as easily have been "The Ladies' Table" or "Mrs. Hale's Thoughts"; the title refers to a job description rather than to a gendered persona and thus does not refer to the writer as a man or woman. Hale uses this strategically ambiguous site in the magazine to define her textual body, utilizing her facility with words to construct a multilayered and variously manifesting textual self.

One of Hale's primary techniques for shaping her textual body in order to allow herself the greatest freedom from constraining stereotypes involves using mini-dramatizations or conversations to characterize her editorial work. This conversational metaphor allowed Hale to complicate her own embodiment within the magazine's pages. She utilizes the model of the conversation regularly in her "Editors' Tables," actually writing conversations and thus expressing her editorial opinions through the voices of multiple fictional characters in discussion. These dramatizations have the effect of dissecting or diffusing Hale's editorial presence; rather than being identified with one person, male or female, Hale becomes embodied in multiple characters. For instance, in several columns she creates mini-plays for her readers with two characters, the Editor and the secretary, looking through manuscripts. Neither character is gendered; although the reader may assume that the Editor is Hale, this character has no other identification than the ambiguous title of "Editor."[68] The readers are encouraged to imagine an Editor and a secretary sitting at desks, speaking to one another; their conversation reveals the typical material of Hale's column, noticing those manuscripts which have been accepted and rejected and touching on such issues of the day as influential speakers. Using these characters, Hale could voice strong opinions and could vary her tone, so that she has the Editor say of one performer of magnetism, "She is no more in the magnetic sleep when she pretends to be, than I am at this moment. I wish she could be placed under a shower-bath when she is in one of her pretended magic slumbers."[69] This comical comment, neither polite nor particularly feminine, demonstrates the assertive enactments of her public voice Hale could develop through her role as Editor.

In 1842, Hale printed a series of columns which she called "Conversations at the Editors' Table." In these columns the editor's table becomes a literal entity, with three characters sitting around it—a young girl, her schoolmaster, and her mother. These columns offer the image of Hale's editorial voice embodied in three characters of differing age, education, gender, and authority; all three state opinions which coincide with Hale's own assertions. Through their conversations over a nine-month period, these characters assess the contributions made to the magazine and discuss relevant cultural issues. For instance, in one column, the young girl tells her schoolmaster that due to lack of space in the magazine, "The writers must be thankful if we give the titles of their articles a place," and in another the mother reports on the state of subscriptions by explaining, "Our western friends find it almost impossible to pay their subscriptions now, on account, as they say, of the disordered state of the exchanges. So we shall make little effort to enlarge our list till better times."[70] Each character has a distinct voice and bodily presence, but all three ultimately speak for Hale. The model of the conversation allowed Hale to construct a complex and powerful textual presence. Rather than linking her identity simplistically to a dramatization of herself as editor, Hale kept her identity fragmented, thus keeping her body malleable and connected to the *Lady's Book* as a whole.

In addition, even when not dramatizing conversations, Hale's first person assertions in the "Editors' Tables" were always made in the plural; she always said "we" rather than "I." This "editorial we" was probably her acknowledgment of the fact that she was not the only editor; Lydia Sigourney and others were listed as contributing editors of the magazine, although their editorship was in name only. However, more than simply an acknowledgment of other editorial presences, this manner of writing had the effect of further complicating Hale's editorial identity. A reader could not be entirely certain how to envision the "we" that was writing to him or her.[71] This kind of ambiguity is powerful. Rather than being tied to a set of stereotypes and expectations that accompany either masculinity or femininity, Hale, in her editorial identity, is able to exist somewhere in between the two.

Hale's use of ambiguous pronouns allowed her to evoke her own power without stating it outright. For instance, in an 1846 "Editors' Table," Hale asks, "What has our Lady's Book done?" She then attributes the rise in women's education to the magazine, which she calls "the pioneer in all these improvements." In response to her next question, "What more can the Lady's Book do?," Hale answers, "We see to make ours emphatically the Lady's Book. No other periodical does or can compare with it in appropriateness for our own sex."[72] She then takes this ambitious statement as the basis for her description of an increasingly heroic role; in this description, the pronoun "we" is a broad referent, encompassing Hale and the magazine as a conjoined entity: "We only want a wider sphere, a broader field, to enable us to carry out all these plans of perfection. We wish to commence the New-Year with fifty-thousand subscribers. Will not every lady who takes the 'Book' use her good offices in its behalf, and send us the name of one friend? We should then feel sure that the 'progression' of our own sex in this country was rapidly advancing."[73]

The *Lady's Book* and Hale seem jointly responsible for the "progression" of women in America. According to Hale, they are the force that has promoted women's education successfully and that meets the needs of women readers more than any other magazine. Their massive subscription lists are both evidence of their popularity and a sign of their power to influence great numbers of readers over a long period of time. More than a single book, the *Lady's Book*, which reappeared in homes month after month, had the opportunity to affect people's thinking and behavior. It seems significant that while the *Lady's Book* advocated separate spheres, Hale would argue that the magazine needed "a wider sphere"; the magazine remained a lady's book, notable for its "appropriateness" within women's sphere, but Hale pushed for that sphere to be larger, even to be transformed from a sphere into "a broader field." By suggesting the alternative metaphor of field, Hale suggests a lack of constraint or boundaries and the possibility for expansion and movement, both for the magazine and for herself. Indeed, given the authority and mobility Hale commanded because of her identification with the *Lady's Book*, a broad field seems a more fitting metaphor for her "place" than a sphere. In this way Hale articulates the decommissioning of the spheres binary that the *Lady's Book* and the larger world of popular print culture have enabled.

In addition to describing herself as multiple identities in conversation, Hale utilizes the model of the conversation to characterize the magazine as a whole. In her first article for the *Lady's Book*, Hale figured her editorial role and the whole magazine as a conversation: "We intend our work as a 'Conversazione' of the highest character, to which we invite every lady in our land."[74] In the same article she describes the merger of the *Lady's Book* with the *Ladies' Magazine* as a joining of two voices—in other words, a conversation. This metaphor of conversation is a corporeal one, allowing Hale to embody her own ideas and to personify differing points of view.[75] By imagining the magazine as a conversation, Hale makes the magazine into an embodied space, implicitly connecting the text to bodies in general and to her body specifically. She often continued with this metaphor in her columns, beginning a column by inviting her readers to join her for a discussion. This technique highlights the kind of power Hale discovered through the magazine. The magazine allowed Hale to engage in conversations around the country; tens of thousands of women, sitting in their homes, could be simultaneously involved in a "conversation" with Hale, being influenced by her words and opinions and contributing their own through letters and submissions.

To further corporealize the image of women in conversation with Hale through the *Lady's Book*, Hale regularly identifies the magazine itself as a woman. This is a point Hale makes obliquely in many of her "Editors' Tables"; any time Hale defends the dignity or standards of the *Lady's Book*, she is contributing to her readers' sense of the magazine itself as a female friend. Hale articulates this point of view directly in an "Editors' Table" in 1843; or, rather, she has a fictional character in the act of conversation articulate it: "Our LADY'S BOOK is the only PERIODICAL in the world which embodies the piety, genius, intelligence and refinement of perfect womanhood. It is consecrated to the promotion of those pure virtues and moral influences which constitute woman's mission. It is her work; and nobly will the sex sustain it."[76] By way of an advertisement for the *Lady's Book*, Hale defines the magazine as a lady.

In characterizing the magazine this way, Hale articulates a particular kind of print embodiment which was aligned with her larger view of men's and women's sexual differences. She argues that women are men's spiritual and moral superiors and that this superiority places responsibilities on both men and women. For instance, she explains in a 1859 column that "God has made woman more spiritual, more tender, more conscientious than man. It is her province to modify the harsher features of man's character."[77] In characterizing women in this way, Hale, by extension, gives a particular shape to the female body that is the *Lady's Book*. Her belief in women's piety and purity upholds her identification of the magazine as a virtuous woman: if women can be embodied in print culture, this embodiment need not be oppressive or culturally inappropriate but may provide a venue for the women to enact the spiritual, conscientious traits which are their primary features. Indeed, by defining the magazine in such terms, Hale suggested a broader envisioning of print culture and the print marketplace as spaces that should be inhabited by female bodies and female values.

Again, in another column, she writes, "We have endeavored to make the 'Book' an emblem of what human life should be—progressive in excellence." In another she explains, "the 'Lady's Book' came as a pleasant friend to amuse as well as instruct."[78] Thus the magazine itself is a being, a body, with whom readers can converse. It is a virtuous female friend who is invited into the home and whose ideas are taken seriously. Hale, of course, as the voice of the magazine, as a presence permeating the text, is, ultimately, that female friend. By utilizing the model of the conversation to characterize her own editorial body and the magazine's relationship to its readers, Hale constructed an editorial identity that was often not classifiable in terms of gender. If gender was implied, it was generally in relation to the magazine as a whole rather than to its editor. This ambiguity gave Hale agency; her power to shape her print embodiment, while not unlimited, allowed her to negotiate with and move beyond stereotypes of femininity. These conversations also demonstrate one way Hale used the *Lady's Book* to complicate the spheres binary: Hale's print body was engaged in a perfectly appropriate private sphere activity of female conversation. Because her body was a magazine with huge circulations, however, she was simultaneously taking part in an emphatically public activity.

Hale's readers seem to have responded to the *Lady's Book* as a lady. The magazine arrived on the first weekday of the month at houses across the nation, and according to letters readers wrote to Hale, its arrival was eagerly awaited. Hale noted readers' irritation when the magazine was late; for example, she announces in the surrogate editorial voice of the fictional Mrs. Marvin, "And yet, if the 'Lady's Book' were not furnished promptly by the day promised, what complaints we should hear!"[79] The fact that subscribers knew the day when the magazine was to come and would be irritated if it was delayed suggests that the magazine played an important role in the lives of its readers. While it is difficult to document readers' responses to many of the texts they encounter, the *Lady's Book* does provide a written record of responses in the form of letters to the editor, which Hale regularly printed.[80] These letters discuss readers' approval of the magazine, their frustrations when it was borrowed, and their own meditations on issues raised in the magazine; readers would also write to share recipes and to ask about concerns such as how to dye red hair. Their letters demonstrate a thoughtful engagement with the magazine; and the fact that they wrote to share their own ideas for inclusion suggests that at least some readers considered the magazine a friend with whom one would exchange household hints.

Critics have often misidentified the character of the female friend which is the *Lady's Book*. Just as Hale moved beyond stereotypes of femininity for her own self-representation within the *Lady's Book*, the magazine's contents were not always stereotypically feminine. Many twentieth-century critics, however, seem to overlook this fact in their assessment of the magazine. The *Lady's Book* has been the focus of extensive negative criticism in the twentieth century, much of it unearned. Like Fred Lewis Pattee's misguided vilification of Fanny Fern as "the most tearful and convulsingly 'female' moralizer" of her time, the criticisms of the *Lady's Book* lead a modern reader familiar with the magazine to wonder if these critics have read the material they lambast.[81] For instance, in 1930 Frank Luther Mott argued of the magazine's stories, "The characters are often so pious and good that we hate them heartily."[82]

This and many other criticisms posit the magazine as a stereotypically sentimental—and thus overwrought, poorly written, and emotionally excessive—publication.[83] In fact, a quick reading of almost any issue will counteract this assumption, because the *Lady's Book* presents a variety of different styles and generic approaches, from sentimental stories to humorous essays, from biographical sketches of prominent women to reviews of current books. The magazine strove for quality, featuring many, if not most, of the prominent authors of the day. The articles are, perhaps surprisingly, often witty and sarcastic, like Hale's "A Chapter of Inferences," which suggests, "When you hear a subscriber for the Lady's Book, or any other good periodical, declare that the work is not worth reading—infer that the subscription has not been regularly and punctually paid."[84]

The magazine featured such material as "Health and Beauty" columns by Hale and later a "Health Department" written by physicians; these columns warned women of potential health risks and offered preventative measures such as exercise.[85] The magazine also offered readers drawing lessons, recipes and household tips, and opinion pieces by Hale and others on marriage laws, women's education, and how to survive a husband's financial failure. In addition, of course, the *Lady's Book* featured a number of poems and stories in each issue, ranging from the sentimental to the comical to the sensational.[86] While many critics have identified the magazine as a stronghold for a kind of sentimental literary approach that the critics wish to denigrate, their criticisms do not accurately reflect the content and format of the magazine. One of the means by which the *Lady's Book* could become an empowering site was through its discussions of a larger realm of material than that enabled by sentimental fiction.

Ultimately, Hale's work demonstrates the ways in which a woman could identify with the material constructs of print culture and thus utilize a surrogate embodiment, one which was public and malleable. Hale's strategic construction of her ambiguous editorial identity allowed her a certain degree of control over the shaping of her body and behavior; her work demonstrates that print was not a site free of constraints but that a woman invested in print culture could manipulate those constraints. In addition, Hale's recourse to the material foundations of the magazine, including her descriptions of the laboring bodies creating the magazine, situated her as a laboring body while protecting her from the dangers material bodies faced. The *Lady's Book* was a site that provided Hale with public embodiment; the tensions that traversed the magazine—Hale's desires in competition with the magazine's material needs, the demands of the marketplace in conflict with the money forthcoming from subscribers—were formative of the complicated syncretic space of print culture.

Each woman analyzed within this book has used rhetoric to describe and define her own embodiment; Mowatt constructed her sensational womanhood through her *Autobiography*, Eddy erased the female body in *Science and Health*, Truth constructed her tall-tale body through her speeches and reports about her, and Wells configured black women's bodies in terms of citizenship in her antilynching pamphlets. This book has made arguments about these women's bodies, bodies that are articulated and that articulate themselves. Although each woman examined here employed different means to define her corporeality, all their corporeal configurations have ultimately taken place at the level of language. Hale's work is in some ways the logical extension of Mowatt's, Eddy's, Truth's, and Wells's bodily self-constructions: Hale not only defined herself through words and rhetoric, she also identified her body with print culture. Print culture was not only the means by which she defined herself but also acted in many cases as the content of her self-definition. She takes the rhetorical construction of the female body to its logical extreme and in so doing reveals the complexity of women's involvement in nineteenth-century print culture.

By identifying her corporeality with the *Lady's Book*, Hale was able to command a tremendous influence over hundreds of thousands of American readers. Her surrogate body traveled across the nation, entering houses, and beginning conversations with readers; Hale was thus able to speak to more Americans than Mowatt, Eddy, Truth, or Wells and to speak to them in a setting of intimacy and confidence. She was the ultimate traveler even though—or perhaps because—she was "always at home."

EPILOGUE

Nineteenth-Century Women's Writing and Public Embodiment

A Prospectus

> *If such women as are here described have once existed, be no longer astonished then, my brethren and friends, that God at this eventful period should raise up your own females to strive, by their example both in public and private, to assist those who are endeavoring to stop the strong current of prejudice that flows so profusely against us at present. No longer ridicule their efforts, it will be counted for sin. For God makes use of feeble means sometimes, to bring about his most exalted purposes.*
>
> —Maria W. Stewart, "Farewell Address to Her Friends in the City of Boston," 1833

> *One needs both leisure and money to make a successful book. There is material among us for the broadest comedies and the deepest tragedies, but, besides money and leisure, it needs patience, perseverance, courage, and the hand of an artist to weave it into the literature of the country.*
>
> —Frances E. W. Harper, *Iola Leroy*, 1893

The canonical figures of nineteenth-century American women's literature have become overly familiar through readings propelled by particular binaric constructions: public versus private, agent versus victim, appropriate versus deviant. The figures this book has examined—Anna Cora Mowatt, Mary Baker Eddy, Sojourner Truth, Ida B. Wells, and Sarah Josepha Hale—along with popular nineteenth-century images of women's athleticism provide an excellent heuristic by which to return to these canonical texts with new readings. These women provide a set of models and strategies by which to reinterpret familiar works of nineteenth-century literature; they offer a continuum of visible, embodied modalities that destabilize the familiar binaries. The flaming ballet girl, transcendent Mind, tall-tale hero, and other forms of embodiment described in *Out in Public* do not negate the familiar image of domesticated womanhood; instead, the women studied here construct their bodies strategically within and against competing discourses. They provide the groundwork for a reinterpretation of nineteenth-century literary womanhood based on the body in public.

The embodied modalities deployed here include pleasure. Pleasure is a recurring theme throughout the lives and writing of several of the women studied in *Out in Public*. Pleasure is here revealed as a destabilizing corporeal energy, not legible within simplistic binary categories; it foregrounds a woman's experience of her own embodiment and ruptures the notion of a woman's body as an object that serves others. While I have noted the descriptions and manifestations of pleasure in Mowatt's text, particularly in her discussions of her travels, the radical potential of pleasure may be most clearly seen in Truth's speeches. By voicing pleasure, as in the moment when she raises her right arm in her speech at the 1851 Woman Rights Convention, "showing its tremendous muscular power," Truth asserts the integrity and autonomy of her bodily existence. She physically demonstrates the emergence of agency within a context of victimization based on race, class, and gender. Truth's use of the tall-tale genre also connects her embodiment to the destabilizing energy of pleasure, because tall tales are comedic and therefore measure their success based on a physical reaction of pleasure—laughter. This reclaiming and releasing of the body through pleasure can be seen, as well, in Hale's use of humor in her columns in *Godey's Lady's Book*. When Hale threatens to throw a batch of writers' submissions into the fire, or proclaims of a performer of magnetism, "I wish she could be placed under a shower-bath," she is utilizing comedic energy—the embodied energy of pleasure—to disrupt the script of domesticated womanhood and appropriate femininity.[1]

Pleasure is one part of a bodily continuum that includes other categories that also destabilize binaries; illness is another point on that continuum. *Out in Public* offers many glimpses of the ways women writers could utilize illness—both as an idea and as an embodied experience—in order to enact agency. For instance, Mowatt and Eddy both received a great deal of familial support, including financial support, because of their illnesses. That Eddy and Mowatt were both middle-class white women is not coincidental in this regard: nineteenth-century women's ability to enact agency via illness is finely keyed to performances of race and class. While Mowatt could leverage her illnesses for power, using it to fortify her public presence as properly feminized, Truth gained more from downplaying her bodily weaknesses, such as her injured hand and her aging body, and instead emphasizing strength and heroism. However, illness cannot be simplistically mapped onto the bodies of white, middle-class women, since women like Eddy and Hale combated the image of the properly weak, ill, and therefore domesticated, female body. Although their arguments were very differently grounded—Eddy's emphasizing erasure of the body, Hale's suggesting a new version of appropriate femininity—both women advocated for a female body not empowered by conforming to debilitating societal mandates. In this way, Eddy and Hale's presentation of the female body is congruent with Truth's; they were offering an image of health and bodily vitality.

Race is another embodied modality that can destabilize the binaries of public and private, agent and victim. Of the writers studied in *Out in Public*, Truth and Wells are the most attuned to the way racial identity affects their embodiment and that of their white contemporaries. It is not surprising that Mowatt, Eddy, and Hale are, for the most part, oblivious to their own whiteness. However, regardless of the women's level of awareness, racial categories were central to the versions of womanhood being produced in the nineteenth century, and each of the women studied here participated in a complex performance of gendered race and raced gender. Rather than viewing these women in terms of another binary—seeing them as simplistically complicit or transgressive in regard to race and racism—*Out in Public* offers a complicated vision of the interpenetration of resistance and collusion. For instance, some authors made strategic use of certain racist stereotypes in order to combat others, as when Wells portrayed black men as bodily disempowered and victimized in order to destabilize race and gender norms. For the most part, the identities of the white women studied here seem to have been thoroughly invested in whiteness: Hale's performance of femininity was grounded in a magazine that relentlessly promoted a white ideal, including many visual representations of appropriate femininity for which whiteness was a crucial component; and after the publication of her *Autobiography*, Mowatt married a slave owner and became a plantation mistress. Eddy's production of femininity, however, was less tied to a specific notion of race; indeed, although *Science and Health* does not interrogate racism, Eddy's decommissioning of the material body enables a decommissioning of perceived racial distinctions.

The complex, often multivalent female bodies deployed by the women studied here offer ways to reexamine canonical texts. For instance, the health and bodily substance of such characters as Nancy Vawse and the bodily insubstantiality of such characters as Alice Humphreys in *The Wide, Wide World* may assume greater complexity of meaning in relation to Eddy's writings. The bodily mortification Harriet Jacobs experiences in her attic enclosure in *Incidents in the Life of a Slave Girl* (1861) can be read alongside Mowatt's and Truth's negotiations with the embodied concept of the freak. Vigorously physical characters such as Nancy Vawse and Jo March may appear to be part of a community of athletic women when viewed in conjunction with images of woman archers, equestrians, and baseball players. Edna Pontellier's attempts to assert ownership of her own body and its desires in Chopin's *The Awakening* suggest a broader cultural significance when read alongside Wells's pamphlets. Emily Dickinson's poem "Publication—is the Auction / Of the Mind of Man—", in which she characterizes writers and their writing as thought's "Corporeal illustration," gains greater legibility through comparison with Hale's engagement with the corporeality of text. Truth's marshalling of the tall tale tradition in her self-representation provides a broader context for Capitola Black, the cross-dressing, heroic heroine of E. D. E. N. Southworth's *The Hidden Hand* (1859). Similarly, Mowatt's deployment of fire imagery as a nexus of passion, victimization, potential freakishness, and performative power deepens the meaning of fire imagery in Alcott's sensation stories like "Which Wins?" (1869) or "La Belle Bayadere" (1870) as well as in *Little Women*. Mowatt's articulation of a multivalent sensational womanhood may add deeper meaning to Maria Stewart's passionate public speeches.

In 1986, critic Estelle Jelinek asserted, "The female identity is not a heroic one. For the most part, women do not see themselves as legends or representatives of their times."[2] Over the last two decades, critics have been formulating a picture of nineteenth-century womanhood which expands beyond Jelinek's assertion. One important means to do so is to analyze women whose lives and writings do not fit within more familiar models of women's behavior; this is the job *Out in Public* has undertaken. The women analyzed here present texts saturated with heroism, adventure, violence, activism, and outspoken professional assertion, characteristics not always apparent to late twentieth-century readers in their assessments of women's writing. In fact, these traits—and these women themselves—are often invisible to late twentieth-century readers who may see heroic or sensational female identities as anomalous. The women examined here often present themselves in the very terms that more familiar readings of womanhood preclude and position themselves as simultaneously public and private, enacting agency even in the midst of oppression and limitations.

Now that these new models of womanhood are apparent, the time has come to apply them by reexamining works of fiction which have shaped familiar configurations of American womanhood. The writings of Mowatt, Eddy, Truth, Wells, and Hale are documents which present the publicly enacted female body as a crucial component of nineteenth-century culture; they can play an important role in this reexamination. As they and texts like them are brought into readings with the canonical female-authored texts of the nineteenth century, scholars may begin to see ironies, slippages, and polyvocality in familiar texts, and these textual sites will reveal "untold stories."[3] One story they will reveal is that easy binaries cannot contain the range of material and discursive energies available to women in the nineteenth century. A different kind of female body can then begin to emerge from the fissures in the binary framework, a body that registers dramatic as well as subtle differences of racial, historical, and class positioning, a body that may surprise us.

APPENDIX

Sojourner Truth's "Ar'n't I a Woman?" Speech as Recorded by Frances Gage

Frances Gage published an article called "Sojourner Truth" in *The Independent*, April 23, 1863. The version of Truth's 1851 speech that was included in that article follows.

The leaders of the movement, staggering under the weight of disapprobation already laid upon them, and tremblingly alive to every appearance of evil that might spring up in their midst, were many of them almost thrown into panics on the first day of the meeting, by seeing a tall, gaunt black woman in a gray dress and white turban, surmounted by an uncouth sun-bonnet, march deliberately into the church, walk with the air of a queen up the aisle, and take her seat upon the pulpit steps. A buzz of disapprobation was heard all over the house, and such words as these fell upon listening ears:

"An abolition affair!" "Women's Rights and niggers!" "We told you so. Go it, old darkey!"

I chanced upon that occasion to wear my first laurels in public life, as president of the meeting. At my request, order was restored, and the business of the hour went on. The morning session closed; the afternoon session was held; the evening exercises came and went; old Sojourner, quiet and reticent as the "Libyan Statue," sat crouched against the wall on a corner of the pulpit stairs, her sun-bonnet shading her eyes, her elbow on her knee, and her chin resting on her broad, hard palm.

At intermissions she was busy selling the "Life of Sojourner Truth," a narrative of her own strange and adventurous life.

Again and again timorous and trembling ones came to me and said with earnestness, "Don't let her speak, Mrs. G. It will ruin us. Every newspaper in the land will have our cause mixed with abolition and niggers, and we shall be utterly denounced." My only answer was, "We shall see when the time comes."

The second day the work waxed warm. Methodist, Baptist, Episcopal, Presbyterian, and Universalist ministers came in to hear and discuss the resolutions brought forth. One claimed superior rights and privileges for man because of superior intellect; another because of the manhood of Christ. If God had desired the equality of woman, he would have given some token of his will through the birth, life, and death of the Savior. Another gave us a theological view of the awful sin of our first mother. There were few women in those days that dared to "speak in meeting," and the august teachers of the people, with long-winded bombast, were seeming to get the better of us, while the boys in the galleries and sneerers among the pews were enjoying hugely the discomfiture, as they supposed, of the strong-minded. Some of the tender-skinned friends were growing indignant and on the point of losing dignity, and the atmosphere of the convention betokened a storm.

Slowly from her seat in the corner rose Sojourner Truth, who, till now, had hardly lifted her head. "Don't let her speak," gasped a half-dozen in my ear. She moved slowly and solemnly to the front; laid her old bonnet at her feet, and turned her great speaking eyes to me.

There was a hissing sound of disapprobation above and below. I rose and announced, "Sojourner Truth," and begged the audience to keep silence for a few moments. The tumult subsided at once, and every eye was fixed on this almost Amazon form, which stood nearly six feet high, head erect, and eye piercing the upper air like one in a dream. At her first word there was a profound hush. She spoke in deep tones, which, though not loud, reached every ear in the house, and away through the throng at the doors and windows.

"Well, chilern, whar dar's so much racket dar must be something out o'kilter. I tink dat, 'twixt de niggers of de South and de women at de Norf, all a-talking 'bout rights, de white men will be in a fix pretty soon. But what's all this here talking 'bout? Dat man ober dar say dat women needs to be helped into carriages, and lifted over ditches, and to have de best place eberywhar. Nobody eber helps me into carriages, or ober mud-puddles, or gives me any best place;" and, raising herself to her full hight [*sic*], and her voice to a pitch like rolling thunder, she asked, "And ar'n't I a woman? Look at me. Look at my arm," and she bared her right arm to the shoulder, showing its tremendous muscular power. "I have plowed and planted and gathered into barns, and no man could head me—and ar'n't I a woman? I could work as much and eat as much as a man (when I could get it,) and bear de lash as well—and ar'n't I a woman? I have borne thirteen chillen, and seen 'em mos' all sold off into slavery, and when I cried out with a mother's grief, none but Jesus heard—and ar'n't I a woman? Den dey talks 'bout dis ting in de head. What dis dey call it?" "Intellect," whispered some one near. "Dat's it honey. What's dat got to do with woman's rights or niggers' rights? If my cup won't hold but a pint and yourn holds a quart, wouldn't ye be mean not to let me have my little half-measure full?" and she pointed her significant finger and sent a keen glance at the minister who had made the argument. The cheering was long and loud. "Den dat little man in black dar, he say woman can't have as much right as man, cause Christ wa'n't a woman. *Whar did your Christ come from?*"

Rolling thunder could not have stilled that crowd as did those deep wonderful tones, as she stood there with outstretched arms and eye of fire. Raising her voice still louder, she repeated,

"Whar did your Christ come from? From God and a woman. Man had nothing to do with him." Oh! what a rebuke she gave the little man. Turning again to another objector, she took up the defense of Mother Eve. I cannot follow her through it all. It was pointed and witty and solemn, eliciting at almost every sentence deafening applause; and she ended by asserting "that if de fust woman God ever made was strong enough to turn de world upside down all her one lone, all dese togeder," and she glanced her eye over us, "ought to be able to turn it back and git it right side up again, and now dey is asking to, de men better let 'em." (Long continued cheering.) "'Bleeged to ye for hearin' on me, and now ole Sojourner ha'n't got nothing more to say."

Amid roars of applause she turned to her corner, leaving more than one of us with streaming eyes and hearts beating with gratitude. She had taken us up in her great strong arms and carried us safely over the slough of difficulty, turning the whole tide in our favor.

I have given but a faint sketch of her speech. I have never in my life seen anything like the magical influence that subdued the mobbish spirit of the day and turned the jibes and sneers of an excited crowd into notes of respect and admiration. Hundreds rushed up to shake hands and congratulate the glorious old mother, and bid her "God-speed" on her mission of "testifying agin concernin the wickedness of this here people."

NOTES

INTRODUCTION

1. This book's title invokes the revealing of a previously hidden sexual identity—"outing," coming out of the closet—and this implication is not accidental. Although *Out in Public* does not consider the sexual orientation or practices of the five women studied here, sexuality and publicity were connected for women in the nineteenth century. Female visibility connoted sexual availability, as many scholars have observed, and thus being "out" as a woman was an implicitly sexualized status.

2. Nineteenth-century women's literature's complicity with or resistance to dominant cultural mores has been central to what has been called the Douglas-Tompkins debate, mapped out originally in Douglas's *Feminization of American Culture* and Tompkins's *Sensational Designs* and revisited in other critical works.

3. Ryan, *Women in Public*, 4.

4. Hazel Carby (*Reconstructing Womanhood*) notes the extent to which the model of the spheres obscures or negates the influence of race in determining women's and men's status and roles, and bell hooks continues this argument in *Feminist Theory* and other texts, asserting repeatedly that feminists and others concerned with oppression must recognize and attempt to dismantle all relationships of domination (based on class, race, or gender) because they are intimately interconnected. Similarly, Peterson's *"Doers of the Word"* systematically challenges the notion of separate spheres, analyzing the public work of African American women in the north. Although she remains wedded to a notion of the private and public spheres, she expands the idea of the public sphere to include women. Critics Claudia Tate (*Domestic Allegories of Political Desire*) and Ann duCille (*The Coupling Convention*) take another approach, arguing that domesticity need not always be associated with limiting, private-sphere constraints; these critics examine the conventions of domesticity as offering African American women writers a means to leverage political power.

5. For example, critics have begun complicating notions of the public and private spheres by examining the economics of women's authorship and the political involvement of nineteenth-century women novelists. See Coultrap-McQuin, *Doing Literary Business*, and Harris, *Redefining the Political Novel*.

6. For discussions of the sentimental as a nationalistic project, see Samuels, *The Culture of Sentiment*, and for an analysis of the formation of the individual, see Brown, *Domestic Individualism*.

7. Barbara Welter's 1966 essay on the cult of true womanhood was one of the first twentieth-century critical texts to analyze nineteenth-century women's lives in terms of the private sphere, and many more followed. Kelley's *Private Woman, Public Stage* is an example of the kind of critical text which has fully examined and explicated the idea of the spheres. Kelley's analysis of the separation of women's private world from the men's public realm is central to her discussion of nineteenth-century women novelists; her framework—that of the private and public spheres—allows her to examine the pressures affecting women writers.

8. In the 1970s and 1980s, critics like Carroll Smith-Rosenberg (*Disorderly Conduct*) and Nina Baym (*Woman's Fiction*) began reevaluating the notion of the spheres, arguing that women were able to use their consignment to the private sphere as a positive good. Smith-Rosenberg discusses the "female world of love and ritual" that developed from women's domestic lives, and Baym argues that, in their fictional writing, women promoted positive identity-formation for their women readers, thus using their female experiences to form a common female community of writers, readers, and characters. Jane Tompkins (*Sensational Designs*, 1985) proposes that sentimental literature was a politically active genre, allowing writers to construct alternative formulations for society. Works like these began the process of destabilizing the binaries structuring nineteenth-century literary studies even as they established those binaries.

9. Davidson, "Preface," 445.

10. Cathy Davidson edited the special issue of *American Literature* and coedited, with Jessamyn Hatcher, the book *No More Separate Spheres*.

11. For example, even as she expands the definition of the domestic in a recent study, Amy Kaplan reinscribes women as "the center of the home" (582).

12. Davidson and Hatcher, *No More Separate Spheres*, 17.

13. Cane and Feinsod, *"The Only Efficient Instrument,"* 4.

14. Grosz argues, "Subjects cannot be understood as powerless, oppressed, defeated, marginalized, and stripped of action; nor conversely can they be affirmed as self-contained and pregiven agents, agents who control their actions, their effects, their social milieu. . . . [B]oth concepts of the subject conceived as victim and the subject conceived as agent are equally fictitious . . ." Grosz, "Histories," 13–14.

15. My understanding of the pervasiveness of dichotomous thinking and the ways in which particular dichotomies are used by authors and critics to stabilize power relations has been greatly informed by the work of Lora Romero. As she notes, "gender's surplus of binary energies" is significant in that it may affect and shape other binaries. Romero, *Home Fronts*, 110.

16. Nelson, "Women," 38.

17. Mahoney, "Victimization or Oppression," 64. Mahoney's work, which addresses the legal challenges surrounding a feminist interpretation of domestic violence, was foundational to my own thinking. Mahoney notes that "All work with subordinated people confronts, at least to some extent, the

challenge of analyzing structures of oppression while including an account of the resistance, struggles, and achievements of the oppressed" (59). She notes the conflicts that have surrounded feminist attempts to document the oppression women face and have faced, currently and historically, and she contends that the particular configuration of victimization and agency that she identifies is responsible for the criticism feminist work has faced for "disempowering" women (the 1990s spate of books and articles discussing "victim feminism" is a case in point). Mahoney asserts, "Feminists need to identify the structures and stereotypes that cause even complex accounts of women's lives to be understood as accounts of victimization" (61).

18. Lest I be seen as unwittingly contradicting my previous contention that applying current stereotypes retroactively to the nineteenth century is ineffective, let me clarify. I do not claim that as scholars we must somehow divest ourselves of all current thinking in order to examine the nineteenth century; however, I do contend that there may be more effective models available for our assessments of this period. Recent reexaminations of victimization provide such models.

19. Carol Gilligan's *The Birth of Pleasure* has been influential to my own thinking. Gilligan notes that "pleasure is a sensation. It is written into our bodies; it is our experience of delight, of joy. . . . Pleasure will become a marker, a compass pointing to emotional true north" (159). She argues that women's experiences of pleasure are transgressive within male-dominated cultures and that pleasure allows women to disrupt the normal social scripts they are taught.

20. The body has been a popular subject for academic study for much of the twentieth century. The work of scholars such as Mary Douglas and Michel Foucault has been foundational; current criticism branches from their seminal work to a broad field of scholars who have provided a theoretical framework for understanding the body as a central component of culture and as a carrier of meaning. Douglas approached the body from an anthropological stance and argued for an understanding of the body as symbolically significant, representative of society. Foucault's work developed this concept: he argued that the body is socially constructed and is therefore a site where history displays itself and works itself out. Foucault explains, "We believe . . . that the body obeys the exclusive laws of physiology and that it escapes the influence of history, but this too is false. The body is molded by a great many distinct regimes; it is broken down by the rhythms of work, rest, and holidays; it is poisoned by food or values, through eating habits or moral laws; it constructs resistances." Foucault, "Nietzsche," 153. The body, thus, becomes a text in which scholars may read the history not only of the individual but also of the larger culture. Foucault's conceptions of the body have been controversial, with many—particularly anthropologists—critiquing the fact that the Foucauldian body is immaterial and apparently lacks agency. His presentation of the body as a "palimpsestic space," however, is crucial to an understanding of the complex meanings of the body, particularly the meanings the

body accrues as a site that bridges the private and the public. Punday, "Foucault's Body Tropes," 514.

21. Judith Butler articulates the interconnectedness of body and text, explaining, "To claim that discourse is formative is not to claim that it originates, causes, or exhaustively composes that which it concedes; rather, it is to claim that there is no reference to a pure body which is not at the same time a further formation of that body." Butler, *Bodies That Matter*, 10.

22. Fuss, *Essential Speaking*, 5.

23. Bordo, *Twilight Zones*, 185.

24. As Mikhail Bakhtin articulates, different languages and discourses compete for representational authority. Bakhtin, *Dialogic*, 278. Vicki Kirby, too, articulates the constraints and empowerment offered by the interconnectedness of the text and the body, arguing that the body itself is one of the heteroglot voices entering into its own construction. She offers useful correctives to the field of poststructuralist body theory as she contends that "the body is unstable—a shifting scene of inscription that both writes and is written." Kirby, *Telling Flesh*, 61. Rhetorical constructedness does not somehow free the body from all constraints. Language is not a purely freeing space. By asserting that the body itself is a voice, a writer, Kirby both prevents the body from being seen as a kind of tabula rasa and offers a corrective to potential assumptions that the body's constructedness offers total freedom.

25. Of course, the idea of passing has been widely studied and was a threatening and much discussed dynamic in the nineteenth century and well into the twentieth. Further, Truth herself was identified and "read" as a man at least once during a public performance, although not because of her attempt consciously to "pass."

26. Bordo, *Twilight Zones*, 181. Jacquelyn Zita, too, notes that the body's physicality interacts with other aspects of its "materialization" to make it a site that has limits, but limits which "are not always absolutely fixed." Zita continues, "As others have argued, the body is a *materialization*, a socially mediated formation, lived individually and in communities as *real effects*. The *physicality* of the body establishes some of the limits for what we can do with our bodies, but these limits are not always absolutely fixed. The social world enters the physical body as we develop skills and capacities, altering even the body's molecular structures, its anatomy, physiology, and metabolism. The body is thus a sturdy but fragile thing, an historical matter of political struggle." Zita, *Body Talk*, 4.

27. Kristeva, *Powers of Horror*, 4. See Thomson, *Freakery*, especially essays by Rosemarie Garland Thomson, Elizabeth Grosz, and Robert Bogdan. See also Chapter 1, below.

28. Even in Muir's case, however, the freakishness is mitigated by the fact that she is redeemed at the end of the story, protected by the love of a powerful man, and incorporated into the Coventry family.

29. Foucault, "Nietzsche," 148.

30. See Hargreaves, *Sporting Females*; Stanley, *Rise and Fall*; and, for a more popular view of the subject, Smith, *Nike Is a Goddess*.

CHAPTER ONE

1. Mowatt, *Autobiography*, 312.

2. Elsom, *Erotic Theatre*, 31.

3. Davis, "Actress in Victorian Pornography," 306; Taylor, "Rhetoric of Self-Fashioning," 76.

4. Mowatt, *Autobiography*, 313–4.

5. Ibid., 316.

6. In *Beneath the American Renaissance*, David Reynolds distinguishes these two forms even as he analyzes the popularity and influence of sensation fiction. Susan Griffin argues, "The celebration of [sensation novels'] subversive excesses, both in their depictions of violence and sexuality (and violent sexuality) and in their stylistic outrageousness, is underscored by contrast to what is assumed to be the constricted realm and tone of domestic fiction." Griffin, "'Dark Stranger,'" 14. As Mowatt's writing demonstrates, these two genres could also bleed into one another; the female gothic, for instance, is a site in which the sensational and the sentimental often merge. As Teresa Goddu argues, "the sentimental and the gothic are interdependent, not essentially different." Goddu, *Gothic America*, 96.

7. Taylor, "Rhetoric of Self-Fashioning," 42.

8. Garff B. Wilson explains, "Mowatt's very presence on the stage, whatever her style of performance, did great service to the profession of acting and helped to weaken the Puritan hostility toward the American theatre. Being a well known woman of wealth, education, and social position, Mrs. Mowatt's decision to go on the stage invoked the wrath of countless puritanical people. Yet for nine years she conducted herself with all the virtue, dignity, and graciousness of a born lady, and when she retired thousands of people throughout the nation had revised their opinions of the sinfulness of the theatre." Wilson, *History of American Acting*, 117. Similarly, Howard Taubman argues, "She was a woman of determination and courage. Her credentials of respectability helped the theatre on its path to acceptance as a tolerable, even honorable profession." Taubman, *American Theatre*, 76. Margaret Opsata states the case most emphatically when she asserts, "Her successes mark the point at which acting and theatergoing became respectable in the United States." Opsata, "Genteel Iconoclast," 41. See also Thompson, "Early Actress-Readers," 634.

9. Taylor, "Rhetoric of Self-Fashioning," 64.

10. Smith, *Subjectivity, Identity, and the Body*, 28.

11. Dudden, *Women in the American Theatre*, 23.

12. Elsom, *Erotic Theatre*, 27.

13. Fowler, *Revelations of Self*, xi.

14. Theater historian Garff B. Wilson explains that *Fashion* is "still admired as one of America's best satirical comedies and a worthy successor to *The Contrast*." Wilson, *Three Hundred Years*, 76. According to Doris Abramson, "*Fashion* is the most frequently anthologized of all plays by nineteenth-century women playwrights," and Mowatt is "the preeminent woman playwright of the century. . . . Only *Fashion* is securely in the canon of American dramatic

literature." Abramson, "'The New Path,'" (38–39). For other theater historians' assessments of *Fashion*, see Hornblow, *History of the Theatre in America*; Hughes, *History of the American Theatre*; Moody, *America Takes the Stage*; Taubman, *American Theatre*; and Mordden, *American Theatre*.

15. See Wilson, *History of American Acting*; Johnson, *American Actresses*; Dudden, *Women in the American Theatre*; and Bank, *Theatre Culture in America*.

16. See Fowler, *Revelations of Self*; Jelinek, *Tradition of Women's Autobiography*; and Conway, *When Memory Speaks*.

17. The only book-length biography of Mowatt is Barnes, *Anna Cora*, which is now out of print, as is Mowatt's autobiography. Barnes's biography provides useful glosses on many of the people and events Mowatt discusses in her autobiography, but it is a problematic document because of the extent to which Barnes takes Mowatt's autobiography at face value, recording its narratives as historical fact. He also regularly plagiarizes Mowatt's autobiography and skews events that Mowatt reports without explanation; for instance, in her autobiography, Mowatt describes pawning her watch to a "Jewish-looking man." When Barnes relates this event, he describes the pawnshop owner as "a somewhat frightening individual with a large nose and sharp eyes." Barnes, *Anna Cora*, 51, 40. This silent reinterpretation of Mowatt's words occurs throughout the biography, limiting the text's usefulness.

18. Jelinek, *Tradition of Women's Autobiography*, 93.

19. Conway, *When Memory Speaks*, 88.

20. Male readers from England had toured the United States in the years preceding Mowatt's first performance, and several other women orators, including Frances Wright, Maria Stewart, and the Grimké sisters, had begun making public speeches, but Mowatt was the first to undertake public readings. Because of her class status and the fact that she was reading in order to support her family, she was greeted much more warmly than most female public speakers.

21. Moses and Brown, *American Theatre*, 61.

22. Mowatt, *Autobiography*, 233.

23. Lerner, *Grimké Sisters*, 170.

24. Jelinek explains, "From the number of such accounts . . . we can see that the public had an insatiable curiosity for these titillating life stories by women engaged in activities unusual for their sex." Jelinek, *Tradition of Women's Autobiography*, 77.

25. Wilson, *History*, 108.

26. While Mowatt began her career as a star, women in other circumstances would typically begin in lesser roles. Alcott's *Work* shows Christie moving through the ranks of a theater company in the way that was more common than Mowatt's approach.

27. As Abigail Adams wrote to her husband in the 1770s, "Women . . . inherit an Eaquel Share of curiosity with the other Sex, yet but few are hardy eno' to venture abroad, and explore the amazing variety of distant lands. The Natural tenderness and Delicacy of our Constitutions, added to the many Dangers we are subject to from your Sex, renders it almost impossible for

a Single Lady to travel without injury to her character." Adams, *Selected Letters*, 50.

28. Foster, *Written by Herself*, 72.

29. Cohen, "Women at Large," 48.

30. Patricia Cline Cohen explains that by the early 1800s, "[t]he speed, convenience and regularity of travel (compared to earlier years) enticed many more passengers to take to the roads, among them large numbers of women," and Mary Suzanne Schriber explains, "during the nineteenth century, American women, the majority of them white and middle or upper class, began to travel abroad in significant numbers for the first time in history." Cohen, "Women at Large," 44; Schriber, *Telling Travels*, xi.

31. Cohen, "Safety and Danger," 119.

32. Schriber, *Telling Travels*, xv.

33. Smith, *Subjectivity, Identity, and the Body*, 31.

34. Cohen, "Women at Large," 50.

35. Travel, especially alone, was often much more perilous and uncomfortable for women of color than it was for white women; as Schriber explains, "For African American women, the voyage itself was painful, no matter how luxurious." Schriber, *Telling Travels*, xix, xx. Peterson's *Doers of the Word* examines black women's written records of their travels in the nineteenth century.

36. Mowatt, *Autobiography*, 383.

37. Ibid., 384, 388.

38. Ibid., 385.

39. Ibid., 387–88.

40. Ibid., 388.

41. Interestingly, Mowatt chooses to enact a cross-gender identification—identifying herself with the men who will "get on"—rather than a cross-racial identification—identifying herself with the Indian squaw who is the only woman who could brave the travel. Rather than erasing this potential comparison altogether, Mowatt leaves it in the pilot's quotation so that it lingers, enhancing the frontier heroism of Mowatt's journey and possibly calling to her reader's minds a similarity to another "travel" genre written by women: the captivity narrative. This moment also calls to mind Butler's contention throughout *Bodies That Matter* that the body—including gender and race—is performative.

42. Mowatt, *Autobiography*, 394.

43. Ibid., 391.

44. Ibid., 392.

45. Ibid., 393.

46. Ibid., 397.

47. Ibid., 398.

48. Ibid., 141.

49. Dudden, *Women in the American Theatre*, 14.

50. McConachie, *Melodramatic Formations*, 112.

51. Mowatt, *Autobiography*, 219.

52. The upper body was the area often targeted by health reformers as

being weak in women. Sarah Hale, in particular, writes at length about the dangers that can come from women's underdeveloped upper bodies, including poor posture, poor support of the spine, and even consumption; the very first "Health and Beauty" column in *Godey's Lady's Book* addressed this topic. By describing her efforts to strengthen her upper body, Mowatt may have been distinguishing herself from the average woman whose weak upper body kept her from enacting sensational strength and endurance.

53. This approach is reminiscent of Sojourner Truth's emphasis on her own strength to counteract the concept of true-womanly weakness in her "Ar'n't I a Woman?" speech; see Chapter 3, below.

54. Mowatt, *Autobiography*, 234.

55. Cogan describes the ideal of Real Womanhood as "a popular, middle-of-the-road image that recognized the disparities and the dangers presented by early feminists but tried to deal with those ugly realities in what it saw as a 'female' way." Cogan, *All-American Girl*, 4. She draws distinctions between true womanhood, Real Womanhood, and feminism. At this point in the criticism of nineteenth-century American women, the distinctions Cogan makes seem somewhat arbitrary, as though there were only three camps for the women she studies, when in fact there were many more options available to nineteenth-century women and many gradations between and combinations of concepts like "true womanhood" and "feminism." While Real Womanhood is a useful formulation of the kinds of "pragmatic feminism" Baym describes in *Woman's Fiction*, it does not describe the kinds of behavior and activity Mowatt discusses in her autobiography. While Mowatt partakes of some elements of Real Womanhood, she takes them *beyond* the boundaries Cogan describes.

56. Beecher, *Letters*, 116, 26.

57. Hale, *Godey's* 59:84.

58. Ibid., 35:112.

59. Wilson, "Health Department," 84.

60. Hale, *Godey's* 38:144–45.

61. Greenwood, "My First Hunting and Fishing," 11.

62. For more on sentimental invalidism, see Chapter 2, below.

63. For a more complete analysis of nineteenth-century literature promoting exercise for women, see Cogan, *All-American Girl*, chap. 1.

64. Hale, *Godey's* 38:214.

65. Ibid., 38:363.

66. Johnson, *American Actresses*, 130.

67. Mowatt, *Autobiography*, 262.

68. See introduction to Csordas, *Embodiment and Experience*.

69. See Chapter 2, below.

70. Mowatt, *Autobiography*, 154.

71. Ibid., 171.

72. Ibid., 173–74.

73. All of chapter 9 of the *Autobiography* addresses Mowatt's experiences with mesmerism, including her apparent increased spiritual knowledge and

her telepathic powers while in mesmeric trances. Dawn Keetley examines Mowatt's experience of mesmerism as a parallel to Mowatt's ability to "lose herself" onstage; she loses her conscious self when she is mesmerized. Keetley, "Power of 'Personation,'" 197. Mowatt's discussions of her unconscious state and the different woman she became while under the influence of mesmerism are outside the realm of this study, but they deserve further critical attention.

74. Mowatt, *Autobiography*, 421.

75. Ibid., 278–79.

76. Scarry, *Body in Pain*, 217.

77. Hiram Powers's *The Greek Slave* is an example of one of the very popular statues which was displayed in many cities in the mid-century. For further discussion of the popular statues of the nineteenth century, see Kasson, *Marble Queens and Captives*.

78. Like Scarry, medical anthropologist E. Valentine Daniel notes that metaphor is one of the first ways pain and analogous experiences like terror become representable or speakable. Daniel, "Individual in Terror," 244.

79. Quoted in Lerner, *Grimké Sisters*, 5.

80. Mowatt, *Autobiography*, 147.

81. Neither illness nor stage fright was exclusively a woman's disorder in the nineteenth century, but in Mowatt's narrative both affect her specifically by forcing her body to conform to societal standards for women.

82. Mowatt, *Autobiography*, 222.

83. This reading of Mowatt as a self-appointed hero directly contradicts Jelinek's argument that "the female identity is not a heroic one. For the most part, women do not see themselves as legends or representatives of their times. . . . On the contrary, what we glean from women's autobiography of [the nineteenth] century is a sense of the female identity as a 'local' one—personal and 'different.'" Jelinek, *Tradition of Women's Autobiography*, 102. Mowatt does not put herself forward as a legendary or representative figure to the extent that someone like Sojourner Truth does; however, an element of the heroic emerges in several instances in Mowatt's autobiography, a fact which contradicts many of the overarching assertions made by critics like Jelinek about women's autobiography.

84. Grosz, "Intolerable Ambiguity," 56.

85. Dennett, *Weird and Wonderful*, 76.

86. Thomson, *Freakery*, 5–7.

87. Ibid., 4.

88. Dennett, *Weird and Wonderful*, 68.

89. This is another example of bodies created discursively and read as texts; Barnum's audiences would return to correct their misreadings.

90. Fretz, *Freakery*, 101.

91. For information about freaks throughout human history and the varieties of human disabilities classified as freakish, see Fiedler, *Freaks*. For further information about nineteenth-century freak shows, see Thomson, *Freakery* and Dennett, *Weird and Wonderful*.

92. Mowatt, *Autobiography*, 255.

93. Ibid., 288–89.

94. Sara Ahmed notes that, because the skin can break and feel, it is a unique boundary: "Although the skin appears to be the matter which separates and contains the body, it allows us to consider how the materialisation of bodies involves, not containment, but an affective opening out of bodies to other bodies, in the sense that skin registers how bodies are touched by other bodies." Ahmed, "Embodying Strangers," 91.

95. So, for instance, Zenobia from Hawthorne's *Blithedale Romance* enacts a sexuality that allows her to exceed the bounds of true womanly behavior, but she is later not only a victim of drowning but her body is pierced by the hooks the men use to dredge the pool searching for her. Her body's permeability ultimately becomes her body's victimization.

96. Grosz, *Volatile Bodies*, 193.

97. Fiedler, *Freaks*, 24.

98. Mowatt, *Autobiography*, 289.

99. See Reynolds, *Beneath the American Renaissance*, 213, and Smith-Rosenberg, *Disorderly Conduct*, 105.

100. Fiedler, *Freaks*, 18.

101. Dennett, *Weird and Wonderful*, 82–83.

102. Cassuto, *Freakery*, 240.

103. Braunberger, "Revolting Bodies," 9.

104. Mowatt, *Autobiography*, 388.

105. Quoted in ibid., 155–56.

106. Ibid., 326.

107. Thomson, *Extraordinary Bodies*, 71. For more information about the lives and deaths of Pastrana and Baartman, see *Extraordinary Bodies*, chap. 3. It is also worth noting that not all women in freak shows forever crossed a boundary separating them from respectable womanhood; tattooed women, in particular, never had their faces or hands tattooed so that, when wearing certain clothing, they could "pass" as nonfreaks. Braunberger, "Revolting Bodies," 12.

108. Mowatt, *Autobiography*, 425–26.

CHAPTER TWO

1. Quoted in Peel, *Mary Baker Eddy*, 44.

2. Quoted in Gill, *Mary Baker Eddy*, 95.

3. While many critics refer to Eddy's "fits," these seizures are difficult to document. Recent biographer Gillian Gill contends that the fits, attributed by many critics to hysteria, are a critical construction. Gill, *Mary Baker Eddy*, 43. Gill and other critics do agree, however, that as an adult Eddy suffered from recurrent periods of paralysis.

4. Mowatt, *Autobiography*, 418.

5. Eddy, *Science and Health*, 84.

6. Fox, "Protest in Piety," 410.

7. Eddy, *Science and Health*, 143. For Eddy, Mind is nearly synonymous with God. She refers to Mind not in the ordinary sense of the part of a human that thinks but in a broader sense, as "divine Principle, substance, Life, Truth, Love." *Science and Health*, 591.

8. Beryl Satter notes that New Thought groups "were united by their shared engagement in a pervasive but now forgotten late nineteenth-century contest over whether the key to progress, civilization, and race perfection was (Anglo-Saxon) male desire or female virtue. Was the nation in need of male rationality or female spirituality?" Satter identifies Eddy's contribution to this larger discourse as her inversion of the usual association of women with matter and men with mind. For Eddy, women had full access to Mind—indeed, arguably better access than men had. Satter, *Each Mind a Kingdom*, 9, 69.

9. Gill maps out the controversies surrounding Eddy and Christian Science, particularly as those controversies have influenced critical assessment of Eddy.

10. See Satter, *Each Mind a Kingdom*. Satter notes that "from the 1880s on, there were so many influential New Thought teachers that it is historically more accurate to view Mary Baker Eddy as an important contributor to the turn-of-the-century New Thought movement than to view New Thought as the long-forgotten context for Eddy's Christian Science." *Each Mind a Kingdom*, 3.

11. See Herndl, *Invalid Women*, 31–32 for a description of the major alternative medicines available in the nineteenth century and a description of each one's philosophy.

12. As her biographer Robert Peel notes, Eddy tried electrical treatments, morphine, homeopathy, hydropathy, Grahamism, and mesmerism, and she worked extensively with mesmerist Phineas P. Quimby. Peel, *Mary Baker Eddy*, 111. Quimby's mesmerism was the first alternative medical treatment that truly relieved Eddy's pain for a prolonged period. Many critics have suggested that Quimby's death in 1866 inspired Eddy to begin her own healing movement based in many ways on Quimby's work. Eddy herself denied Quimby's influence, saying of the Great Discovery that Quimby "was in no wise connected with this event." Eddy, *Retrospection*, 24.

13. Twain, *Christian Science*, 102.

14. See Gill's "Research Note" for a narrative explaining the difficulties she faced in writing a biography of Eddy. *Mary Baker Eddy*, 557–62.

15. Tibbetts, *Women Who Were Called*, 144.

16. Her religious upbringing links Eddy to other nineteenth-century women, including Harriet Beecher Stowe and Fanny Fern, who sought to soften the Calvinistic doctrines of their fathers.

17. Eddy, *Retrospection*, 24; quoted in Gill, *Mary Baker Eddy*, 161.

18. Peel, *Mary Baker Eddy*, 197.

19. Eddy, *Retrospection*, 24. Some doubt exists as to the seriousness of Eddy's injuries in the first place; her physician later stated that he did not

think she was badly hurt. His testimony, solicited by scholars who sought to discredit Eddy, was given forty years after Eddy's accident and is therefore not entirely credible. See Gill, *Mary Baker Eddy*, chap. 9. Whether or not Eddy's life was actually threatened, however, her perception was that she had discovered the way to heal herself.

20. Eddy, *Retrospection*, 24.

21. See chapter 4 for a more thorough discussion of the interpenetration of discourses of race and gender in the late nineteenth century.

22. See Satter, *Each Mind a Kingdom*, 10–11. Satter also notes, "White middle-class women were . . . understood as the opposites of working-class women and nonwhite women. If working-class and nonwhite women were animalistic, strong, and active, then white middle-class women were passionless, weak, and passive." *Each Mind a Kingdom*, 30.

23. Eddy, *Science and Health*, 273.

24. Martin Gardner is the most recent example of the kinds of critics who cannot take *Science and Health* or Christian Science seriously. Gardner insists that Eddy engaged in "outrageous lying" (46), and he argues that "you can't escape from the reality of sin, sickness, pain, and matter by the verbal trick of redefining them as dreams" (55). His scorn for Christian Science in a book he accurately characterizes as an "attack" on the religion (11) prevents him from achieving any useful insights about Christian Science, its origins, or its continuing popularity. Along with other hostile critics, including Georgine Milmine and Edwin Dakin in the early twentieth century, Gardner has helped put forth a view of Eddy and Christian Science as ridiculous at best, villainous at worst. Gardner, *Healing Revelations*, 46, 55, 11.

25. Millingen, *Lectures*, 169.

26. Smith-Rosenberg, "Female Animal," 14.

27. Ibid., 13–14.

28. Eddy, *Science and Health*, 109, 468.

29. Ibid., 143.

30. Scarry, *Body in Pain*, 14, 127.

31. Ibid., 14.

32. Eddy, *Retrospection*, 26.

33. Eddy, *Science and Health*, 268.

34. Gill, *Mary Baker Eddy*, xvii.

35. Mitchell, *Wear and Tear*, 33; Eddy, *Science and Health*, 124–25.

36. Scarry, *Body in Pain*, 14.

37. Eddy, *Science and Health*, 372.

38. Ibid., 256, 530, 517.

39. Ibid., 332.

40. Gill, *Mary Baker Eddy*, 344.

41. Fox, "Protest in Piety," 412.

42. Beecher, *Letters*, 111.

43. See Herndl, *Invalid Women*.

44. Quoted in Herndl, *Invalid Women*, 20–21; quoted in Gilbert and Gubar, *Madwoman in the Attic*, 45.

45. Beecher, *Letters*, 121; Woolson, *Women in American Society*, 189.

46. For example, see Smith-Rosenberg, *Disorderly Conduct*, King, *Transformations in American Medicine*, and Wood, "'Fashionable Diseases.'"

47. Herndl, *Invalid Women*, 21–22.

48. Wood, "'Fashionable Diseases,'" 26–27.

49. Stowe, *Uncle Tom's Cabin*, 289, 293.

50. Evans, *Beulah*, 172.

51. Warner, *Wide, Wide World*, 170.

52. In the four literary examples I have provided, the woman who becomes ill is not the novel's protagonist. This model of a healthy but less virtuous protagonist in connection to a virtuous but sickly friend may demand further examination.

53. Davis, *Life in the Iron Mills*, 17, 21.

54. Indeed, they often reinforced the invisible association of illness with white, middle-class status, making pronouncements about "women" without consideration of *which* women. Current critics of nineteenth-century sentimental invalidism often do exactly the same thing.

55. Eddy, *Science and Health*, 175.

56. Woolson, *Women in American Society*, 193.

57. Quoted in Gilbert and Gubar, *Madwoman in the Attic*, 55.

58. Herndl, *Invalid Women*, 111.

59. Beecher, *Letters*, 7.

60. Gilbert and Gubar, *Madwoman in the Attic*, 53.

61. Hale, *Godey's* 18:142. Hale so firmly believed that women's inappropriate clothing was the cause of widespread sickness and death that she repeated the quote, "Lady, wrap your cloak around / Pale consumption's in the sky" many times in the course of her editorship of the *Lady's Book*. She and other health reformers also argued that clothing should be selected on the basis of health and comfort rather than fashion.

62. See Tompkins, *Sensational Designs*; Douglas, *Feminization of American Culture*, 92; and Herndl, *Invalid Women*, 30.

63. Poovey, "Scenes of an Indelicate Character," discusses this invalidation of women's health care as it occurred in the competing fields of midwifery and gynecological and obstetrical medicine in the nineteenth century.

64. Herndl, *Invalid Women*, 33.

65. Eddy, *Science and Health*, 150–51.

66. Ibid., 175, 179. Eddy was not alone in her conviction that medicine actually promoted illness. Sylvester Graham, whose dietary regimen was a popular form of alternative health care in the early and mid-nineteenth century, said, "All medicine, as such, is itself an evil." Quoted in Numbers, "Ministries of Healing," 377. Catharine Beecher, too, warned women against visiting regular physicians because their medicines could be poison and their physical manipulations of the female body could be very dangerous. Beecher, *Letters*, 152, 39–40.

67. Smith-Rosenberg, "Female Animal," 12.

68. Wiltbank, *Introductory Lecture*, 7; Hollick, *Diseases of Women*, 205.

69. Goodell, *Lessons in Gynecology*, 369, 373.

70. Hodge, *On Diseases*, 20, 21, 31.

71. Wood, "'Fashionable Diseases,'" 37.

72. Mitchell, *Fat and Blood*, 41, 50.

73. It may be worth noting that Mitchell and his colleagues had no conscious agenda to harm nineteenth-century women; they were simultaneously creators and creations of their culture, shaped by the dominant ideologies of womanhood just as they were shaping these very ideologies in their practice of medicine.

74. Eddy, *Science and Health*, 162–63.

75. Ibid., 162.

76. Ibid., 165.

77. Ibid., 152.

78. Ibid., 601.

79. Ibid., 384–85.

80. Cassedy, *American Medicine*, 69.

81. Osler, "Medicine," 177 (emphasis Osler's); Billings, "Progress of Medicine," 175–76.

82. Experimentation was a controversial component of the medical field throughout the middle of the nineteenth century, gaining greater acceptance as the century progressed. Experimental science, particularly within the field of bacteriology, seemed to compete directly with the sanitarian approach to medicine, which identified the origins of disease not in particles of matter but in communities that were unclean and lifestyles that involved little exercise or fresh air. As Regina Markell Morantz explains, between the 1840s and the 1860s, "Medicine as an occupation began to merge with medicine as a science," and this merger did not always occur smoothly within the medical community. Morantz, "Feminism, Pluralism, and Germs," 461. Morantz cites Elizabeth Blackwell and Mary Putnam Jacobi as examples of two physician colleagues on different sides of this conflict; Blackwell belonged to the older sanitarian approach, while Jacobi advocated experimentation. By the time Eddy was writing *Science and Health*, experimental medicine was gaining widespread acceptability.

83. Wrobel, *Pseudo-Science and Society*, 6.

84. Ibid., 3.

85. Homeopathy gained credibility through the shortcomings of allopathic medicine. "The biggest boost to homeopathy's popularity came during the cholera epidemic of 1832, when conventional bleeding and purging devastated those already weakened by the wasting disease. Homeopathic treatments appeared to cure simply because they lowered the death rate by not further debilitating the patient." Floyd, *From Quackery to Bacteriology*.

86. Wood, "'Fashionable Diseases,'" 44.

87. Hunt, *Glances and Glimpses*, 152.

88. Ibid., 156, 157.

89. Woolson, *Women in American Society*, 194.

90. Wood, "'Fashionable Diseases,'" 49.

91. Not all female physicians can be identified as "incipient Christian Scientists" or even as overt critics of the dominant medical establishment. Mary Putnam Jacobi, for instance, was a female physician whose work was closely aligned with the dominant trends in nineteenth-century medicine. See Morantz, "Feminism, Pluralism, and Germs."

92. Eddy, *Science and Health*, 174.

93. Ibid., 101.

94. Ibid., 475.

95. Ibid., 370–71.

96. Ibid., 184–85.

97. Chapple, *Science and Literature*, 7.

98. Bruce, *Launching of Modern American Science*, 115.

99. Chapple, *Science and Literature*, 160.

100. King, *Transformations in American Medicine*, 209.

101. Eddy, *Science and Health*, 122–23.

102. Mendenhall, "Physics," 329.

103. Lockyer, "Astronomy," 105.

104. Eddy, *Science and Health*, 128–9.

105. Ibid., 277.

106. Ibid., 273.

107. Ibid., 171, 147.

108. Eddy is known, for instance, to have cut articles from a Boston newspaper about a series of Darwinist lectures in 1869. Peel, *Mary Baker Eddy*, 246.

109. Eddy, *Science and Health*, 123–24, 128.

110. Ibid., 174.

CHAPTER THREE

1. Truth's use of the tall tale to define her body is true of her speeches, but her public life in print was more complex. She utilized images of domesticity to define her body in her many *cartes de visite*, photographs of herself which she sold and distributed at her speeches and later in lieu of speeches when she was too ill to travel. These photographs show Truth wearing plain, attractive clothing and sitting by a table with a vase of flowers, knitting needles in her lap or in her hands. She utilizes domestic imagery to inscribe her body within a realm of leisured femininity rather than within the realm of labor.

2. Peterson, *"Doers of the Word,"* 20. See also White, *Ar'n't I a Woman?*, and Carby, *Reconstructing Womanhood*.

3. Nudelman, "Harriet Jacobs," 941.

4. Truth, *Narrative*, 71–72.

5. Nell Irvin Painter suggests that Truth was sexually abused by Sally Dumont when she was a slave of the Dumont family in her early teenage years. Painter, *Sojourner Truth*, 14–17. While slave women most often suffered sexual abuse at the hands of their masters, Truth explained that her sufferings were "unnatural." Truth, *Narrative*, 82.

6. Carby, *Reconstructing Womanhood*, 32.

7. Peterson, *"Doers of the Word,"* 31. This is a reasonable step to take, to portray black women as eternally, and justifiably, railing against the cultural standards that imprison them. The excellent work, however, by such scholars as Carby and Hortense Spillers has not only positioned black and white women's texts in a binary opposition but has predisposed readers to regard all such texts in the same terms. This approach works well in the case of many authors, but not Truth.

8. Carlton Mabee's *Sojourner Truth: Slave, Prophet, Legend*, the subtitle expressing its emphasis, offered the 1990s' first serious historical study of Truth, while Erlene Stetson and Linda David's *Glorying in Tribulation: The Lifework of Sojourner Truth* analyzes Truth's life in the context of her illiteracy. Painter's *Sojourner Truth: A Life, a Symbol*, as the subtitle suggests, investigates the way in which Truth became a cultural symbol. Painter analyzes the layers of nineteenth- and twentieth-century formulations of Truth, from Truth's construction of her own persona during her life to the recent uses of her image on T-shirts, posters, and postcards as a politically correct representative of powerful black womanhood. Most recently, Suzanne Pullon Fitch and Roseann M. Mandziuk's *Sojourner Truth as Orator: Wit, Story, and Song* combines an analysis of Truth's oratorical techniques with an extensive anthology of her speeches.

9. Peterson, *"Doers of the Word,"* 23.

10. Truth, *Narrative*, 178. Painter explains of this incident that it is one of "four incidents now constituting the symbolic Sojourner Truth: 'Frederick, is God dead?'; 'ar'n't I a woman?' at Akron; breast-baring in Indiana; and the warm welcome from President Lincoln." Painter, *Sojourner*, 266.

11. Stetson, *Glorying in Tribulation*, 12. Fitch and Mandziuk's recent full-length study of Truth's oratory gives evidence of Truth's status as a preeminent orator.

12. The two versions of Truth's speech I will discuss are "Women's Rights Convention: Sojourner Truth," hereafter referred to as the *Bugle* version, and Gage, "Sojourner Truth," hereafter referred to as the Gage version.

13. While Mabee and Painter consider the historical authenticity of each version, Peterson compares the two in order to interrogate Truth's use of African tropes and the influence of racism on a white woman's version of Truth.

14. Jay, "American Literature," 242.

15. Painter, *Sojourner Truth*, 174.

16. "Women's Rights Convention: Sojourner Truth." This version of Truth's speech is now also available in Ripley, *Black Abolitionist Papers*, and in Fitch and Mandziuk's *Sojourner Truth as Orator*.

17. Stewart, *Narrative*, xxxiv.

18. Gage's version is different in style, form, and even some content from the version the *Bugle* printed. In fact, it is stylistically different than many of the quotations from Truth printed elsewhere in her narrative. (Gage's version, which is much more widely available than the *Bugle* version, is quoted in full in the appendix to this book.) In Gage's version appears the refrain,

"Ar'n't I a woman?" Gage represents Truth as continually referring to blacks as "niggers" throughout the speech (something she does nowhere else in her narrative or *Book of Life* and something that surely would have been repellent to her), and she portrays Truth as a feisty but somewhat stupid woman.

19. One of the most troubling aspects of Gage's version of the speech is that she transfers the whole speech into a Southern black dialect reminiscent of Joel Chandler Harris's "Uncle Remus," creating the most dramatically stereotypical element of the speech and almost certainly the most inaccurate, since Truth was a Northern woman whose first language was Dutch. There are two possible explanations for Gage's choice of stilted Southern dialect for her representation of Truth: Gage may have felt the accent enhanced Truth's story's sense of authenticity, or this may have been how she heard Truth's voice. See Stewart, *Narrative*, xxxiv–xxxv. Both explanations point to the significance of this transformation of Truth's language: the cultural assumptions about how a black person speaks were stronger than the actual way an individual black person might speak. Certain white-constructed cultural models of black speech gained tremendous influence in the nineteenth century. For instance, Joel Chandler Harris's *Uncle Remus* became a model by which all other representations of black language were judged well into the twentieth century. While *Uncle Remus* was not published until 1880, seventeen years after Gage's version of Truth's 1851 speech, white representations of black speech had been prevalent in the popular culture since much earlier. Harriet Beecher Stowe's novel *Uncle Tom's Cabin* (1852) almost certainly contributed to Gage's use of dialect in representing Truth's speech. *Uncle Tom's Cabin* was so popular and influential in the years after its publication that the dialect spoken by the black characters in the novel became a kind of standard of realism, especially for abolitionist writers. Additionally, as Nell Painter discusses in several articles, Gage wrote her report of Truth's speech after Stowe published "The Libyan Sibyl" (1863), a sentimental portrait of Truth which became a defining description of Truth in the nineteenth century. Thus, Gage was probably dually influenced by Stowe as she represented Truth. See Painter, "Representing Truth" and "Sojourner Truth."

20. Gage's version of the speech appeared in Elizabeth Cady Stanton's *History of Women Suffrage* in 1881, and a recent children's book about Truth by Patricia C. and Frederick McKissack is called *Sojourner Truth: Ain't I a Woman?* (1992). In addition, both Deborah Gray White and bell hooks have used the phrase "ain't I a woman?" or "ar'n't I a woman?" in the titles of critical books. The phrase has become so widely known that it has appeared in James Hynes's parody of academia, *The Lecturer's Tale* (165), and antisweatshop activists have used it in campaigns.

21. In the chapter of Truth's biography entitled "Ar'n't I a Woman?," Painter discusses Gage's motivation in crafting her version of Truth's speech as she did.

22. Painter, *Sojourner Truth*, 284.

23. In fact, very little critical discussion exists on either fictional women

represented in tall tales or actual women who utilized the techniques of tall talk and tall humor in representing themselves. See Lofaro, "Riproarious Shemales," 148–49 (nn. 6–7) for a listing of the works that have been done.

24. Wonham, *Mark Twain*, 21.

25. In this way tall humor resembles the jeremiad, another form which notes the discrepancies between the ideal and the real America. Truth uses both forms.

26. Mabee, *Sojourner Truth*, 65.

27. Blair, *Crockett*, 3.

28. Dorson, *Davy Crockett*, xxiv. For more information on tall tales and American folklore in general, see such texts as Dorson, *America in Legend*.

29. Smith-Rosenberg, *Disorderly Conduct*, 97.

30. For instance, Sam Patch was an extremely well-known man in the 1830s and 1840s because of his skills as a jumper. He jumped from roofs and into rivers, and he solidified his fame in 1829 when he successfully jumped from Niagara Falls in front of a crowd. Later that same year he jumped from Genesee Falls and died, but his death marked the beginning of his fame as a tall-tale hero rather than the end. Reports of his survival, including a report that he sank through the earth and emerged in the South Sea, appeared in newspapers and comic almanacs. Botkin, *Treasury of New England Folklore*, 221. Similarly, Mike Fink was an actual early nineteenth-century boatman whose real and fictional exploits appeared in comic almanacs and who became a folk hero. While Paul Bunyan is perhaps one of the better-known tall-tale heroes today, his tall tales have recently been debunked by folklorists because they were the creation of a lumber company attempting to advertise itself rather than an authentic folk tale. See Wonham, *Mark Twain* and Lofaro, *Davy Crockett*. On authentic early nineteenth-century American folk heroes, see Dorson, *America in Legend*.

31. Lofaro, "Hidden 'Hero,'" 47.

32. Because Crockett's tall tales have been the subject of a substantial base of research, something which Truth's tall-tale persona has not, the Crockett legend offers useful critical apparatus which may be applied to Truth.

33. Mabee, *Sojourner Truth*, 68; Painter, "Representing Truth," 470. Although Painter here refers particularly to Truth's selling of her *cartes de visite*, her discussion of Truth's marketing of herself relates more broadly to Truth's public presence.

34. Peterson, *"Doers of the Word,"* 29.

35. Quoted in Dorson, *America in Legend*, 77.

36. Dorson, *Davy Crockett*, 29. Dorson's book remains the most widely used anthology of Crockett's almanac stories. As an interesting comment on the variety of ways in which Crockett's legend was created, this boast was initially Col. Nimrod's line in Paulding's *The Lion of the West* and was later adopted into the Crockett legend.

37. Quoted in Lofaro, "The Hidden 'Hero,'" 55.

38. Dorson, *Davy Crockett*, 6.

39. Carby, *Reconstructing Womanhood*, 25.

40. Truth, *Narrative*, 33.
41. Stowe, "Libyan Sibyl," 151.
42. Dorson, *Davy Crockett*, 39, 47, 22.
43. Truth, *Narrative*, xii.
44. Dorson, *Davy Crockett*, 19.
45. Truth, *Narrative*, 146–47.
46. Mabee, *Sojourner Truth*, 70.
47. Truth, *Narrative*, 149.
48. Quoted in Lofaro, *Tall Tales*, xxix.
49. Racism is not a feature of all tall tales. For instance, the railroad hero John Henry and his wife, Polly Ann, were both black. Both are represented positively, and Polly Ann, one of few black female tall-tale characters, shows a physical strength that is comparable to John Henry's. According to one version of the song that immortalized them, she did John Henry's job for him when he was sick and "drove steel like a man." See Williams, *John Henry*. Because the legend of John Henry was developing near the end of Truth's life, in the 1870s and 1880s, the story of Polly Ann was probably not a direct influence on her self-presentation. However, Polly Ann's very existence as a character suggests that Truth was not an anomaly but instead that certain cultural models were developing that presented less racially oppressive versions of the tall tale.
50. Lofaro, "Riproarious Shemales," 123.
51. Dorson, *Davy Crockett*, 49, 50.
52. According to this tale, a stranger arrives to fight strong man Johnny McNiel, but he is not at home. His wife says, "'And troth, mon . . . Johnny's gone, but I'm not the woman to see ye disappointed: an' I think if ye'll try, mon, I'll throw ye myself.' The stranger, not liking to be bantered by a woman, accepted the challenge; and, sure enough, Christian tripped his heels and threw him upon the ground. The stranger, upon getting up, thought he would not wait for 'Johnny'; but left, without deigning to leave his name." Dorson, *Jonathan Draws the Long Bow*, 122–25. The stranger makes the mistake of using traditional stereotypes of womanhood to interpret McNiel, and she shows him his error.
53. Lofaro, "Riproarious Shemales," 129.
54. Ibid., 132.
55. Ibid., 127.
56. Smith-Rosenberg, *Disorderly Conduct*, 104.
57. Lofaro, "Riproarious Shemales," 123.
58. For instance, Henry Wonham argues that the tall tale, when told rather than written, is a communal act of consensus-building; this articulation of a community's values becomes more difficult when the tale is written. Wonham, *Mark Twain*, 25–28.
59. Dorson, *Davy Crockett*, 30.
60. Kirkham, *Essay on Elocution*, xiii.
61. Johnson, "Popularization of Nineteenth-Century Rhetoric," 139–40.
62. Ibid., 145.

63. Stetson, *Glorying in Tribulation*, 11. Stewart suggests that Truth may have been able to write her own story, but she may have chosen Olive Gilbert to write it for her to give it more cultural validity or weight. "Sojourner was astute enough to realize that having a white woman tell her story would lend credibility to her accomplishments. . . . Sojourner may have believed that Gilbert would give her story a more authoritative voice." Stewart, *Narrative*, xxxix.

64. See Peterson, *"Doers of the Word,"* 45.

65. Clark, *Oratorical Culture*, 24.

66. Johnson, "Popularization of Nineteenth-Century Rhetoric," 139.

67. See Chapter 1, above.

68. Quoted in O'Connor, *Pioneer Women Orators*, 26–27, see also 24. See also Hedrick, *Harriet Beecher Stowe*, 238.

69. Truth, *Narrative*, 45.

70. Fitch and Mandziuk, *Sojourner Truth as Orator*, 90.

71. Peterson, *"Doers of the Word,"* 48. Peterson does an excellent job of drawing connections between Truth's oratory and African and African American cultural models.

72. A few models available during Truth's lifetime did show the possibility of women speaking. One of these, a cultural image which to some degree stood against that of true womanhood, was the image of the Amazon Queen, which appeared as a representation of America as early as 1581 and which became "a monumental figure of moral righteousness." Banta, *Imagining American Women*, 486–88. Gage, in fact, refers to Truth as "this almost Amazon form" as she begins her description of the Akron speech. A possible subset of the Amazon Queen model is the image of Republican Motherhood, an eighteenth-century, Revolutionary War concept which represented good women as those who stood up for American values and had a responsibility for the virtue of the nation. Republican Mothers took an active role in public life. In addition, religious women had also established a precedent for women's speech. Painter explains, "As an itinerant female preacher, [Truth] belonged to an established tradition of women evangelists, Quakers and Methodists. . . . Prohibited by church discipline to head established churches, these female prophets heeded the divine calling to preach and reached wide, heterogeneous audiences." Painter, "Sojourner Truth," 5. The Woman Rights Convention, as well, presented models of virtuous women speaking, because this was a convention run by women for women. However, the 1851 Akron Woman Rights Convention was the first in which women spoke to a male and female audience.

73. Truth, *Narrative*, 225, 241.

74. An exceptionally powerful voice is often attributed to tall-tale characters. Crockett describes himself as "a screamer" and explains that he can "yell like an Indian." In fact, yelling or crowing is often an integral part of a fight in the Crockett almanacs; in one story, Crockett is insulted by a rival, and he describes his response: "I . . . squealed with all my might. After I had done squealing, I screamed; then I begun to holler; and, at last, I jumped

up and crowed!" Women tall-tale characters have powerful voices as well; Katy Goodgrit, for example, was trapped by wolves, and to save herself, "she stuck up her head, and crowed, till she crowed and screamed all the wolves deaf." Tall-tale voices, then, can be weaponry; they are another excessive and powerful part of the characters' bodies. Perhaps the clearest representation of the materiality and violent power of the tall-tale voice comes through Crockett's description of Ben Hardin. Crockett writes, "He had a voice that was so ruff, I can't rite it down, but have had a cut made to pictur it out." The woodcut shows a man in profile, his mouth open and a cone of sharp shards emerging, suggesting arrowheads or knife blades. This is an unusual take on the assertion that words alone are not adequate to convey the experience of hearing a person's voice. Hardin's voice can be better understood through a visual representation as a weapon-like material substance. Dorson, *Davy Crockett*, 29, 30, 35, 53, 67.

75. Truth, *Narrative*, 138.

76. Ibid., 115, 116.

77. Ibid., 116–17.

78. Ibid., 117–18, 119.

79. Stowe, "Libyan Sibyl," 473. According to Fitch and Mandziuk, the story of Truth's naming was more popular with those who wrote about her than it was with Truth herself.

CHAPTER FOUR

1. Critic Dana Nelson argues that white male identity and unity were created in the early national period through "imagined and actual excavations of multiple others," including blacks and women; Wells's work delineates a similar dynamic in the late nineteenth century. Nelson, *National Manhood*, 17. Similarly, Robyn Wiegman argues that the specular scene "communalizes white power while territorializing the black body." Wiegman, *American Anatomies*, 13.

2. Martha Hodes's social history, *White Women, Black Men*, traces the social response to sex between white women and black men from the colonial era through post-Reconstruction. She notes that such illicit sex did not come to be seen as a public threat necessitating violence until after Reconstruction had begun. Her study effectively connects sex and sexuality to larger questions of national and racial identity.

3. Tolnay and Beck, *Festival of Violence*, ix.

4. Shapiro, *White Violence*, 31. Current critics offer dissenting opinions on what motivated lynchings. Many critics agree with Wells's assessment that lynchings were a means of economic control of the black community, occurring when economic or social gains had been made and functioning to terrorize blacks and "keep them in their place." Joel Williamson and Trudier Harris share a psychoanalytic view of lynchings. Williamson argues that lynchings were a "psychic compensation" for Southern white men's declining economic

power and guilt at having sex with their wives. He argues, "White men were projecting upon black men extravagant sexual behavior because they were, at varying levels, denying ordinary sexual behavior to themselves. . . . To paint the black man as ugly and then to destroy him was to destroy the evil within themselves." Similarly, Trudier Harris sees a psychological dynamic in the stylized rituals of lynchings, arguing, for instance, "White American males castrated black men presumably in an effort to eliminate the threat of black sexuality to white women, and, . . . perhaps in an effort to transfer some of that sexuality to themselves." Harris, however, also emphasizes the societal and political consequences of lynching; while Williamson seems to believe that lynchings could serve as a form of justice, Harris sees lynchings as an elaborate means of social and political control. She argues, "Ultimately, lynching and burning rituals functioned to sustain a belief in racial, economic, psychological, and moral superiority in whites and to reinforce a clearly designate concept of place for Blacks. Deviation meant death." Williamson, *Rage for Order*, 82, 189, 125; Harris, *Exorcising Blackness*, 15, 18–19. In a more recent historical analysis of lynchings, Stewart Tolnay and E. M. Beck argue that evidence suggests that lynchings were most likely to occur when blacks threatened white status. They assert, "Free blacks threatened southern whites and their caste system in a way that slaves never could, and lynching was one of the mechanisms to neutralize that threat." Tolnay and Beck, *Festival of Violence*, 247. Significantly, their assessment validates Wells's own conclusions about lynching.

5. Bederman, "'Civilization,'" 14.

6. Wiegman, *American Anatomies*, 96; Gunning, *Race, Rape, and Lynching*, 10.

7. Royster, "Introduction," 3; Wells, *Crusade for Justice*, 65.

8. See, for instance, Carby, *Reconstructing Womanhood*, and Foster, *Written by Herself*, for examples of Wells's inclusion in texts considering black women's writing. Painter, *Standing at Armageddon*, shows Wells's inclusion in historical studies of the post-Reconstruction period.

9. See Shapiro, *White Violence*, and Tolnay and Beck, *Festival of Violence*.

10. The Schomburg series, of course, publishes Wells's writings, and a combined edition of *Southern Horrors, A Red Record*, and *Mob Rule in New Orleans* is available as part of the Bedford Series in History and Culture.

11. Carby explains, "She has been measured by historians and declared a dwarf in relation to the giants of Du Bois and Washington; subject to such comparison, her political ideas, strategies, tactics, and analyses have been totally subordinated to and understood only in relation to the achievements of these men." Carby, *Reconstructing Womanhood*, 108. Similarly, Wells's biographer Linda O. McMurry has convincingly suggested that Wells is the natural philosophical inheritor of the mantle of Frederick Douglass, but because she was female, historians have not considered her.

12. Rogers M. Smith addresses these historical blind spots at length in the introduction to *Civic Ideals*.

13. Wald, *Constituting Americans*, 1.

14. See, for instance, Harris, *Exorcising Blackness*; Sundquist, *To Wake the Nations*; Wiegman, *American Anatomies*; and Bederman, *Manliness and Civilization*.

15. See Cott, "Marriage and Women's Citizenship"; Isenberg, *Sex and Citizenship*; and Kerber, *No Constitutional Right to Be Ladies*.

16. Scholars including Lauren Berlant, Carla Peterson, Hazel Carby, Nell Painter, and Sander Gilman consider the intersection of race and gender in the lives of black women in the nineteenth and twentieth centuries. Not all of this work concerns citizenship specifically.

17. The notion of *civilization* as a concept to be deployed and aligned with particular configurations of race and gender has been effectively explored in Bederman, *Manliness and Civilization*. Bederman notes the interarticulation of race and gender; gender norms, particularly manhood, were predicated on specific racial configurations. Her analysis of Wells has been influential on this study.

18. Wells, *Crusade for Justice*, 37.

19. Robyn Wiegman also articulates the significance of rhetoric, particularly written, as a means of transforming black bodies: "The written . . . displaces the text of black inferiority crafted by scientific and popular discourses, offering instead a black textuality that attempts to remake the flesh by asserting to the privilege accorded the word throughout the Anglophilic West." Wiegman, *American Anatomies*, 63.

20. Wells, *Southern Horrors*, 36.

21. She routinely quoted extensive descriptions of lynchings from white newspapers, and got much of her raw data on yearly numbers of lynchings and the justifications given for them from the *Chicago Tribune*. In this way, she both protected herself from charges of exaggeration and falsifying the facts and revealed the hypocrisy of the white community. Significantly, Wells's own voice was never overwhelmed by the white newspaper reports she printed; instead, she was able to use those excerpts, speak through them, almost ventriloquize them. By embedding these quotes in her own writing and by occasionally inserting editorial comments—often a parenthetical question mark after a description or word she found problematic—Wells reconfigured hegemonic white narratives of lynching and of racial and sexual identity. For an effective close reading and analysis of Wells's use of parenthetical commentary, see Davis, "'Weak Race.'"

22. The ideal of objectivity in journalism was being developed in the late nineteenth century, and Wells was one of the practitioners who worked within this emerging professional construct. According to a historian of journalism, "Ida B. Wells, through careful research and impassioned pleas, confronted 'objectivity' and showed that mainstream journalists, while professing their 'objectivity,' were operating under flawed and culturally biased assumptions." Mindich, *Just the Facts*, 136.

23. Lisa Duggan, too, refers to the "lynching narrative" in *Sapphic Slashers*; Jacquelyn Dowd Hall was probably the first critic to map out the contours of this "dramatization of cultural themes." Martha Hodes identifies "powerful

stories about black men and white women" that "white Southerners began to tell themselves and each other" after Reconstruction. Hall, "'Mind That Burns,'" 335; Hodes, *White Women, Black Men*, 177.

24. Wells, *Crusade for Justice*, 64.

25. Carby, *Reconstructing Womanhood*, 18.

26. Kerber, "Meanings of Citizenship," 833; Cott, "Marriage," 1440; Ginzberg, "Pernicious Heresies," 141. Smith, *Civic Ideals*, and Holland, *Body Politic*, are texts that explore and historically map out notions of citizenship and how they developed through the nineteenth century, particularly in relation to black men and all women.

27. Schechter, *Ida B. Wells-Barnett*, 82.

28. *Dred Scott v. Sandford*, 60 U.S. 393, 405.

29. As Eric Sundquist explains, the *Slaughterhouse* cases of 1873 established dual citizenship, national and state: "Separating national from state rights, the Court insisted that, while it could prevent a *state* from abridging civil rights, only states themselves could prevent *individuals* from denying blacks their rights." Sundquist, *To Wake the Nations*, 238. Similarly, the *Civil Rights* cases of 1883 "suggest that when racial discrimination fell short of chattel slavery or violation of a few basic rights, it was not only constitutional but uncontroversial." Smith, *Civic Ideals*, 376.

30. Immigration laws were propagated in the late nineteenth century and were typically very exclusionary, particularly toward Chinese immigrants, who were in 1882 categorically denied access to American naturalization.

31. Dole, *American Citizen*, 260; Smith, *Civic Ideals*, 31.

32. Political scientist Rogers M. Smith defines a civic myth as "a myth used to explain why persons form a people, usually indicating how a political community originated, who is eligible for membership, who is not and why, and what the community's values and aims are." Smith, *Civic Ideals*, 33. Lauren Berlant explains national fantasy: "By 'fantasy' I mean to designate how national culture becomes local—through the images, narratives, monuments, and sites that circulate through personal/collective consciousness." Berlant, *Anatomy of National Fantasy*, 5.

33. Wald, *Constituting Americans*, 2.

34. Grosz, *Volatile Bodies*, 142.

35. Wald, *Constituting Americans*, 10, 1.

36. For instance, British sociologist T. H. Marshall offered a widely accepted definition of social citizenship in 1949 as "the right to share to the full in the social heritage and to live the life of a civilized being according to the standards prevailing in the society." Quoted in Kerber, "Meanings of Citizenship," 843. American historian Philip Gleason contends in another widely known description that the American citizen "did not have to be of any particular national, linguistic, religious, or ethnic background. All he had to do was commit himself to the political ideology centered on the abstract ideals of liberty, equality, and republicanism." Gleason, "American Identity," 62–63. Both of these definitions emphasize "abstract ideals"—"rights," "social heritage," "liberty, equality, and republicanism"—rather than the material bodies

and experiences of those who are or will be citizens, and such definitions do not acknowledge that *ideas* of citizenship are based on embodied notions.

37. Root, *Citizen's Part*, 123; Dole, *American Citizen*, 257.

38. Grosz, *Volatile Bodies*, 142.

39. Historian David Roediger contends that in the antebellum period blacks were not only noncitizens but were actually understood as "anticitizens," and this status had lasting implications. Roediger, *Wages of Whiteness*, 57. According to Sander Gilman, notions of disembodied, rational white citizenship and civilization were built on and contrasted to the bodies of blacks. He explains that to late nineteenth-century whites in America and Europe, "[blacks'] presence in the contemporary world served as an indicator of how far mankind had come in establishing control over his world and himself. The loss of control was marked by a regression into this dark past—a degeneracy into the primitive expression of emotions in the form of either madness or unrestrained sexuality." Gilman, "Black Bodies," 248–50. Robyn Wiegman posits the nineteenth-century emphasis on the embodiment of blacks and women as a way of fortifying the ideal of the disembodied white masculine and explains that the white male citizen was thereby "'freed' from the corporeality that might otherwise impede his insertion into the larger body of national identity." Wiegman, *American Anatomies*, 88–89, 94. Gunning, too, identifies the role of black bodies as a screen on which white male citizenship was projected. Gunning, *Race, Rape, and Lynching*, 7. The civic myths which made white men's bodies the image of American citizenship have often been invisible even to current historians and cultural critics. Berlant explains, "When a given symbolic national body signifies as *normal*—straight, white, middle-class, and heterosexual—hardly anyone asks critical questions about its representativeness." Berlant, *Queen of America*, 36.

40. Roediger, *Wages of Whiteness*, 57.

41. See Gunning, *Race, Rape, and Lynching*, 7, and Duggan, *Sapphic Slashers*, 36.

42. Berlant, *Anatomy of National Fantasy*, 34.

43. Wald, *Constituting Americans*, 1.

44. Wells-Barnett, *Southern Horrors*, 17.

45. Ibid., 18.

46. Ibid.

47. Ibid.

48. This does not mean, however, that black women's bodies were not implicated in the white supremacist violence that constituted lynchings. The gender slippage Wells exposes in the *Scimitar* editorial does in fact suggest the danger to black women's bodies. In this case, as in many, the violence was not simply rhetorical. Sandra Gunning notes that Wells's reprinting of the *Scimitar* article "argues into public consciousness the black female body itself as a primary site of white aggression, because the retelling of the events . . . forces the reader to contemplate what the mob answering the white press's call would have done had it found Wells at the *Free Speech* headquarters." Gunning, *Race, Rape, and Lynching*, 85.

49. Particularly Thomas Moss, Calvin McDowell, and Henry Stewart, the three Memphis businessmen whose lynching began Wells's crusade.

50. Gunning and Duggan mention black female victims, but this is not their focus. Schechter offers more attention to women victims, comparing Wells's writings on women to those of her contemporaries Anna Julia Cooper and Frederick Douglass.

51. Wells-Barnett, *Southern Horrors*, 44. In *Southern Horrors* she also refers to "a little Afro-American girl" who was raped, again repeating the adjective "little" which is a central component of sentimental descriptions of women.

52. Gunning, *Race, Rape, and Lynching*, 86.

53. Wells, "Afro-Americans," 176.

54. Wells, *Crusade for Justice*, 79, 80.

55. Ibid., 149.

56. Ibid., 80; Schechter, *Ida B. Wells-Barnett*, 22.

57. Wells's biographer Linda O. McMurry notes that Wells "sought to counteract the sensational nature of her material by adopting a dispassionate mode of speaking." McMurry, *To Keep the Waters Troubled*, 216.

58. Wells-Barnett, *Red Record*, 220.

59. Aptheker, *Woman's Legacy*, 54; Gunning, *Race, Rape, and Lynching*, 76.

60. Wells-Barnett, *Red Record*, 147.

61. Interestingly, racist scientist Nathaniel Shaler, in an 1890 article in *Atlantic Monthly*, identifies a variety of skin colors and body types of American blacks, explaining, "It is not uncommon to find [in the South] faces and limbs which depart widely from the Guinea coast type, and closely approach the aspect of the Arab." Shaler, "Science," 39. His explanation for these differences is that they result from origins in different parts of Africa; he completely ignores the possibility that some of this variety results from "miscegenation," primarily in the form of white men's rape of black women.

62. Wells-Barnett, *Southern Horrors*, 27, 28; Wells-Barnett, *Red Record*, 213, 239–40, 211.

63. Schechter, *Ida B. Wells-Barnett*, 87.

64. Quoted in Wells-Barnett, *Southern Horrors*, 22.

65. Ibid., 20–21.

66. Wells-Barnett, *Red Record*, 145.

67. Martha Hodes traces the historical development of this particular component of the lynch narrative, the assertion that no consensual sex is possible between black men and white women.

68. Sander Gilman notes that the bodies of black women "[come] to serve as an icon for black sexuality in general" in the nineteenth century. Gilman, "Black Bodies," 231.

69. Hammonds, "Toward a Genealogy," 173.

70. Wells-Barnett, *Southern Horrors*, 14.

71. Duggan, *Sapphic Slashers*, 21.

72. Schechter, too, compares Wells's writing with that of Chopin and Dreiser.

73. Duggan, *Sapphic Slashers*, 2.

74. The 1875 Supreme Court case *Minor v. Happersett* explicitly decided this issue, ruling that women have "membership of a nation and nothing more." Quoted in Holland, *Body Politic*, 100.

75. Wells-Barnett, *Southern Horrors*, 18.

76. Wells-Barnett, *Red Record*, 161.

77. Ibid., 162, 164.

78. Ibid., 165. According to Bederman, the savagery of the white mobs was a cause of anxiety among many who worked to strengthen white manliness. However, this savagery was not universally seen as a problem, as is evidenced by a statement from South Carolina Senator Ben Tillman, who said in a 1907 speech that when a white man is confronted with a rape of a white woman, "Civilization peels off us, and any and all of us who are men, and we revert to the original savage type whose impulses under any and all circumstances has always been to 'kill! kill! kill!'" Quoted in Gunning, *Race, Rape, and Lynching*, 5.

79. Wells-Barnett, *Red Record*, 166.

80. Spillers explains that the terms by which we refer to black bodies are overdetermined and yet simultaneously emptied of individual significance so that "every feature of social and human differentiation disappears in public discourses regarding the African-American person." Thus, in order to function "properly" in the white newspaper article, Smith must be emptied of social and human categories of differentiation and appear as a cipher to be filled with whatever symbolic meaning the dominant discourse demands. When his story is placed within Wells's text, however, that emptiness becomes noteworthy and no longer operates in support of the white narrative. Spillers, "Mama's Baby," 78.

81. Wells-Barnett, *Red Record*, 167–68. Wiegman asserts that these detailed reports in white papers helped to propagate the lynch narrative. She explains, "Such accounts extended the function of lynching as a mode of surveillance by reiterating its performative qualities, carving up the black body in the specular refiguration of slavery's initial, dismembering scene." Wiegman, *American Anatomies*, 91.

82. *Plessy v. Ferguson*, 163 U.S. 537, 551–52.

83. As Sundquist explains, "*Plessy* was a landmark case not because it drastically altered the direction of legislation and judicial thought but because it concluded the process of transfiguring dual *constitutional* citizenship into dual *racial* citizenship which had unfolded since the end of Reconstruction." Sundquist, *To Wake the Nations*, 241.

84. Ibid., 426; Bederman, *Manliness and Civilization*, 26.

85. Wells-Barnett, *Southern Horrors*, 17.

86. Hodes, *White Women, Black Men*, 201; Nelson, *National Manhood*, 142.

87. The description of Lee Walker's lynching was first printed in Wells-Barnett, *Reason Why* and then was reprinted in her *Red Record*.

88. Quoted in Wells-Barnett, *Red Record*, 193.

89. Ibid., 194, 196.

90. Trudier Harris and Robyn Wiegman, in particular, provide smart psy-

choanalytical readings of the white mob's collection of black victims' body parts.

91. Even Douglass's support was not unqualified; while Wells was on her second public speaking tour in England, Douglass was initially wary of offering her his full support. See McMurry, *To Keep the Waters Troubled*, 208–9.

92. See McMurry, *To Keep the Waters Troubled*, 115–17, 232.

93. Beam, "Flower," 71.

94. McMurry, *To Keep the Waters Troubled*, 232.

95. Walker, for instance, was accused variously of assault on white women and rape, but Wells reports that "no woman was harmed, no serious indignity suffered." Wells-Barnett, *Red Record*, 191. Walker accosted two women in a wagon, and although his story differed from the women's—he claimed he only asked them for something to eat, while they accused him of attempted assault—none of the participants in the actual event claimed that rape had occurred. Wells does not absolve Walker of all wrongdoing—she does report that some encounter between Walker and the white women occurred—but she makes it clear to her readers that the charges and the response of the lynch mob were far out of proportion to the actual crime committed. Wells's determination to present the facts fairly is even more evident in her portrayal of Henry Smith. Wells presents him as a criminal; she claims that the facts supported the allegation that Smith killed the four-year-old daughter of a police officer in Paris, Texas.

96. Wells's picture of black male victimization is mitigated by such cases as that of C. J. Miller, a man wrongly accused of a crime. Miller *is* innocent, and more than that, he is extremely articulate, reasonable, and rational, embodying all the civilized virtues that the dominant ideology attributes to white men. He makes a statement to the lynch mob, telling them his name, and arguing, "I stand here surrounded by men who are excited, men who are not willing to let the law take its course, and as far as the crime is concerned, I have committed no crime, and certainly no crime gross enough to deprive me of my life and liberty to walk upon the green earth." Wells-Barnett, *Red Record*, 180. As he appears in Wells's text, he manifests self-control and an ability to express himself that supersedes that of many of the whites whose words appear. These characteristics do not save Miller, however, and neither does the significant evidence that he was not the man who committed the crime. Like the other black male victims Wells describes, Miller ultimately is powerless to stop the mob, and he is killed.

97. Wells-Barnett, *Reason Why*, 61.

98. For more information on these photographs, see Allen, *Without Sanctuary*.

99. Tate, *Domestic Allegories*, 97, see also 63. See also DuCille, *Coupling Convention*, 50, and Beam, "Flower," 71–72.

100. Schechter, *Ida B. Wells-Barnett*, 250–51.

101. Hammonds, "Toward a Genealogy," 174.

102. Berlant, *Queen of America*, 88.

103. Ibid., 223.

104. Berlant discusses Harriet Jacobs, Frances Harper, and Anita Hill as her examples of Diva Citizens.

105. As Melba Joyce Boyd explains in her exploration of Wells's entry into the American history canon, Wells's expulsion from the train and lawsuit against the railroad company is considered one of the crucial events of Wells's life in most biographical accounts. See Boyd, "Canon Configurations."

106. Wells, *Crusade for Justice*, 18–19.

107. Sundquist, *To Wake the Nations*, 439. *Plessy v. Ferguson*, it should be remembered, centered on a black man's attempt to ride in a segregated train car.

108. Simone Davis asserts, "[Wells] refuses to enact the Otherness—the savagery, the unruliness, the carnality, the animal incoherence—that the Black individual must embody if whites are to claim the opposing virtues as their own." Davis, "'Weak Race,'" 86.

109. McMurry, *To Keep the Waters Troubled*, 238. In her diary, Wells reports an event early in her public career, when a man implied that she was not a respectable woman. She explains, "I was so angry I foamed at the mouth, bit my lips and then recognized my impotence—ended in a fit of crying." Quoted in ibid., 44–45. This emphatic bodily response to injustice was not characteristic of Wells's speaking career, but does suggest how implicated her own body was in her fight for social—and personal—justice.

110. Wells-Barnett, *Southern Horrors*, 37.

111. Gunning, *Race, Rape, and Lynching*, 87. Bederman, too, makes this assertion.

112. Wells-Barnett, *Red Record*, 144.

113. Ibid.

114. Quoted in Thompson, *Ida B. Wells-Barnett*, 65.

115. Wells, "Afro-Americans and Africa," 165.

116. These terms certainly conjure images of slavery as well, and the two phenomena are not entirely distinct either historically or linguistically; as Hortense Spillers notes, the language surrounding the experience of blacks in America "remains grounded in the originating metaphors of captivity and mutilation so that it is as if neither time nor history, nor historiography and its topics, shows movement, as the human subject is 'murdered' over and over again . . ." Although slavery had ended, Wells writes in a time in which blacks are still "captive flesh" and are therefore subject to bodily mortification which is an extension of the control and torture of black bodies under slavery. Spillers, "Mama's Baby," 68, 67.

CHAPTER FIVE

1. Kirby describes the speaking body graphically, speculating that one might be able to read "the peristaltic movements of the viscera, the mitosis of cells, the electrical activity that plays across a synapse, the itinerary of a virus. . . . In other words, is this a 'text' and a 'writing' whose tissue includes all the

oozings and pulsings that literally and figuratively make up the differential stuff of the body's extra-ordinary circuitry?" Kirby, *Telling Flesh*, 61, 76.

2. Hale, "'Conversazione,'" 5.

3. Her home office was quite busy; according to her grandson, "I remember streams of people going upstairs to grandmother's room. Everybody who came to Philadelphia must have called on her, and of course there were always many local friends and the endless authors and artists who contributed to the magazine." Quoted in Finley, *Lady of Godey's*, 307.

4. While critics often refer to *Godey's Lady's Book* as *Godey's*, this shorthand inappropriately prioritizes Louis Godey, the publisher, at the expense of Hale. During Hale's editorship of the magazine, it was more often referred to by readers as "Mrs. Hale's magazine" or "the book." Hale herself referred to the magazine as the *Lady's Book*, and that is how I have chosen to refer to it throughout this chapter.

5. Godey, "Notes," 293.

6. Warner, *Letters of the Republic* and Looby, *Voicing America* both examine the male print culture that obtained during the Revolutionary and early nationalist periods of American history and literature. Warner, in fact, ends his study precisely at the point when women began writing in greater numbers.

7. Baym, "Between Enlightenment and Victorian," 25; Tonkovich, "Rhetorical Power," 162.

8. See Bordo, *Twilight Zones*, 185.

9. The idea of the body as printed text appears throughout American literature, from Bradstreet and Franklin to Ray Bradbury's *Fahrenheit 451*, which describes a culture of rebels who memorize and thus actually come to embody books.

10. Marcus, "Shakespeare's Computer," 12.

11. Franklin, too, was borrowing from early modern configurations of the body as text; his epitaph shows striking similarities to the elegy for John Cotton in Cotton Mather's *Magnalia Christi Americana*.

12. Marcus, "Shakespeare's Computer," 12.

13. Quoted in Zboray, "Antebellum Reading," 183.

14. Lehuu, *Carnival on the Page*, 3, 10.

15. Ibid., 110–11.

16. Isabelle Entrikin argues that Hale was "one of the foremost women of her day" whose "influence extended into the lives of almost every middle class household in the United States." Ann Douglas calls Hale "the most important arbiter of feminine opinion of her day." Caroline Bird argues, "It is hard to think of another individual of her time who exerted influence over so many areas for so many years." Bardes and Gossett refer to Hale as "arguably the most prominent woman engaged in literary enterprise in the middle of the nineteenth century." Entrikin, *Sarah Josepha Hale*, v; Douglas, *Feminization of American Culture*, 45; Bird, *Enterprising Women*, 60; Bardes and Gossett, "Sarah J. Hale," 18.

17. Most critics, including Baym, focus on Hale's independent texts, in-

cluding her novel, *Northwood* (1827), and her compendious *Woman's Record* (1863). The first book-length study of Hale's editorial career, Patricia Okker's excellent *Our Sister Editors*, did not appear until 1995. While Hale's books certainly deserve critical attention, I suspect that the neglect of Hale's editorial work stems in part from the vast terrain that must be covered to address this topic. A single book is more easily pinned down for analysis than forty years of magazines. This difficulty, however, must not prevent critics from analyzing this work, which is ultimately much more important for Hale's historical significance, and her influence on women of her time, than her books are.

18. Criticism of Hale has tended to fall into two camps: those critics who see Hale as a damaging force whose work hurt women, and those who celebrate Hale, either to confirm her status as an important American person or, more recently, as an attempt to wrest her from obscurity. Hale's early biographers and critics celebrate her work as an exception to the kinds of writing being done in the nineteenth century. From 1928 to 1931, critics Lawrence Martin, Bertha Stearns, and Ruth Finley described Hale as "sensible" and her publications as works "that actually did much to make women intelligent readers." These early writings posit Hale as an exceptional, even unique woman of the nineteenth century. Martin, "Genesis," 54; Stearns, "Early New England Magazines," 450.

With the rise of feminist criticism in the 1970s, Hale became the target of feminist critique, portrayed as a pawn for the dominant cultural values that oppressed women. Ann Douglas and Barbara Welter are key voices in this critical camp; Hale is seen as the ultimate purveyor of true womanhood. Nicole Tonkovich, Bardes and Gossett, and Nina Baym in recent years have begun a critical reclamation of Hale, attempting to elevate her status by counteracting feminist critics who condemn Hale as antifeminist and apolitical. Baym argues of Hale's approach to woman's rights and abolition, "Hale was very much an active political writer, at least in the decade before the Civil War. The problem, of course, is that from 'our' point of view she argued for the wrong side in both instances." Baym, "Sarah Hale," 168.

19. Romero, *Home Fronts*, 87.

20. Bardes and Gossett, "Sarah J. Hale," 21.

21. Warner, *Wide, Wide World*, 333.

22. Sicherman, "Sense and Sensibility," 202.

23. Hale, *Woman's Record*, 687.

24. Ibid.

25. Fern, *Ruth Hall*, 290.

26. Tonkovich, *Domesticity*, 51.

27. Melville, "Tartarus of Maids," 221.

28. As was discussed in Chapter 4, above, Sojourner Truth argued for the connection of her voice and her body, and her audience often recognized this connection. In an extended discussion of voice, Christopher Looby notes the many bodily organs which construct voice: "Linguists speak of those speech sounds in which the vocal chords are clenched and the larynx is thereby made to vibrate as voiced phenomes. . . . Thus the same positions of the tongue,

lips, and teeth will produce quite different sounds depending on the open or closed position of the glottis." Body theorist Vicki Kirby, too, unifies voice and body by arguing that the body is a voice. Looby, *Voicing America*, 4; Kirby, *Telling Flesh*, 154.

29. Hale, *Godey's* 16:46.

30. Ibid., 16:96.

31. Ibid., 21:285.

32. Louis Godey actually began instituting this policy in the *Lady's Book* a year or so before Hale became editor; critics generally interpret this as a deliberate imitation of the *Ladies' Magazine* and part of his attempt to convince Hale to become editor of the *Lady's Book*.

33. Hale, *Godey's* 19:284, 21:143, 24:239.

34. Ibid., 21:143, 238, 18:47.

35. For a thorough discussion of Hale's role in promoting the professionalization of authorship through her editorship of the *Lady's Book*, see Okker, *Our Sister Editors*, chap. 4.

36. Ibid., 97.

37. Hale, *Godey's* 16:46.

38. Ibid., 25:306.

39. Moylan and Stiles, *Reading Books*, 12. Lehuu, too, emphasizes the materiality of print culture: "Between the text and readers lies the material appearance of printed artifacts." Lehuu, *Carnival on the Page*, 61.

40. Apparently the *Lady's Book* was more successful than most nineteenth-century magazines at recouping debts from subscribers because Okker notes that the demands for money in the *Lady's Book* were less frequent and less desperate than those in many other magazines. Okker, *Our Sister Editors*, 57.

41. Hale, *Godey's* 17:190.

42. Ibid.

43. Ibid.

44. Ibid.

45. As historians like David Hall note, eighteenth-century print culture was characterized by scarcity and respect; the number of printed texts available in a given family or community was small, and thus reading was an activity that was undertaken carefully and respectfully, typically for devotional purposes. By the late eighteenth century, this was changing. One printer wrote in 1850 that it was "an era of literary affluence, almost amounting to surfeit." Hale herself experienced this change; she writes of her childhood, "The books to which I had access were few, very few, in comparison with the number given children now-a-days; but they were such as required to be studied—and I did study them." Hall, *Cultures of Print*, 56–57, 71; Hale, *Woman's Record*, 686.

46. While the eighteenth-century printer had been a local artisan, producing and selling printed material to the local community, the nineteenth century saw a decrease in the number of small, local printers and a growing number of large publishing houses which catered to the country as a mass market. For more information on the publishing marketplace of the nine-

teenth century, see Hall, *Cultures of Print*; Coultrap-McQuin, *Doing Literary Business*; and Lehuu, *Carnival on the Page*.

47. See Zboray, "Antebellum Reading," 182.

48. Indeed, as the Civil War approached, Hale saw the *Lady's Book* as a potential means for unification; she used its pages as a space to call for the country's unity by presenting stories and editorials which showed the nation as an integrated whole. For example, Hale's extended campaign to institute a national Thanksgiving Day celebration emphasized national unity. For twenty years, Hale offered her readers reiterated images of families across the country sitting down at the same time, on the same day, to eat a Thanksgiving meal.

49. Okker reports that the Southern Literary Messenger had a subscription list of 4,000 in the 1840s. Okker, *Our Sister Editors*, 56.

50. In 1840, Hale published a letter from a subscriber who details the abuses her magazine suffers from the "five or six families in the area" who are "as eager to get the numbers as we are, and watch the post office as carefully." When the magazine is borrowed, it is returned with "the plates torn, or soiled with grease and dirt, and the cover commonly gone; no longer fit to occupy its place on the centre table or in the library." This letter reveals the demand for the magazine as well as the esteem the magazine could hold as an attractive center table book in a family home or library. *Godey's* 20:46.

51. *Peterson's Magazine* could boast an equal or greater number of subscribers after the war.

52. Hale, *Godey's* 19:46.

53. Ibid., 42:380.

54. Hale's pride in the magazine's success and, implicitly, in her work as an editor and writer may be surprising to twentieth-century readers whose understanding of nineteenth-century women writers has been shaped by arguments like Mary Kelley's in *Private Woman, Public Stage* that women writers suffered from anxiety and attempted to keep their writing as secretive an activity as possible. Hale's textual life is not legible within this model of anxiety; instead, her work within the Lady's Book and her pride in her work may become more intelligible when seen within the larger context of the business of print in the nineteenth century. As Susan Coultrap-McQuin has demonstrated convincingly in *Doing Literary Business*, many women considered themselves literary professionals in the nineteenth century; the professional environment surrounding publishing in this period contributed to their comfort. As Coultrap-McQuin explains, the literary market structured itself around personal relationships and Victorian morality, "The atmosphere of the literary marketplace was not particularly alienating to women who could successfully integrate their female values and behaviors into the pursuit of their literary careers." Coultrap-McQuin, *Doing Literary Business*, xii. Hale was certainly one of these women who found a way to integrate her status as a woman with her role as a successful literary figure. Hale, of course, worked both sides of this equation; she was both an author and a liaison to the world of the magazine's "Gentleman Publisher," Louis Godey. Like the

"Gentleman Publishers" of the mid-century, Hale considered her work to have greater value than simply that of making a commercial success; she felt that her magazine was making important intellectual and moral contributions to her society. More importantly, by identifying herself with the magazine, Hale could represent herself as making these contributions. As she asks what the *Lady's Book* has done, she answers, "We are thankful that we have been able to aid in directing public sentiment on this subject [women's education]." Hale, *Godey's* 33:236. By leaving the pronoun ambiguous, Hale herself can claim responsibility for changing the thoughts of the nation on this issue and others.

55. For instance, Ruth Hall's publishers fanned the flames of public outrage over Fanny Fern's semi-autobiographical text by printing advertisements which asked, "Who is Ruth Hall?"

56. Richard Brodhead explains that novels in the 1850s changed the meaning of popular, "a term that now came to denote not just 'well-liked' or 'widely-read' but specifically production into a certain market status through the commercial management of a book's public life. The new promotional campaigns mounted by the publishers of such works to an altogether new extent produced public demand for them, demand which was then republicized as a way of creating further demand." Brodhead, *Cultures of Letters*, 57. See also Zboray, "Antebellum Reading," 189.

57. Lehuu, *Carnival on the Page*, 63.

58. The highest-quality engravings were done on plates of copper or steel; these could be very detailed and were the most expensive. Less detailed engravings were often done on wood. The wood engravings used in the *Lady's Book* were "usually utilitarian rather than artistic, and very crude into the bargain." Mott, *History of American Magazines*, 523.

59. Hale, *Godey's* 21:285.

60. Mott, *History of American Magazines*, 519.

61. The increased length of magazines like *Harper's* and the *Atlantic Monthly* in the late 1850s probably has partially to do with the cost of paper; in the eighteenth century, paper was made from rags, and good cotton or linen rags were always in short supply in America, which made paper quite expensive. In 1828, a technique was developed to make paper from straw pulp, which reduced the demand for rags somewhat, but it was not until the mid-1850s that paper began being produced from wood pulp which finally reduced the price considerably and made it feasible for magazine publishers to increase the length of their texts. In addition, in the 1830s publishers began to use rolls of paper, which were much less expensive than individual sheets. See Neuberg, "Chapbooks," 83–84, and Zboray, "Antebellum Reading," 189.

62. Lehuu, *Carnival on the Page*, 34.

63. According to Lehuu, "Although printed materials were increasingly customized separately for men and women in order to satisfy the tastes of various publics, the public sphere was threatened to be no longer the exclusive domain of men. As a result, the distinction between the public and private blurred, and in the midst of border-crossers and ambiguous categories,

two antagonistic spheres of cultural production took shape: the legitimate and the popular." Lehuu, *Carnival on the Page*, 34. While the *Lady's Book* was clearly a legitimate publication, locating itself as appropriately middle-class, its extraordinary popular appeal and large circulation numbers suggest that it made use of some of the strategies of more popular publications and took advantage of the popular market.

64. Baym, "Onward Christian Women," 249, n. 1.

65. Tonkovich, *Domesticity*, 82.

66. Bardes and Gossett, "Sarah J. Hale," 25. Bird, for instance, says of Hale's sustained campaign to nationalize Thanksgiving that Hale "*nagged* Abraham Lincoln into making Thanksgiving a national holiday . . ." Bird, *Enterprising Women*, 64 (italics mine). Bird and other critics like her thus deflect attention from the political and financial significance of Hale's actions by describing these actions in stereotypically feminine terms.

67. Okker, *Our Sister Editors*, 98.

68. In fact, the reader might well assume that this "Editor" is male since Hale herself argued that women in business roles should go by specifically female titles such as editress.

69. Hale, *Godey's* 16:47.

70. Ibid., 24:238, 25:107.

71. Critics have had this problem, as well; many early critics of the *Lady's Book*, including Mott and Satterwhite, assumed that the "Editors' Tables" were written by Godey.

72. Hale, *Godey's* 33:236.

73. Ibid., 33:236–37.

74. Hale, "'Conversazione,'" 2.

75. As Marcus explains, this model of reading as conversation emerged in the early modern period as part of the identification of texts with bodies; for instance, readers would often characterize reading ancient texts as a conversation with the ancient authors. Marcus, "Shakespeare's Computer," 17.

76. Hale, *Godey's* 26:58.

77. Ibid., 60:465.

78. Ibid., 39:463, 33:236.

79. Ibid., 25:306.

80. Cathy Davidson notes that studies of reading are difficult to enact because of the lack of written records; she explains, "Except for surviving chance observations and marginal comments in the works themselves, it is virtually impossible to know how past readers evaluated and understood particular books." Davidson, "Toward a History of Books," 19.

81. Pattee, *Feminine Fifties*, 110.

82. Mott, *History of American Magazines*, 588. Ruth Finley, too, argues, "Turning through the files of Godey's Lady's Book, one wonders how any mind that could read the words could bring itself to peruse the meaningless trash scribbled by the majority." Joseph Satterwhite describes the tastes of the *Lady's Book*'s readers as running "to sickly sentiment and mawkish melodrama," and he explains that for the magazine, "a good story was one

that made the reader cry and wait." Finley, *Lady of Godey's*, 128; Satterwhite, "Tremulous Formula," 99, 106.

83. Okker identifies this early twentieth-century "tradition of using sentimentalism as a derogatory rather than a descriptive term" with an attempt to make a clear distinction between modernism and popular literature. Okker, *Our Sister Editors*, 2.

84. Hale, "Chapter of Inferences," 33.

85. See illustrations titled "Health and Beauty" and "Hints on Equestrianism," in Chapter 1, above.

86. Laura McCall's systematic analysis of the fiction in a random sampling of *Lady's Books* demonstrates convincingly that the female characters in the magazine are not, in fact, "pious and good" and did not fit the true womanhood model; as McCall argues, "The women in Godey's fiction were not passive, purity did not connote asexuality, piety was understated, and home was not the only sphere to which a woman aspired." McCall, "'Reign of Brute Force,'" 236.

EPILOGUE

1. Hale, *Godey's* 16:47.
2. Jelinek, *Tradition of Women's Autobiography*, 102.
3. Wald, *Constituting Americans*, 1.

BIBLIOGRAPHY

Abramson, Doris. "'The New Path': Nineteenth-Century American Women Playwrights." In *Modern American Drama: The Female Canon*, edited by June Schlueter, 38–51. Rutherford, N.J.: Fairleigh Dickinson University Press, 1990.

Abzug, Robert H. *Cosmos Crumbling: American Reform and the Religious Imagination*. New York: Oxford University Press, 1994.

Adams, Abigail, and John Adams. *The Book of Abigail and John: Selected Letters of the Adams Family, 1762–1784*. Cambridge, Mass.: Harvard University Press, 1975.

Ahmed, Sara. "Embodying Strangers." In *Body Matters: Feminism, Textuality, and Corporeality*, edited by Avril Horner and Angela Keane, 85–96. Manchester, Eng.: Manchester University Press, 2000.

Alcott, Louisa May. "La Belle Bayadere." In *The Lost Stories of Louisa May Alcott*, edited by Madeline B. Stern, 145–62. New York: Citadel Press, 1993.

———. *Little Women*. 1868. Reprint. New York: Penguin Books, 1989.

———. "Which Wins?" In *The Lost Stories of Louisa May Alcott*, edited by Madeline B. Stern, 75–91. New York: Citadel Press, 1993.

———. *Work*. 1873. Reprint. New York: Penguin Books, 1994.

Allen, James, et al. *Without Sanctuary: Lynching Photography in America*. Santa Fe, N.M.: Twin Palms Publishers, 2000.

Aptheker, Bettina. *Woman's Legacy: Essays on Race, Sex, and Class in American History*. Amherst: University of Massachusetts Press, 1982.

Bakhtin, M. M. *The Dialogic Imagination: Four Essays*. Edited by Michael Holquist. Austin: University of Texas Press, 1981.

Bank, Rosemarie K. *Theatre Culture in America, 1825–1860*. Cambridge: Cambridge University Press, 1997.

Banta, Martha. *Imaging American Women: Idea and Ideals in Cultural History*. New York: Columbia University Press, 1987.

Bardes, Barbara, and Suzanne Gossett. *Declarations of Independence: Women and Political Power in Nineteenth-Century American Fiction*. New Brunswick, N.J.: Rutgers University Press, 1990.

———. "Sarah J. Hale, Selective Promoter of Her Sex." In *A Living of Words: American Women in Print Culture*, edited by Susan Albertine, 18–34. Knoxville: University of Tennessee Press, 1995.

Barnes, Eric Wollencott. *Anna Cora: The Life and Theatre of Anna Cora Mowatt*. London: Secker and Warburg, 1954.

Baym, Nina. *American Women of Letters and the Nineteenth-Century Sciences: Styles of Affiliation*. New Brunswick, N.J.: Rutgers University Press, 2002.

———. *American Women Writers and the Work of History, 1790–1860*. New Brunswick, N.J.: Rutgers University Press, 1995.

———. "Between Enlightenment and Victorian: Toward a Narrative of American Women Writers Writing History." *Critical Inquiry* 18 (1991): 22–41.

———. "Onward Christian Women: Sarah J. Hale's History of the World." *New England Quarterly* 63 (1990): 249–70.

———. "Sarah Hale, Political Writer." *Feminism and American Literary History: Essays*. New Brunswick, N.J.: Rutgers University Press, 1992: 167–82.

———. *Woman's Fiction: A Guide to Novels by and about Women in America, 1820–1870*. Ithaca, N.Y.: Cornell University Press, 1978.

Beam, Dori Rabung. "The Flower of Black Female Sexuality in Pauline Hopkins's *Winona*." In *Recovering the Black Female Body*, edited by Michael Bennett and Vanessa D. Dickerson, 71–96. New Brunswick, N.J.: Rutgers University Press, 2001.

Beauchamp, Edward R. "Boxing." In *International Encyclopedia of Women and Sports*, edited by Karen Christensen et al., 167–75. New York: Macmillan Reference USA, 2000.

Bederman, Gail. "'Civilization,' the Decline of Middle-Class Manliness, and Ida B. Wells' Antilynching Campaign." *Radical History Review* 52 (1992): 5–30.

———. *Manliness and Civilization: A Cultural History of Gender and Race in the United States, 1880–1917*. Chicago: University of Chicago Press, 1995.

Beecher, Catharine. *Letters to the People on Health and Happiness*. New York: Harper and Brothers, 1856.

———. *A Treatise on Domestic Economy*. 1841. Reprint. New York: Source Book Press, 1970.

Berlage, Gai Ingham. "Baseball." In *International Encyclopedia of Women and Sports*, edited by Karen Christensen et al., 95–101. New York: Macmillan Reference USA, 2000.

Berlant, Lauren. *The Anatomy of National Fantasy: Hawthorne, Utopia, and Everyday Life*. Chicago: University of Chicago Press, 1991.

———. *The Queen of America Goes to Washington City: Essays on Sex and Citizenship*. Durham, N.C.: Duke University Press, 1997.

Billings, John Shaw. "The Progress of Medicine in the Nineteenth Century." In *Little Masterpieces of Science*, edited by George Iles, 161–76. New York: Doubleday, Page, and Co., 1902.

Bingham, Caleb. *The Columbian Orator*. Baltimore, Md.: Philip H. Nicklin and Company, 1797.

Bird, Caroline. *Enterprising Women*. New York: W. W. Norton and Company, 1976.

Blair, Walter. Introduction to *Crockett at 200: New Perspectives on the Man and the Myth*, edited by Michael A. Lofaro and Joe Cummings, 3–6. Knoxville: University of Tennessee Press, 1989.

Bogdan, Robert. "The Social Construction of Freaks." In *Freakery: Cultural Spectacles of the Extraordinary Body*, edited by Rosemarie Garland Thomson, 23–37. New York: New York University Press, 1996.

Bordo, Susan. *Twilight Zones: The Hidden Life of Cultural Images from Plato to O. J.* Berkeley: University of California Press, 1997.

Botkin, B. A. *A Treasury of New England Folklore*. New York: Crown Publishers, 1947.

Boyd, Melba Joyce. "Canon Configurations for Ida B. Wells-Barnett." *Black Scholar* 24 (1988): 8–13.

Braunberger, Christine. "Revolting Bodies: The Monster Beauty of Tattooed Women." *NWSA Journal* 12 (2000): 1–23.

Brodhead, Richard. *Cultures of Letters: Scenes of Reading and Writing in Nineteenth-Century America*. Chicago: University of Chicago Press, 1993.

Brodzki, Bella, and Celeste Schenk. Introduction to *Life/Lines: Theorizing Women's Autobiography*, edited by Brodski and Schenk, 1–15. Ithaca, N.Y.: Cornell University Press, 1988.

Broughton, T. L. "Women's Autobiography: The Self at Stake?" In *Autobiography and Questions of Gender*, edited by Shirley Neuman, 76–94. London: Frank Cass and Co., 1991.

Brown, Carolyn. *The Tall Tale in American Folklore and Literature*. Knoxville: University of Tennessee Press, 1987.

Brown, Gillian. *Domestic Individualism: Imagining Self in Nineteenth-Century America*. Berkeley: University of California Press, 1990.

Bruce, Robert V. *The Launching of Modern American Science, 1846–1876*. New York: Alfred A. Knopf, 1987.

Butler, Judith. *Bodies That Matter: On the Discursive Limits of "Sex."* New York: Routledge, 1993.

Campbell, David, ed. *The Graham Journal of Health and Longevity*. Boston: David Campbell, 1837–39.

Cane, Aleta Feinsod, and Susan Alves. Introduction to *"The Only Efficient Instrument": American Women Writers and the Periodical, 1837–1916*, edited by Feinsod and Alves, 1–19. Iowa City: University of Iowa Press, 2001.

Carby, Hazel. "'On the Threshold of Woman's Era': Lynching, Empire, and Sexuality in Black Feminist Theory." In *"Race," Writing, and Difference*, edited by Henry Louis Gates Jr., 301–16. Chicago: University of Chicago Press, 1986.

———. *Reconstructing Womanhood: The Emergence of the Afro-American Woman Novelist*. New York: Oxford University Press, 1987.

Cassedy, James H. *American Medicine and Statistical Thinking, 1800–1860*. Cambridge, Mass.: Harvard University Press, 1993.

Cassuto, Leonard. "'What an Object He Would Have Made of Me!': Tattooing and the Racial Freak in Melville's *Typee*." In *Freakery: Cultural Spectacles of the Extraordinary Body*, edited by Rosemarie Garland Thomson, 234–47. New York: New York University Press, 1996.

Chapple, J. A. V. *Science and Literature in the Nineteenth Century*. London: Macmillan, 1986.

Clark, Gregory, and S. Michael Halloran, eds. *Oratorical Culture in Nineteenth-Century America: Transformations in the Theory and Practice of Rhetoric*. Carbondale: Southern Illinois University Press, 1993.

Cogan, Frances B. *All-American Girl: The Ideal of Real Womanhood in Mid-Nineteenth-Century America*. Athens: University of Georgia Press, 1989.

Cohen, Jeffrey Jerome, and Gail Weiss. "Introduction: Bodies at the Limit." In *Thinking the Limits of the Body*, edited by Jeffrey Jerome Cohen and Gail Weiss, 1–10. Albany: State University of New York Press, 2003.

Cohen, Patricia Cline. "Safety and Danger: Women on American Public Transport, 1750–1850." In *Gendered Domain: Rethinking Public and Private in Women's History*, edited by Dorothy O. Helly and Susan M. Reverby, 109–22. Ithaca, N.Y.: Cornell University Press, 1992.

———. "Women at Large: Travel in Antebellum America." *History Today* 44 (1994): 44–50.

Coleman, Linda S. Introduction to *Women's Life-Writing: Finding Voice/Building Community*, edited by Linda S. Coleman, 1–7. Bowling Green, Ohio: Bowling Green State University Popular Press, 1997.

Conway, Jill Ker. *When Memory Speaks: Reflections on Autobiography*. New York: Alfred A. Knopf, 1998.

Cott, Nancy. "Marriage and Women's Citizenship in the United States, 1830–1934." *American Historical Review* 103 (1998): 1440–74.

Coultrap-McQuin, Susan. *Doing Literary Business: American Women Writers in the Nineteenth Century*. Chapel Hill: University of North Carolina Press, 1990.

Crawford, Scott. "Oakley, Annie." In *International Encyclopedia of Women and Sports*, edited by Karen Christensen et al., 815–16. New York: Macmillan Reference USA, 2000.

Csordas, Thomas J., ed. *Embodiment and Experience: The Existential Ground of Culture and Self*. Cambridge: Cambridge University Press, 1994.

Daniel, E. Valentine. "The Individual in Terror." In *Embodiment and Experience*, edited by Thomas J. Csordas, 229–47. Cambridge: Cambridge University Press, 1994.

Davidson, Cathy N. "Preface: No More Separate Spheres!" *American Literature* 70 (1998): 443–63.

———. "Toward a History of Books and Readers." In *Reading in America: Literature and Social History*, edited by Cathy N. Davidson, 1–26. Baltimore, Md.: Johns Hopkins University Press, 1989.

Davidson, Cathy N., and Jessamyn Hatcher. Introduction to *No More Separate Spheres!*, edited by Davidson and Hatcher, 7–26. Durham, N.C.: Duke University Press, 2002.

Davis, Rebecca Harding. *Life in the Iron Mills and Other Stories*. Edited by Tillie Olsen. New York: Feminist Press, 1985.

Davis, Simone W. "The 'Weak Race' and the Winchester: Political Voices in the Pamphlets of Ida B. Wells-Barnett." *Legacy* 12.2 (1995): 77–97.

Davis, Tracy C. "The Actress in Victorian Pornography." *Theatre Journal* 41 (1989): 294–315.
Dennett, Andrea Stulman. *Weird and Wonderful: The Dime Museum in America*. New York: New York University Press, 1997.
Dickinson, Emily. *The Complete Poems of Emily Dickinson*. Boston: Little, Brown, 1960.
Dole, Charles F. *The American Citizen*. Boston: D. C. Heath, 1892.
Dorson, Richard. *America in Legend: Folklore from the Colonial Period to the Present*. New York: Pantheon Books, 1973.
———. *Davy Crockett: American Comic Legend*. New York: Arno Press, 1977.
———. *Jonathan Draws the Long Bow: New England Popular Tales and Legends*. Cambridge, Mass.: Harvard University Press, 1946.
Douglas, Ann. *The Feminization of American Culture*. New York: Alfred A. Knopf, 1977.
Douglas, Mary. *Purity and Danger: An Analysis of the Concepts of Pollution and Taboo*. London: Ark Paperbacks, 1966.
DuCille, Ann. *The Coupling Convention: Sex, Text, and Tradition in Black Women's Fiction*. New York: Oxford University Press, 1993.
Dudden, Faye E. *Women in the American Theatre: Actresses and Audiences, 1790–1870*. New Haven, Conn.: Yale University Press, 1994.
Duggan, Lisa. *Sapphic Slashers: Sex, Violence, and American Modernity*. Durham, N.C.: Duke University Press, 2000.
Eddy, Mary Baker. *Retrospection and Introspection*. Boston: Christian Science Publishing Society, 1891.
———. *Science and Health with Key to the Scriptures*. 1875. Reprint. Boston: First Church of Christ, Scientist, 1994.
Elsom, John. *Erotic Theatre*. New York: Taplinger Publishing Co, 1974.
Entrikin, Isabelle Webb. *Sarah Josepha Hale and Godey's Lady's Book*. Philadelphia: University of Pennsylvania Press, 1946.
Evans, Augusta Jane. *Beulah*. Baton Rouge: Louisiana State University Press, 1992.
Fern, Fanny. *Ruth Hall and Other Writings*. Edited by Joyce W. Warren. New Brunswick, N.J.: Rutgers University Press, 1994.
Fetterley, Judith. "'My Sister! My Sister!': The Rhetoric of Catharine Sedgwick's *Hope Leslie*." *American Literature* 70 (1998): 491–516.
Fiedler, Leslie. *Freaks: Myths and Images of the Secret Self*. New York: Simon and Schuster, 1978.
Finley, Ruth E. *The Lady of Godey's: Sarah Josepha Hale*. 1931. Reprint. New York: Arno Press, 1974.
Fitch, Suzanne Pullon, and Roseann M. Mandziuk. *Sojourner Truth as Orator: Wit, Story, and Song*. Westport, Conn.: Greenwood Press, 1997.
Floyd, Barbara. *From Quackery to Bacteriology: The Emergence of Modern Medicine in Nineteenth-Century America: An Exhibition*. University of Toledo Libraries. <http://www.cl.utoledo.edu/canaday/quackery/quack1.html>. 7 June 1999.
Foster, Frances Smith. *Written by Herself: Literary Production by African*

American Women, 1746–1892. Bloomington: Indiana University Press, 1993.

Foucault, Michel. "Nietzsche, Genealogy, and History." In *Language, Counter-Memory, Practice: Selected Essays and Interviews*, edited by Daniel Bouchard, 139–64. Ithaca, N.Y.: Cornell University Press, 1977.

Fowler, Lois J., and David H. Fowler. Introduction to *Revelations of Self: American Women in Autobiography*, edited by Fowler and Fowler, xi–xxiv. Albany: State University of New York Press, 1990.

Fox, Margery. "Protest in Piety: Christian Science Revisited." *International Journal of Women's Studies* 1 (1978): 401–16.

Fretz, Eric. "P. T. Barnum's Theatrical Selfhood in the Nineteenth-Century Culture of Exhibition." In *Freakery: Cultural Spectacles of the Extraordinary Body*, edited by Rosemarie Garland Thomson, 97–107. New York: New York University Press, 1996.

Fuss, Diana. *Essentially Speaking: Feminism, Nature, and Difference*. New York: Routledge, 1989.

Gage, Mrs. F. D. "Sojourner Truth." *Independent*, 23 April 1863: 1.

Gardner, Martin. *The Healing Revelations of Mary Baker Eddy: The Rise and Fall of Christian Science*. New York: Prometheus Books, 1993.

Gilbert, Sandra M. and Susan Gubar. *The Madwoman in the Attic: The Woman Writer and the Nineteenth-Century Literary Imagination*. New Haven, Conn.: Yale University Press, 1979.

Gill, Gillian. *Mary Baker Eddy*. Reading, Mass.: Perseus Books, 1998.

Gilligan, Carol. *The Birth of Pleasure*. New York: Alfred A. Knopf, 2002.

Gilman, Sander L. "Black Bodies, White Bodies: Toward an Iconography of Female Sexuality in Late Nineteenth-Century Art, Medicine, and Literature." In *"Race," Writing, and Difference*, edited by Henry Louis Gates Jr., 223–61. Chicago: University of Chicago Press, 1986.

Gilmore, Leigh. *Autobiographics: A Feminist Theory of Women's Self-Representation*. Ithaca, N.Y.: Cornell University Press, 1994.

Ginzberg, Lori D. "Pernicious Heresies: Female Citizenship and Sexual Respectability in the Nineteenth Century." In *Women and the Unstable State in Nineteenth-Century America*, edited by Alison M. Parker and Stephanie Cole, 139–61. College Station: Texas A & M University Press, 2000.

Gleason, Philip. "American Identity and Americanization." In *Concepts of Ethnicity*, edited by William Petersen, Michael Novak, and Philip Gleason. Cambridge, Mass.: Harvard University Press, 1982.

Goddu, Teresa. *Gothic America: Narrative, History, and Nation*. New York: Columbia University Press, 1997.

Godey, Louis. "Notes from the Editor's Armchair." *Godey's Lady's Book* 23 (December 1841): 293.

Goodell, William, M.D. *Lessons in Gynecology*. Philadelphia: D. G. Brinton, 1879.

Greenwood, Grace. "My First Hunting and Fishing." *Godey's Lady's Book* 35 (January 1847): 9–11.

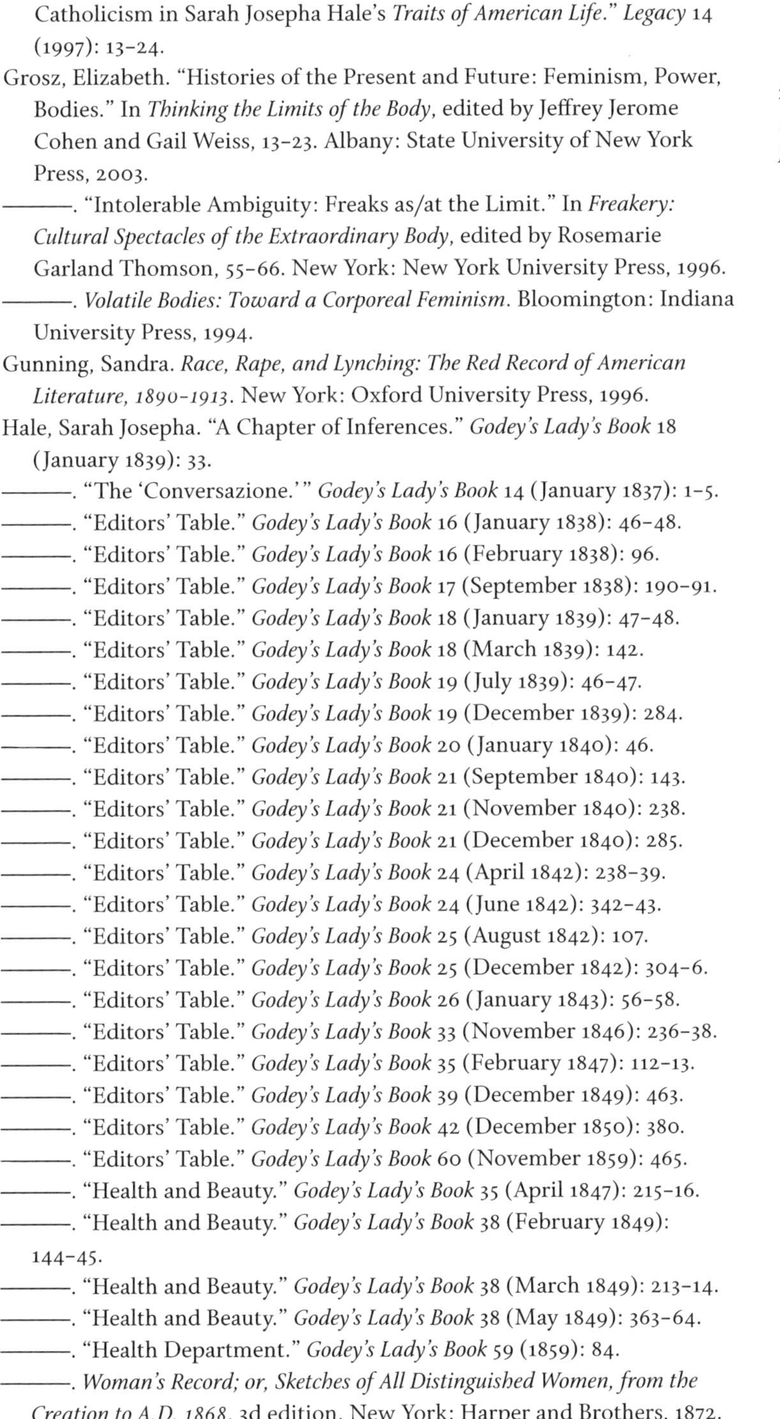

Griffin, Susan M. "'The Dark Stranger': Sensationalism and Anti-Catholicism in Sarah Josepha Hale's *Traits of American Life*." *Legacy* 14 (1997): 13–24.

Grosz, Elizabeth. "Histories of the Present and Future: Feminism, Power, Bodies." In *Thinking the Limits of the Body*, edited by Jeffrey Jerome Cohen and Gail Weiss, 13–23. Albany: State University of New York Press, 2003.

———. "Intolerable Ambiguity: Freaks as/at the Limit." In *Freakery: Cultural Spectacles of the Extraordinary Body*, edited by Rosemarie Garland Thomson, 55–66. New York: New York University Press, 1996.

———. *Volatile Bodies: Toward a Corporeal Feminism*. Bloomington: Indiana University Press, 1994.

Gunning, Sandra. *Race, Rape, and Lynching: The Red Record of American Literature, 1890–1913*. New York: Oxford University Press, 1996.

Hale, Sarah Josepha. "A Chapter of Inferences." *Godey's Lady's Book* 18 (January 1839): 33.

———. "The 'Conversazione.'" *Godey's Lady's Book* 14 (January 1837): 1–5.

———. "Editors' Table." *Godey's Lady's Book* 16 (January 1838): 46–48.

———. "Editors' Table." *Godey's Lady's Book* 16 (February 1838): 96.

———. "Editors' Table." *Godey's Lady's Book* 17 (September 1838): 190–91.

———. "Editors' Table." *Godey's Lady's Book* 18 (January 1839): 47–48.

———. "Editors' Table." *Godey's Lady's Book* 18 (March 1839): 142.

———. "Editors' Table." *Godey's Lady's Book* 19 (July 1839): 46–47.

———. "Editors' Table." *Godey's Lady's Book* 19 (December 1839): 284.

———. "Editors' Table." *Godey's Lady's Book* 20 (January 1840): 46.

———. "Editors' Table." *Godey's Lady's Book* 21 (September 1840): 143.

———. "Editors' Table." *Godey's Lady's Book* 21 (November 1840): 238.

———. "Editors' Table." *Godey's Lady's Book* 21 (December 1840): 285.

———. "Editors' Table." *Godey's Lady's Book* 24 (April 1842): 238–39.

———. "Editors' Table." *Godey's Lady's Book* 24 (June 1842): 342–43.

———. "Editors' Table." *Godey's Lady's Book* 25 (August 1842): 107.

———. "Editors' Table." *Godey's Lady's Book* 25 (December 1842): 304–6.

———. "Editors' Table." *Godey's Lady's Book* 26 (January 1843): 56–58.

———. "Editors' Table." *Godey's Lady's Book* 33 (November 1846): 236–38.

———. "Editors' Table." *Godey's Lady's Book* 35 (February 1847): 112–13.

———. "Editors' Table." *Godey's Lady's Book* 39 (December 1849): 463.

———. "Editors' Table." *Godey's Lady's Book* 42 (December 1850): 380.

———. "Editors' Table." *Godey's Lady's Book* 60 (November 1859): 465.

———. "Health and Beauty." *Godey's Lady's Book* 35 (April 1847): 215–16.

———. "Health and Beauty." *Godey's Lady's Book* 38 (February 1849): 144–45.

———. "Health and Beauty." *Godey's Lady's Book* 38 (March 1849): 213–14.

———. "Health and Beauty." *Godey's Lady's Book* 38 (May 1849): 363–64.

———. "Health Department." *Godey's Lady's Book* 59 (1859): 84.

———. *Woman's Record; or, Sketches of All Distinguished Women, from the Creation to A.D. 1868*. 3d edition. New York: Harper and Brothers, 1872.

Hall, David D. *Cultures of Print: Essays in the History of the Book*. Amherst: University of Massachusetts Press, 1996.

Hall, Jacquelyn Dowd. "'The Mind That Burns in Each Body': Women, Rape, and Racial Violence." In *Powers of Desire: The Politics of Sexuality*, edited by Ann Snitow, Christine Stansell, and Sharon Thompson, 328–49. New York: Monthly Review Press, 1983.

Halttunen, Karen. *Confidence Men and Painted Women: A Study of Middle-Class Culture in America, 1830–1870*. New Haven, Conn.: Yale University Press, 1982.

Hamilton, Kristie. *America's Sketchbook: The Cultural Life of a Nineteenth-Century Literary Genre*. Athens: Ohio University Press, 1998.

Hammonds, Evelynn M. "Toward a Genealogy of Black Female Sexuality: The Problematics of Silence." In *Feminist Genealogies, Colonial Legacies, and Democratic Futures*, edited by M. Jacqui Alexander and Chantra T. Mohanty, 170–82. New York: Routledge, 1997.

Hargreaves, Jennifer. *Sporting Females: Critical Issues in the History and Sociology of Women's Sports*. London: Routledge, 1994.

Harris, Sharon. *Redefining the Political Novel: American Women Writers, 1797–1901*. Knoxville: University of Tennessee Press, 1995.

Harris, Trudier. *Exorcising Blackness: Historical and Literary Lynching and Burning Rituals*. Bloomington: Indiana University Press, 1984.

Hauck, Richard Boyd. "The Man in the Buckskin Hunting Shirt: Fact and Fiction in the Crockett Story." In *Davy Crockett: The Man, the Legend, the Legacy, 1786–1986*, edited by Michael A. Lofaro, 3–20. Knoxville: University of Tennessee Press, 1985.

Hedrick, Joan. *Harriet Beecher Stowe: A Life*. New York: Oxford University Press, 1994.

Herndl, Diane Price. *Invalid Women: Figuring Feminine Illness in American Fiction and Culture, 1840–1940*. Chapel Hill: University of North Carolina Press, 1993.

Hodes, Martha. "The Sexualization of Reconstruction Politics: White Women and Black Men in the South after the Civil War." *Journal of the History of Sexuality* 3 (1993): 402–17.

———. *White Women, Black Men: Illicit Sex in the Nineteenth-Century South*. New Haven, Conn.: Yale University Press, 1997.

Hodge, Hugh, M.D. *On Diseases Peculiar to Women*. Philadelphia: Blanchard and Lea, 1860.

Hoffman, Nicole Tonkovich. "*Legacy* Profile: Sarah Josepha Hale (1788–1874)." *Legacy* 7 (1990): 47–55.

Holland, Catherine A. *The Body Politic: Foundings, Citizenship, and Difference in the American Political Imagination*. New York: Routledge, 2001.

Hollick, F., M.D. *The Diseases of Woman, Their Causes and Cure Familiarly Explained*. New York: Burgess, Stringer, and Co., 1847.

hooks, bell. *Feminist Theory: From Margin to Center*. Boston: South End Press, 1984.

Hornblow, Arthur. *A History of the Theatre in America from Its Beginnings to the Present Time*. Philadelphia: J. B. Lippincott, 1919.

Horton, James Oliver. "Freedom's Yoke: Gender Conventions among Antebellum Free Blacks." *Feminist Studies* 12 (1986): 51–76.

Hughes, Glenn. *A History of the American Theatre, 1700–1950*. New York: Samuel French, 1951.

Hunt, Harriot K., M.D. *Glances and Glimpses; or Fifty Years Social, Including Twenty Years Professional Life*. Boston: John P. Jewett and Co., 1856.

Hynes, James. *The Lecturer's Tale*. New York: Picador, 2002.

Isenberg, Nancy. *Sex and Citizenship in Antebellum America*. Chapel Hill: University of North Carolina Press, 1998.

Jackson. "A Word to the Wise." *Godey's Lady's Book* 23 (August 1841): 89–92.

Jacobs, Harriet. *Incidents in the Life of a Slave Girl*. 1855. Reprint. New York: Oxford University Press, 1990.

Jay, Gregory S. "American Literature and the New Historicism: The Example of Frederick Douglass." *boundary 2* 17 (1990): 211–42.

Jelinek, Estelle C. *The Tradition of Women's Autobiography: From Antiquity to the Present*. Boston: Twayne Publishers, 1986.

Johnson, Claudia. *American Actresses: Perspectives on the Nineteenth Century*. Chicago: Nelson-Hall, 1984.

———. "That Guilty Third Tier: Prostitution in Nineteenth-Century American Theaters." *American Quarterly* 27 (1975): 575–684.

Johnson, Nan. "The Popularization of Nineteenth-Century Rhetoric: Elocution and the Private Learner." In *Oratorical Culture in Nineteenth-Century America: Transformations in the Theory and Practice of Rhetoric*, edited by Gregory Clark and S. Michael Halloran, 139–57. Carbondale: Southern Illinois University Press, 1993.

Kaplan, Amy. "Manifest Domesticity." *American Literature* 70 (1998): 581–606.

Kasson, Joy S. *Marble Queens and Captives: Women in Nineteenth-Century American Sculpture*. New Haven, Conn.: Yale University Press, 1990.

Keetley, Dawn. "The Power of 'Personation': Anna Cora Mowatt and the Literature of Women's Public Performance in Nineteenth-Century America." *ATQ* 10 (1996): 187–200.

Kelley, Mary. *Private Woman, Public Stage: Literary Domesticity in Nineteenth-Century America*. New York: Oxford University Press, 1984.

Kelly, Joan. *Women, History, and Theory*. Chicago: University of Chicago Press, 1984.

Kerber, Linda K. "The Meanings of Citizenship." *Journal of American History* 84 (1997): 833–54.

———. *No Constitutional Right to Be Ladies: Women and the Obligations of Citizenship*. New York: Hill and Wang, 1998.

———. "Separate Spheres, Female Worlds, Woman's Place: The Rhetoric of Women's History." *Journal of American History* 75 (1988): 9–39.

Kessler-Harris, Alice. *Out to Work: A History of Wage-Earning Women in the United States*. New York: Oxford University Press, 1982.

Keyser, Elizabeth Lennox. *Whispers in the Dark: The Fiction of Louisa May Alcott*. Knoxville: University of Tennessee Press, 1993.

Kimmel, Michael. *Manhood in America: A Cultural History*. New York: Free Press, 1996.

King, Lester S. *Transformations in American Medicine*. Baltimore, Md.: Johns Hopkins University Press, 1991.

Kirby, Vicki. *Telling Flesh: The Substance of the Corporeal*. New York: Routledge, 1997.

Kirkham, Samuel. *An Essay on Elocution, Designed for the Use of Schools and Private Learners*. Baltimore, Md.: John W. Woods, 1833.

Kristeva, Julia. *Powers of Horror: An Essay on Abjection*. New York: Columbia University Press, 1982.

Kwolek-Folland, Angel. *Incorporating Women: A History of Women and Business in the United States*. New York: Twayne Publishers, 1998.

Lehuu, Isabelle. *Carnival on the Page: Popular Print Media in Antebellum America*. Chapel Hill: University of North Carolina Press, 2000.

———. "Sentimental Figures: Reading *Godey's Lady's Book* in Antebellum America." In *The Culture of Sentiment: Race, Gender, and Sentimentality in Nineteenth-Century America*, edited by Shirley Samuels, 73–91. New York: Oxford University Press, 1992.

Lerner, Gerda. *The Grimké Sisters from South Carolina: Pioneers for Woman's Rights and Abolition*. New York: Oxford University Press, 1998.

Lockyer, Sir Joseph Norman. "Astronomy." In *The Progress of the Century*, by Alfred Russel Wallace et al., 105–44. New York: Harper and Brothers, 1901.

Lofaro, Michael A. "The Hidden 'Hero' of the Nashville Crockett Almanacs." In *Davy Crockett: The Man, the Legend, the Legacy, 1786–1986*, edited by Michael A. Lofaro, 46–79. Knoxville: University of Tennessee Press, 1985.

———. "Riproarious Shemales: Legendary Women in the Tall Tale World of the Davy Crockett Almanacs." In *Crockett at 200: New Perspectives on the Man and the Myth*, edited by Michael A. Lofaro and Joe Cummings, 114–52. Knoxville: University of Tennessee Press, 1989.

———, ed. *The Tall Tales of Davy Crockett: The Second Nashville Series of Crockett Almanacs, 1839–1841*. Knoxville: University of Tennessee Press, 1987.

Looby, Christopher. *Voicing America: Language, Literary Form, and the Origins of the United States*. Chicago: University of Chicago Press, 1996.

Mabee, Carlton. *Sojourner Truth: Slave, Prophet, Legend*. New York: New York University Press, 1993.

Macy, Sue. *Winning Ways: A Photohistory of American Women in Sports*. New York: Henry Holt and Co., 1997.

Mahoney, Martha. "Victimization or Oppression?: Women's Lives, Violence, and Agency." In *The Public Nature of Private Violence: The Discovery of Domestic Abuse*, edited by Martha Albertson Fineman and Roxanne Mykitiuk. New York: Routledge, 1994.

Marcus, Leah. "Shakespeare's Computer: A Lecture in Honor of the Birthday of the Bard." Lecture at Vanderbilt University, 22 April 1999.

Martin, Lawrence. "The Genesis of *Godey's Lady's Book.*" *New England Quarterly* 1 (1928): 41–70.

Mason, Mary G. "The Other Voice: Autobiographies of Women Writers." In *Life/Lines: Theorizing Women's Autobiography*, edited by Bella Brodzki and Celeste Schenk, 19–44. Ithaca, N.Y.: Cornell University Press, 1988.

McCall, Laura. "'The Reign of Brute Force Is Now Over': A Content Analysis of *Godey's Lady's Book*, 1830–1860." *Journal of the Early Republic* 9 (1989): 217–36.

McConachie, Bruce A. *Melodramatic Formations: American Theatre and Society, 1820–1870*. Iowa City: University of Iowa Press, 1992.

McKissack, Patricia C., and Frederick McKissack. *Sojourner Truth: Ain't I a Woman?* New York: Scholastic Press, 1992.

McMurry, Linda O. *To Keep the Waters Troubled: The Life of Ida B. Wells*. New York: Oxford University Press, 1998.

Melville, Herman. "The Paradise of Bachelors and the Tartarus of Maids." In *Great Short Works of Herman Melville*, edited by Warner Berthoff, 202–22. New York: Perennial Library, 1969.

Mendenhall, T. C. "Physics." In *The Progress of the Century*, by Alfred Russel Wallace et al., 303–29. New York: Harper and Brothers, 1901.

Miller, Erika M. *The Other Reconstruction: Where Violence and Womanhood Meet in the Writings of Wells-Barnett, Grimké, and Larsen*. New York: Garland Publishing, 2000.

Millingen, J. G. *Lectures on Diseases of the Uterus, by Waller, Lisfranc and Ingleby, and Aphorisms on Insanity*. Philadelphia: E. Barrington and G. D. Haswell, 1841.

Mills, Sara. *Discourses of Difference: An Analysis of Women's Travel Writing and Colonialism*. London: Routledge, 1991.

Mindich, David T. Z. *Just the Facts: How "Objectivity" Came to Define American Journalism*. New York: New York University Press, 1998.

Mitchell, S. Weir. *Fat and Blood: And How to Make Them*. Philadelphia: J. B. Lippincott and Co., 1878.

———. *Wear and Tear; or, Hints for the Overworked*. Philadelphia: J. B. Lippincott and Co., 1871.

Moody, Richard. *America Takes the Stage: Romanticism in American Drama and Theatre, 1750–1900*. Bloomington: Indiana University Press, 1955.

Morantz, Regina Markell. "Feminism, Pluralism, and Germs: The Thought of Mary Putnam Jacobi and Elizabeth Blackwell." *American Quarterly* 34 (1982): 459–78.

Mordden, Ethan. *The American Theatre*. New York: Oxford University Press, 1981.

Moses, Montrose and John Mason Brown, eds. *The American Theatre as Seen by Its Critics, 1752–1934*. New York: W. W. Norton and Company, 1934.

Mott, Frank Luther. *A History of American Magazines, 1741–1850*. New York: D. Appleton and Co., 1930.

Mowatt, Anna Cora. *Autobiography of an Actress; or, Eight Years on the Stage*. Boston: Ticknor and Fields, 1853.

———. *Fashion: Life in New York, a Comedy in Five Acts*. New York: Samuel French, 1845.

Moylan, Michelle, and Lane Stiles. Introduction to *Reading Books: Essays on the Material Text and Literature in America*, edited by Moylan and Stiles, 1–15. Amherst: University of Massachusetts Press, 1996.

Nelson, Dana D. *National Manhood: Capitalist Citizenship and the Imagined Fraternity of White Men*. Durham, N.C.: Duke University Press, 1998.

———. "Women in Public." In *The Cambridge Companion to Nineteenth-Century American Women's Writing*, edited by Dale M. Bauer and Philip Gould, 38–68. Cambridge: Cambridge University Press, 2001.

Nelson, Mariah Burton. "Introduction: Who We Might Become." In *Nike Is a Goddess: The History of Women in Sports*, edited by Lissa Smith, ix–xix. New York: Atlantic Monthly Press, 1998.

Neuberg, Victor. "Chapbooks in America: Reconstructing the Popular Reading of Early America." In *Reading in America: Literary and Social History*, edited by Cathy N. Davidson, 81–113. Baltimore, Md.: Johns Hopkins University Press, 1989.

Neuman, Shirley. "Autobiography and Questions of Gender: An Introduction." In *Autobiography and Questions of Gender*, edited by Shirley Neuman, 1–11. London: Frank Cass and Co., 1991.

Nudelman, Franny. "Harriet Jacobs and the Sentimental Politics of Female Suffering." *ELH* 59 (1992): 939–64.

Numbers, Ronald L., and Rennie B. Schoepflin. "Ministries of Healing: Mary Baker Eddy, Ellen G. White, and the Religion of Health." In *Women and Health in America: Historical Readings*, edited by Judith W. Leavitt, 376–89. Madison: University of Wisconsin Press, 1984.

O'Connor, Lillian. *Pioneer Women Orators: Rhetoric in the Ante-Bellum Reform Movement*. New York: Columbia University Press, 1954.

Odell, George C. D. *Annals of the New York Stage*. Vol. 5, *1843–1850*. New York: Columbia University Press, 1931.

Okker, Patricia. *Our Sister Editors: Sarah J. Hale and the Tradition of Nineteenth-Century American Women Editors*. Athens: University of Georgia Press, 1995.

Opsata, Margaret. "Genteel Iconoclast." *American History Illustrated* 17 (1983): 40–45.

Osler, William. "Medicine." In *The Progress of the Century*, by Alfred Russel Wallace et al., 173–215. New York: Harper and Brothers, 1901.

Painter, Nell Irvin. "Representing Truth: Sojourner Truth's Knowing and Being Known." *Journal of American History* 81 (1994): 461–92.

———. *Sojourner Truth: A Life, a Symbol*. New York: Oxford University Press, 1996.

———. "Sojourner Truth in Life and Memory: Writing the Biography of an American Exotic." *Gender and History* 2.1 (1990): 3–16.

———. *Southern History across the Color Line*. Chapel Hill: University of North Carolina Press, 2002.

Park, You-me, and Gayle Wald. "Native Daughters in the Promised Land: Gender, Race, and the Question of Separate Spheres." *American Literature* 70 (1998): 607–34.

Parker, Gail. "Mary Baker Eddy and Sentimental Womanhood." *New England Quarterly* 43 (1970): 3–18.

———. *Mind Cure in New England; from the Civil War to World War I*. Hanover, N.H.: University Press of New England, 1973.

Pattee, Fred Lewis. *The Feminine Fifties*. D. Appleton-Century Company, 1940.

Pawelko, Katherine A. "Cycling." In *International Encyclopedia of Women and Sports*, edited by Karen Christensen et al., 291–95. New York: Macmillan Reference USA, 2000.

Peel, Robert. *Mary Baker Eddy: The Years of Discovery*. New York: Holt, Rinehart, and Winston, 1966.

Peterson, Carla. *"Doers of the Word": African-American Women Speakers and Writers in the North (1830-1880)*. New York: Oxford University Press, 1995.

———. "Foreword: Eccentric Bodies." In *Recovering the Black Female Body: Self-Representations by African American Women*, edited by Michael Bennett and Vanessa D. Dickerson, ix–xvi. New Brunswick, N.J.: Rutgers University Press, 2001.

Poovey, Mary. "Scenes of an Indelicate Character." In *The Making of the Modern Body*, edited by Catherine Gallagher and Thomas Laqueur, 137–68. Berkeley: University of California Press, 1987.

Pryse, Marjorie. "Sex, Class, and 'Category Crisis': Reading Jewett's Transitivity." *American Literature* 70 (1998): 517–50.

Punday, Daniel. "Foucault's Body Tropes." *New Literary History* 31 (2000): 509–28.

Reynolds, David S. *Beneath the American Renaissance: The Subversive Imagination in the Age of Emerson and Melville*. New York: Alfred A. Knopf, 1988.

Ripley, C. Peter, ed. *The Black Abolitionist Papers*. 5 vols. Chapel Hill: University of North Carolina Press, 1985.

Roediger, David R. *The Wages of Whiteness: Race and the Making of the American Working Class*. London: Verso, 1991.

Rogers, Sherbrooke. *Sarah Josepha Hale: A New England Pioneer, 1788–1879*. Grantham, N.H.: Tompson and Rutter, 1985.

Romero, Lora. *Home Fronts: Domesticity and Its Critics in the Antebellum United States*. Durham, N.C.: Duke University Press, 1997.

Root, Elihu. *The Citizen's Part in Government*. New Haven, Conn.: Yale University Press, 1907.

Royster, Jacquelyn Jones. "Introduction: Equity and Justice for All." In *Southern Horrors and Other Writings: The Anti-Lynching Campaign of Ida B.*

Wells, 1892–1900, edited by Jacquelyn Jones Royster, 1–41. Boston: Bedford Books, 1997.

Ryan, Mary P. *Women in Public: Between Banners and Ballots, 1825–1880*. Baltimore, Md.: Johns Hopkins University Press, 1990.

Samuels, Shirley, ed. *The Culture of Sentiment: Race, Gender, and Sentimentality in Nineteenth-Century America*. Berkeley: University of California Press, 1990.

Sánchez-Eppler, Karen. *Touching Liberty: Abolition, Feminism, and the Politics of the Body*. Berkeley: University of California Press, 1993.

Satter, Beryl. *Each Mind a Kingdom: American Women, Sexual Purity, and the New Thought Movement, 1875–1920*. Berkeley: University of California Press, 1999.

Satterwhite, Joseph N. "The Tremulous Formula: Form and Technique in *Godey's* Fiction." *American Quarterly* 8 (1956): 99–113.

Scarry, Elaine. *The Body in Pain: The Making and Unmaking of the World*. New York: Oxford University Press, 1985.

Schechter, Patricia. *Ida B. Wells-Barnett and American Reform, 1880–1930*. Chapel Hill: University of North Carolina Press, 2001.

Schriber, Mary Suzanne. Introduction to *Telling Travels: Selected Writings by Nineteenth-Century American Women Abroad*, edited by Mary Suzanne Schriber, xi–xxxi. DeKalb: Northern Illinois University Press, 1995.

Schudson, Michael. *The Good Citizen: A History of American Civic Life*. New York: Free Press, 1998.

Shaler, Nathaniel. "The Negro Problem." *Atlantic Monthly* 54 (1884): 696–709.

———. "Science and the African Problem." *Atlantic Monthly* 66 (1890): 36–45.

Shapiro, Herbert. *White Violence and Black Response: From Reconstruction to Montgomery*. Amherst: University of Massachusetts Press, 1988.

Shew, Joel. *The Hydropathic Family Physician*. New York: Fowlers and Wells, 1855.

Sicherman, Barbara. "Sense and Sensibility: A Case Study of Women's Reading in Late-Victorian America." In *Reading in America: Literature and Social History*, edited by Cathy N. Davidson, 201–25. Baltimore, Md.: Johns Hopkins University Press, 1989.

Six Women's Slave Narratives. New York: Oxford University Press, 1987.

Smith, Gail K. "Who Was That Masked Woman?: Gender and Form in Louisa May Alcott's Confidence Stories." In *American Women Short Story Writers*, edited by Julie Brown, 45–59. New York: Garland Publishing, 1995.

Smith, Lissa, ed. *Nike Is a Goddess: The History of Women in Sports*. New York: Atlantic Monthly Press, 1998.

Smith, Rogers M. *Civic Ideals: Conflicting Visions of Citizenship in United States History*. New Haven, Conn.: Yale University Press, 1997.

Smith, Sidonie. "Resisting the Gaze of Embodiment: Women's Autobiography in the Nineteenth Century." In *American Women's*

Autobiography: Fea(s)ts of Memory, edited by Margo Culley, 75–110. Madison: University of Wisconsin Press, 1992.

———. *Subjectivity, Identity, and the Body: Women's Autobiographical Practices in the Twentieth Century*. Bloomington: Indiana University Press, 1993.

Smith-Rosenberg, Carroll. *Disorderly Conduct: Visions of Gender in Victorian America*. New York: Oxford University Press, 1985.

Smith-Rosenberg, Carroll, and Charles Rosenberg. "The Female Animal: Medical and Biological Views of Woman and Her Role in Nineteenth-Century America." In *Women's Health in America: Historical Readings*, edited by Judith W. Leavitt, 10–25. Madison: University of Wisconsin Press, 1984.

Southworth, E. D. E. N. *The Hidden Hand*. 1859. Reprint. New York: Oxford University Press, 1997.

Spillers, Hortense. "Mama's Baby, Papa's Maybe: An American Grammar Book." *Diacritics* 17.2 (1987): 65–81.

Stanley, Gregory Kent. *The Rise and Fall of the Sportswoman: Women's Health, Fitness, and Athletics, 1860–1940*. New York: Peter Lang, 1996.

Stanton, Domna. "Autogynography: Is the Subject Different?" In *The Female Autograph: Theory and Practice of Autobiography from the Tenth to the Twentieth Century*, edited by Domna Stanton, 3–20. Chicago: University of Chicago Press, 1987.

———. Preface to *The Female Autograph: Theory and Practice of Autobiography from the Tenth to the Twentieth Century*, edited by Domna Stanton, vii–xi. Chicago: University of Chicago Press, 1987.

Stearns, Bertha M. "Early New England Magazines of Ladies." *New England Quarterly* 2 (1929): 420–57.

Stetson, Erlene, and Linda David. *Glorying in Tribulation: The Lifework of Sojourner Truth*. East Lansing: Michigan State University Press, 1994.

Stewart, Jeffrey. Introduction to *Narrative of Sojourner Truth: A Bondswoman of Olden Time, with a History of Her Labors and Correspondence Drawn from Her "Book of Life."* 1878. Reprint. New York: Oxford University Press, 1991.

Stowe, Harriet Beecher. "Sojourner Truth, the Libyan Sibyl." *Atlantic Monthly* 11 (April 1863): 473.

———. *Uncle Tom's Cabin*. 1852. Reprint. New York: Bantam Books, 1981.

Sundquist, Eric J. *To Wake the Nations: Race in the Making of American Literature*. Cambridge, Mass.: Harvard University Press, 1993.

Tait, Peta. "Feminine Free Fall: A Fantasy of Freedom." *Theatre Journal* 48 (1996): 27–34.

Tate, Claudia. *Domestic Allegories of Political Desire: The Black Heroine's Text at the Turn of the Century*. New York: Oxford University Press, 1992.

Taubman, Howard. *The American Theatre*. New York: Coward McCann, 1965.

Taylor, Kelly S. "The Rhetoric of Self-Fashioning in the Works of Anna Cora Mowatt." Ph.D. diss., Louisiana State University, 1994.

Thompson, David W. "Early Actress-Readers: Mowatt, Kemble, and

Cushman." In *Performance of Literature in Historical Perspectives*, edited by David W. Thompson, 629–50. Lanham, Md.: University Press of America, 1983.

Thompson, Mildred I. *Ida B. Wells-Barnett: An Exploratory Study of an American Black Woman, 1893–1930*. Brooklyn: Carlson Publishing, 1990.

Thomson, Rosemarie Garland. *Extraordinary Bodies: Figuring Physical Disability in American Culture and Literature*. New York: Columbia University Press, 1997.

———, ed. *Freakery: Cultural Spectacles of the Extraordinary Body*. New York: New York University Press, 1996.

———. "Introduction: From Wonder to Error—a Genealogy of Freak Discourse in Modernity." In *Freakery: Cultural Spectacles of the Extraordinary Body*, edited by Rosemarie Garland Thomson, 1–19. New York: New York University Press, 1996.

Tibbetts, Joel W. "Women Who Were Called: A Study of the Contributions to American Christianity of Ann Lee, Jemima Wilkinson, Mary Baker Eddy, and Aimee Simple McPherson." Ph.D. diss., Vanderbilt University, 1976.

Tolnay, Stewart E., and E. M. Beck. *A Festival of Violence: An Analysis of Southern Lynchings, 1882–1930*. Urbana: University of Illinois Press, 1995.

Tompkins, Jane. *Sensational Designs: The Cultural Work of American Fiction, 1790–1860*. New York: Oxford University Press, 1985.

Tonkovich, Nicole. *Domesticity with a Difference: The Nonfiction of Catharine Beecher, Sarah J. Hale, Fanny Fern, and Margaret Fuller*. Jackson: University Press of Mississippi, 1997.

———. "Rhetorical Power in the Victorian Parlor: *Godey's Lady's Book* and the Gendering of Nineteenth-Century Rhetoric." In *Oratorical Culture in Nineteenth-Century America: Transformations in the Theory and Practice of Rhetoric*, edited by Gregory Clark and S. Michael Halloran, 158–83. Carbondale: Southern Illinois University Press, 1993.

Truth, Sojourner. *Narrative of Sojourner Truth: A Bondswoman of Olden Time, with a History of Her Labors and Correspondence Drawn from Her "Book of Life."* 1878. Reprint. New York: Oxford University Press, 1991.

Twain, Mark. *Christian Science*. 1907. Reprint. Oxford: Oxford University Press, 1996.

Wald, Priscilla. *Constituting Americans: Cultural Anxiety and Narrative Form*. Durham, N.C.: Duke University Press, 1995.

Walker, John. *Elements of Elocution*. Boston: D. Mallory, 1810.

Warner, Michael. *The Letters of the Republic: Publication and the Public Sphere in Eighteenth-Century America*. Cambridge, Mass.: Harvard University Press, 1990.

Warner, Susan. *The Wide, Wide World*. 1850. Reprint. New York: Feminist Press, 1987.

Watson, Julia, and Sidonie Smith. Introduction to *De/Colonizing the Subject: The Politics of Gender in Women's Autobiography*, edited by Watson and Smith, xi–xxxi. Minneapolis: University of Minnesota Press, 1992.

Webster, Noah. *An American Selection of Lessons*. Albany: Charles R. and George Webster, 1797.

Wells, Ida B. "Afro-Americans and Africa." In *Ida B. Wells-Barnett: An Exploratory Study of an American Black Woman, 1893–1930*, edited by Mildred I. Thompson, 165–69. Brooklyn: Carlson Publishing, 1990.

———. *Crusade for Justice: The Autobiography of Ida B. Wells*. Edited by Alfreda M. Duster. Chicago: University of Chicago Press, 1970.

Wells, Susan. *Out of the Dead House: Nineteenth-Century Women Physicians and the Writing of Medicine*. Madison: University of Wisconsin Press, 2001.

Wells-Barnett, Ida B. *The Reason Why The Colored American Is Not in the World's Columbian Exposition*. In *Selected Works of Ida B. Wells-Barnett*, edited by Trudier Harris. New York: Oxford University Press, 1991.

———. *A Red Record: Tabulated Statistics and Alleged Causes of Lynchings in the United States, 1892–1893–1894*. 1895. Reprinted in *Selected Works of Ida B. Wells-Barnett*, edited by Trudier Harris, 138–252. New York: Oxford University Press, 1991.

———. *Southern Horrors: Lynch Law in All Its Phases*. 1892. Reprinted in *Selected Works of Ida B. Wells-Barnett*, edited by Trudier Harris, 14–45. New York: Oxford University Press, 1991.

Welter, Barbara. "The Cult of True Womanhood: 1800–1860." *American Quarterly* 18 (1966): 151–74.

———. *Dimity Convictions: The American Woman in the Nineteenth Century*. Athens: Ohio University Press, 1976.

White, Deborah Gray. *Ar'n't I a Woman?: Female Slaves in the Plantation South*. New York: W. W. Norton and Company, 1985.

Wiegman, Robyn. *American Anatomies: Theorizing Race and Gender*. Durham, N.C.: Duke University Press, 1995.

Willard, Frances. *A Wheel within a Wheel: How I Learned to Ride the Bicycle, with Some Reflections by the Way*. 1895. Reprint. Bedford, Mass.: Applewood Books, 1997.

Williams, Brett. *John Henry: A Bio-Bibliography*. Westport, Conn.: Greenwood Press, 1983.

Williamson, Joel. *A Rage for Order: Black/White Relations in the American South since Emancipation*. New York: Oxford University Press, 1986.

Wilson, Garff B. *A History of American Acting*. Bloomington: Indiana University Press, 1966.

———. *Three Hundred Years of American Drama and Theatre*. Inglewood Cliffs, N.J.: Prentice Hall, 1982.

Wilson, J. Stainback. "Health Department." *Godey's Lady's Book* 59 (1859): 83–84.

Wiltbank, John. *Introductory Lecture for the Session, 1853–54*. Philadelphia: Edward Grattan, 1854.

"Women's Rights Convention: Sojourner Truth." *Anti-Slavery Bugle*, 21 June 1851.

Wonham, Henry B. *Mark Twain and the Art of the Tall Tale*. New York: Oxford University Press, 1993.

Wood, Ann Douglas. "'The Fashionable Diseases': Women's Complaints and Their Treatment in Nineteenth-Century America." *Journal of Interdisciplinary History*. 4.1 (1973): 25–52.

Woolson, Abba Gould. *Woman in American Society*. Boston: Roberts Brothers, 1873.

Woolum, Janet. *Outstanding Woman Athletes*. Phoenix: Oryx Press, 1998.

Wrobel, Arthur. Introduction to *Pseudo-Science and Society in Nineteenth-Century America*, edited by Arthur Wrobel. Lexington: University Press of Kentucky, 1987.

Yellin, Jean Fagan. *Women and Sisters: The Antislavery Feminists in American Culture*. New Haven, Conn.: Yale University Press, 1989.

Zboray, Ronald J. "Antebellum Reading and the Ironies of Technological Innovation." In *Reading in America: Literature and Social History*, edited by Cathy N. Davidson, 180–200. Baltimore, Md.: Johns Hopkins University Press, 1989.

Zita, Jacqueline N. *Body Talk: Philosophical Reflections on Sex and Gender*. New York: Columbia University Press, 1998.

INDEX